BU

The origins of
Suffolk

Origins of the Shire

general editor
Nick Higham

The origins of
Suffolk

Peter Warner

Manchester University Press
Manchester and New York
Distributed exclusively in the USA and Canada by St. Martin's Press

Published by Manchester University Press
Oxford Road, Manchester M13 9NR, UK
and Room 400, 175 Fifth Avenue, New York, NY 10010, USA
Distributed exclusively in the USA and Canada
by St Martin's Press, Inc., 175 Fifth Avenue, New York,
Ny 10010, USA

British Library Cataloguing-in-Publication Data
A catalogue record for this book is available from the British Library

Library of Congress Cataloging-in-Publication Data
Warner, Peter (Peter M.)
    The origins of Suffolk/Peter Warner.
        p.   cm. – (Origins of the Shire)
    Includes bibliographical references and index.
    ISBN 0–7190–3817–0
    1. Suffolk (England) – History.   2. Land settlement – England – Suffolk –
History.   3. Anglo-Saxons – England – Suffolk.   4. Britons – England –
Suffolk.   5. Romans – England – Suffolk.   I. Title.   II. Series.
    DA670.S9W36   1996
    942.6′4 – dc20   95-33402
                                                                                          CIP

ISBN 0 7190 3817 0 *paperback*

First published 1996

00 99 98 97 96   10 9 8 7 6 5 4 3 2 1

Typeset by Best-set Typesetter Ltd., Hong Kong.
Printed in Great Britain by Bell & Bain Ltd, Glasgow

Contents

Figures

List of figures

List of figures

Plates

1 The medieval diocese of Norwich: the old East Anglian diocese included both counties of Norfolk and Suffolk and extended westwards to the line of the Devil's Dyke and the Isle of Ely; its boundary derives from the frontiers of the old Anglo-Saxon kingdom of East Anglia (Jessopp 1884)

2 The Devil's Dyke: a late Roman or early Anglo-Saxon frontier to the territory which later became the kingdom of East Anglia (P. Warner)

3 Crop-marks of the Fornham cursus and interrupted ditch systems. The narrow parallel lines receding from view in the centre of the picture mark the cursus, while the curving dotted lines in the foreground represent two interrupted ditch systems. Both the ditch systems and the cursus indicate a focus of ritual activity during the early and late Neolithic respectively (Suffolk County Council Archaeological Service)

4 Westhall terrets: found on an small early Roman site in 1854 when new ditches were being dug near the line of the East Suffolk railway. These bronze enamelled terrets represent the best of late Icenian metalwork intended for a decorative chariot or wheeled vehicle (P. Warner)

5 Burgh-by-Woodbridge: although ploughed almost flat the lighter colour of the rectangular banked and ditched enclosure can be clearly seen. The church of Burgh stands in the trees near the centre. This major Iron Age fortification later served as the site of a Roman villa (University of Cambridge Committee for Aerial Photography)

List of plates

Plates appear between pages 94 and 107

General Editor's preface

The shire was the most important single unit of government, justice and social organisation throughout the Later Middle Ages and on into the Modern period. An understanding of the shire is, therefore, fundamental to English history of all types and of all periods – be it conducted on a national, regional or local basis.

This series sets out to explore the origins of each shire in the Early Middle Ages. Archaeological evidence for settlement hierarchies and social territories in later prehistory and the Roman period is necessarily the starting point. The shire and its component parts are then explored in detail during the Anglo-Saxon period. A series of leading scholars, each with a particular regional expertise, have brought together evidence drawn from literary and documentary sources, place-name research and archaeological fieldwork to present a stimulating picture of the territorial history of the English shires, and the parishes, estates and hundreds of which they were formed.

In some instances the results stress the degree of continuity across periods as long as a millennium. Elsewhere, these studies underline the arbitrary nature of the shire and the intentional break with the past, particularly where the West Saxon King, Edward the Elder, imposed his southern ideas concerning local organisation on the regional communities of the English Midlands.

These volumes will each be a great asset to historians and all those interested in their own localities, offering an open door into a period of the past which has for many so far been too difficult or obscure to attempt an entry.

Nick Higham

Preface

This book could not have been written without constant reference to a continuum of Suffolk topographical writing; from Kirby's *Suffolk Traveller* of 1764, to the recently published *Historical Atlas of Suffolk* by Dymond and Martin. The maps are mostly my own work based on other sources and any errors in them must be laid at my door; because of the small page size, it has been necessary to simplify and eliminate all but the most basic information on the maps. Some omissions are therefore deliberate.

It is twenty-three years since Norman Scarfe published his work on *The Suffolk Landscape*, a work which was an inspiration to me as a student. I hope that readers who enjoy Scarfe's scholarly style, so richly interwoven with information and ideas, will not be too disappointed with my text, which does not pretend to match his eloquent prose. Instead I have tried to build on some of Scarfe's work by choosing key themes and to show where modern scholarship has shed light on his ideas. Inevitably, this, the Suffolk volume in the *Origins of the Shire* series will be compared with Tom Williamson's excellent work on *The origins of Norfolk*. I had the advantage of having his work beside me, but I have tried to make the Suffolk volume different in its approach, but at the same time complementary as a work in the same series. I hope that scholars will enjoy the differences and benefit from the approaches of both writers, the one a geographer turned archaeologist, the other an archaeologist turned local historian; readers must draw their own conclusions. If nothing else, I hope they will rush out and buy whichever volume they have not yet read.

I have also tried to incorporate as much new archaeological evidence as possible, particularly where it has a bearing on key issues of settlement history. For this I am deeply indebted to members of the Suffolk Archaeological Unit, in particular Keith Wade, Judith Plouviez, Edward Martin and Bob Carr for their comments on the text. They are the unsung heroes of Suffolk archaeology whose efforts over the last twenty-one years have transformed our understanding of the early county, particularly for the Anglo-Saxon period.

Stanley West, founder of the Suffolk Archaeological Unit and best known for his excavations at West Stow, inspired me as a student attending his evening classes many years ago; without his influence this book could not have been conceived. The work of the Sutton Hoo Project has been a more recent inspiration, and the approach of Martin Carver in particular has been an important stimulus to the archaeology of the county. Readers may recognise some of my own work from East Suffolk which derives from research done in the Department of English Local History at the University of Leicester; I am deeply indebted to Harold Fox, and other members of the department for their guidance with this work. Sandra Raban gave valuable advice on the Domesday chapter.

I am grateful to Homerton College for granting me a term's sabbatical to complete the work and for the use of their reprographic facilities. I am also grateful to Mary Tilney for reading the text and attempting to suppress eccentricities of spelling and grammar; also to Nesta Evans for preparing the index. All subsequent errors are, of course, my own.

1

The natural frame

The South Folk

This book is about the origins of the county of Suffolk and the people who lived and dwelt within it. A county is a living entity with which many of us identify; ask anyone which cricket team they support or where they come from and the chances are you will be given the name of a county. Yet the counties and the shires (there is little difference between the two names) have complex origins. Suffolk was itself composed of a number of older shires which at one time had all the characteristics of separate counties. Indeed, until local government changes in 1974 there were the two counties of East and West Suffolk focused on the two county towns of Ipswich and Bury St Edmunds (Figure 1.1). West Suffolk still retains the elements of a separate county with its police force and Shire Hall situated close to the great Abbey ruins at Bury St Edmunds. West Suffolk, comprising the eight and a half hundreds of Thinghoe, was a 'liberty' or ecclesiastical shire, established in the Late Saxon period to accommodate the power and wealth of the shrine of St Edmund and the abbot who was its spiritual and temporal guardian.

East Suffolk also contained within it another, smaller ecclesiastical shire: the five and a half hundreds of Wicklaw, which belonged to the monastery at Ely. Woodbridge, whose market charter was granted in 1227 as a concession out of the more ancient market at Ipswich, eventually became the focus for this smaller 'liberty'. It

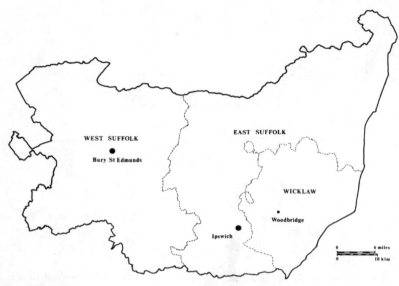

1.1 Suffolk: the shires of West and East Suffolk with the area of the Wicklaw hundreds and their respective shire towns of Bury St Edmunds, Ipswich and Woodbridge

developed from the early thirteenth-century as a miniature county town in its own right, with its own shire courts and later, a separate police force. Ipswich, although the oldest attested Saxon town in Suffolk, if not in England, remained as an urban focus for the 'geldable' hundreds; in other words, all those hundreds lying in East Suffolk that were not part of the Wicklaw territory, and paid their geld or taxation to the Crown rather than to a secular or ecclesiastical lord.

This complex pattern of hundreds and shires within the county is, as we shall see, a very ancient one and pre-dates the emergence of the County of Suffolk itself. Considering the obvious geographical divide formed by the rivers Ouse and Waveney the formal division between the two counties of Norfolk and Suffolk comes surprisingly late, probably at about the time of the Norman Conquest. Indeed, the earldom of East Anglia was not divided into Norfolk and Suffolk until some time after the Conquest and the sheriffs likewise remained the sheriffs of both counties until the time of

Elizabeth I (Warner 1988). The two counties are clearly part of one cohesive territory; the area is perhaps best seen in the ancient diocese of Norwich amply illustrated by Jessopp in 1884 (Plate 1). Both counties reflect the ancient Anglo-Saxon kingdom of East Anglia and in order to understand the essential nature of the County of Suffolk and the folk who were clearly instrumental in its origins the county must be seen as part of the wider territory of East Anglia with its partner, the County of Norfolk.

If the counties of Norfolk and Suffolk were two parts of one cohesive territory, who were the 'folk'? The *Anglo-Saxon Chronicle* tells us that in 1004, Ulfketill, the Earl of East Anglia, attacked Sweyn of Denmark and a Viking army at Thetford and there the flower of the East Anglian *folc* was killed (Barlow 1970, 11). To the Danes East Anglia was 'Ulfketill's Land'; although we only hear of the English defeat, the Danes themselves said that they 'never met harder fighting in England than Ulfketill dealt to them'. Again in 1010, at the Battle of Ringmere in West Suffolk, Ulfketill was defeated by Thorkell the Tall (Thorkell Havi) and Olaf Haraldsson; 'many good thegns and a countless mass of the *folc* were killed' (Garmonsway 1972, 135, 140). The *folc* are equated with the *thingmen*, the freemen that attended the folk-courts or *thing* moots of the hundreds which made up the two counties; they were the levies whose duty it was to muster in defence of their own lands and form the *fyrd* or Anglo-Saxon army. From the time of Alfred the Great and the unification of the English kingdom, provincial leaders were given the title of Earl and could no longer style themselves kings (Pálsson & Edwards 1976, 117). Nevertheless, earls such as Ulfketill were able to inspire leadership within the area of the old kingdom of East Anglia and the loyalty of their *folc* was central to law and order and defence of the region.

The *folc* of the shires which comprised East Anglia were a complex social order. The Domesday survey indicates that in Suffolk freemen comprised some 41% of the listed population (Darby 1952, 168). A small number of freewomen are also mentioned, but in the language of Domesday they are sometimes hard to distinguish from men. In Norfolk, sokemen outnumbered freemen, but in both counties the two classes of men and women existed within a complex pattern of 'commendation' or allegiance to superior freemen and thegns. At least three or four classes of freemen have been recognised in the Domesday survey ranging from the wealthiest landholders to the poorest free peasants (Warner 1987). The survey describes a complex network of loyalties extending from top to bottom of this freeholding society. Thus the *folc* were central to the old East Anglian kingdom; they had the strongest reasons to defend and identify with their territory, to support the established system of lordship and the process of local administration through their folk-courts at hundred and shire.

The East Anglian region

What was it, or is it, that makes the two counties of Norfolk and Suffolk so cohesive in the pre-Conquest period and to a lesser extent today? Geographically, the region, which comprised the two counties, was much more cohesive in the past than it is today due to fundamental environmental and topographical changes that have taken place since the early Middle Ages (Figure 1.2). East Anglia is bordered on its northern and eastern sides by the North Sea or German Ocean and on the west by the fenland basin, a fertile landscape but one which was subject to changes in water-level. At different times the fens have been transformed in part into verdant rich pasture intersected by drainage channels and waterways only to revert to a swampy wasteland teeming with fish and wildfowl.

To the south the central clay plateau of Suffolk and Norfolk extends down into Essex and in the past created an intractable interior, originally densely wooded, sparsely populated and difficult to traverse. However, the claylands are ideally suited to small-scale mixed agriculture: cereal growing combined with dairying and pig-keeping. At different periods, dependent in part on minor climatic changes in rainfall and the subtle balance of population levels and market prices, the claylands have been transformed from waterlogged wood-pasture into well-drained agricultural land.

The East Anglian coast, with its low sandy cliffs, is deeply intersected by estuaries which provide another distinctive habitat of open salt marsh and sandy heath. This was a coastline notorious for smuggling in the eighteenth century because it was so difficult to patrol. The heathlands, although settled in prehistoric times, were sparsely populated in later periods. Barley, sheep and rabbits formed a background economy to fishing. In recent years the North Sea has been over-fished, but there is no doubt that coastal fishing

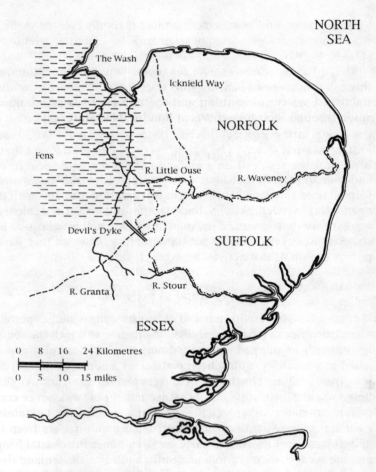

NORTH
SEA

The Wash

Icknield Way

NORFOLK

Fens

R. Little Ouse

R. Waveney

Devil's Dyke

SUFFOLK

R. Granta

R. Stour

ESSEX

```
0    8    16    24 Kilometres
0    5    10    15 miles
```

1.2 The East Anglian region

from the beach as well as the estuary ports was a very important
part of the medieval economy in the region; indeed by the late
Middle Ages there is evidence for long-distance fishing to Iceland,
Shetland and the northern seas (Bailey 1990). The rivers also provided easy access to the lush valleys and more loamy soils of the
clay edge just a few miles up stream. This coast has, of course,
always been subject to erosion, but it has also suffered from human
intervention. Like most of the heathlands in southern England,
including parts of the distinctive Brecklands of West Norfolk and

Suffolk, the coastal heaths were almost certainly created through woodland clearance and over-grazing in remote prehistory (Dimbleby 1962).

The estuaries themselves have been subject to exploitation through drainage and peat-digging, or turbary. What are now open tracts of reed-swamp along the Suffolk coast were prime marsh grazing before the Second World War, and before canalisation of the rivers in the eighteenth century they were mud-flats. When looking at what seems to be a timeless rural scene we forget that it is not just the result of one interaction between ecological forces and human intervention, but that the landscape has been transformed time and again; each human intervention interacts with the one before as well as with both fragile and resilient ecological forces, leaving a complex palimpsest of old and new in juxtaposition. It is this diversity of habitat and cumulative history which gives a region its distinctive character.

East Anglia and its neighbours

It is the changing environmental character of the landscape over many centuries that has determined the degree to which the region has either been merged with neighbouring areas, becoming part of a wider community, or has been isolated as a peninsula jutting out into the southern North Sea. The territory of the East Anglian kingdom, although a peninsula in ancient times, was n￵ pletely isolated geographically; its lengthy coastline and river system provided easy access to settlers and trader and wide. In prehistoric and early medieval times the co and the areas of west Norfolk and Suffolk close to the fe system benefited from their accessibility, but also live fear of unwanted migrants and sea-borne raiders. The i less subject to external influence and settlement mig exception is perhaps in the Roman period when an e￵ tem of roads opened up the claylands to settlement East Anglia into a wider world of the province of Br￵ an outpost of Empire.

There is now evidence to suggest that some clayla￵ been opened up in pre-Roman or very early Roman complex network of small rectangular fields subseque￵ by Roman roads (Williamson 1993). The Romans

---

6

1.3 Neighbours of the East Anglian kingdom

territory with a distinctive tribal identity. Tacitus, writing in the first century AD, and other classical writers have given us the names of tribal groups in Britain; it is the Iceni that are clearly associated with East Anglia.

East Anglia looked out not only over the southern North Sea but also westwards and northwards towards Mercia and Northumbria and beyond them to the late Celtic world (Figure 1.3). The East Anglian kingdom was frequently at war with its neighbours and eventually fell to Mercian supremacy in the mid-seventh century. Celtic influence can be seen in the metalwork of the hanging bowls contained in the ship-burial at Sutton Hoo and at least one Irish saint, Fursey, settled briefly in north-east Suffolk at Burgh Castle. Stories of the early Church retold by Béde point to royal connections with Northumbria. We must not forget that for a period of about one hundred years, until the territory was reconquered by Edward the Elder, East Anglia formed part of the northern Danelaw, before it became, for the first time, part of the wider kingdom of England.

East Anglia lies within a fertile crescent extending around the southern rim of the North Sea: from southern Sweden across the Baltic, to Poland and the Schleswig-Holstein peninsula, the plains of northern Germany, the Low Countries, Belgium, Northern

France and across the Channel into southern England, through East Anglia and up into Lincolnshire. The landscape of this North Sea litoral is composed of the richest farming land in Northern Europe. Although interspersed with areas of fen and salt marsh and upland areas of chalk downland and dry sandy heaths, it is a landscape which can support high population levels dependent on mixed farming and, of course, fishing. By 1086, it would seem that Norfolk, Suffolk, Lincolnshire and Kent were the most densely populated counties in England, with Norfolk and Suffolk being two of the wealthiest (Darby 1952).

It is not surprising, therefore, that long before the County of Suffolk came into being we have evidence for contacts and movements of peoples from nearly all of the areas within this fertile crescent. Recent research suggests that among the Anglo-Saxon cemetery material in East Anglia there were brooches and other artefacts from south Norway (Hines 1992). The seventh-century dynasty of the East Anglian kingdom, the 'Wuffings', was almost certainly of Swedish extraction, the Sutton Hoo ship-burial being an outlier of the Swedish Vendel tradition of burial practice. Migration from the 'Anglian' Danish peninsula of Schleswig-Holstein and the 'Saxon' areas around Hamburg formed the basis of the Anglo-Saxon settlements, more evidenced in some areas than in others perhaps, but none the less formative to settlement patterns and place-names. Later, the conversion of the East Anglian kingdom to Christianity stemmed from contacts with the Frankish world of Merovingian Gaul.

The Normans, like their Viking predecessors, brought continental and Scandinavian influence to the region as they did to other parts of England. The development of towns in the Anglo-Saxon and Norman periods marks, in many respects, the formation of the modern county. Certainly by 1086, the essential urban structure was in place, with the main county towns of Bury St Edmunds and Ipswich together with some of the more important market centres, such as Beccles, Clare, Sudbury and, of course, Dunwich, later to be lost through coastal erosion. The essential administrative structure of the county based on its sub-division into hundreds and shires, or groups of hundreds, was already well established by this date and was not reformed until the late nineteenth century.

The modern county of Suffolk, therefore, retains a territory that is little changed since the time of the Domesday survey. As a

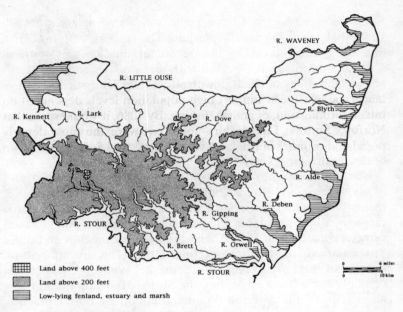

R. WAVENEY

R. LITTLE OUSE

R. Blyth

R. Kennett   R. Lark   R. Dove

R. Alde

R. Deben

R. Gipping

R. STOUR

R. Brett   R. Orwell

R. STOUR

0   6 miles
0   10 km

Land above 400 feet

Land above 200 feet

Low-lying fenland, estuary and marsh

1.4 Suffolk: relief and river systems

county it was relatively unaffected by the Industrial Revolution and
the appearance of new urban centres associated with manufactur-
ing. Even today, although much of the county is within one hundred miles of London, there are no motorways and few rail links;
the flat claylands of central and eastern Suffolk remain pleasantly
rural, but poorly served by public transport. We are therefore able
to study a county which not only retains much of its ancient pattern
of administrative boundaries, but also much of its essential rural
character which has survived into living memory.

Relief, soils and minerals

Suffolk has a very shallow but subtle relief (Figure 1.4). The highest
point, 420 feet (140 metres), is close to the western edge of the
county in the parishes of Chedburgh and Depden, but only one-
third of West Suffolk lies over 300 feet (90 metres) and most of the
rest of the county including almost the whole of East Suffolk lies
under 200 feet (58 metres).

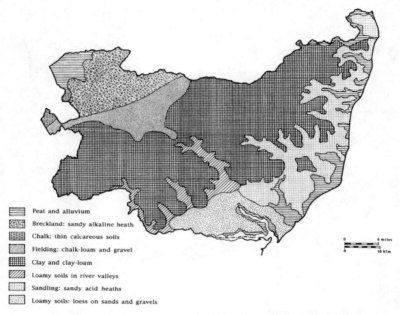

Legend:

- Peat and alluvium
- Breckland: sandy alkaline heath
- Chalk: thin calcareous soils
- Fielding: chalk-loam and gravel
- Clay and clay-loam
- Loamy soils in river valleys
- Sandling: sandy acid heaths
- Loamy soils: loess on sands and gravels

1.5 Suffolk: main soil types (from Trist 1971; Dymond & Martin 1988)

The central landscape of Suffolk is dominated by a flat clay plateau which extends diagonally from Haverhill to Halesworth (Figure 1.5). Although this area is generally referred to as the 'claylands', the soil is variable. The heaviest intractable blue-grey chalky boulder-clay of the Lowestoft till and the sandy coloured Norwich brick-earth, jokingly known to farmers and gardeners as the 'treacle-mines' of Suffolk, contrasts with the mixed loams, pockets of sand and pebble that characterise the clay edge. It is not uncommon to find fields with water-filled clay pits in one corner and dry sand and gravel pits in another. The clays may contain as much as 30–50% chalk nodules and flints, and due to weathering in the late glacial period these frequently appear on the surface as coarse gravel (Corbett & Tatler 1970). Occasionally larger stones appear as glacial erratics on the surface, mostly pulled up by the plough. The upper surface of the clay is by no means consistent, being confused by interglacial deposits, mostly pockets of sands and gravels, which have filled depressions and ice wedges in the

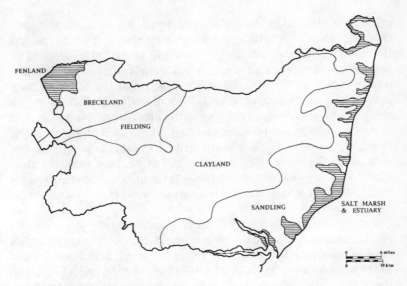

1.6 Suffolk: regions or pays

clay. In consequence the claylands are not easy to cultivate with modern farming methods due to variable moisture retention and pH levels. Underground pipe-drains and mole drains only work with limited success in this difficult subsoil (Curtis *et al*. 1976, 136). In contrast the landscape of West Suffolk is pleasantly hilly, particularly near the border with Cambridgeshire at Lidgate and the chalk downs around Newmarket. Here the soils are sandy loams overlying chalk. With modern deep ploughing, the chalk is frequently exposed; pits to the west of Bury St Edmunds show the chalk at just 1–3 feet below the surface, covered by a coarse loamy sand mixed with flints (Trist 1971, 17). The area north of Bury St Edmunds and south of the Breckland is also more undulating. It is called the Fielding (Figure 1.6) because it lay unenclosed in open strip fields until relatively recent times (Scarfe 1972, 27). Here the depth of the soil varies, and the further north and east of Bury so the soils become more mixed with clay as one moves eastwards towards the pottery kilns of Wattisfield.

West Suffolk sands of the Breckland are also of very low with the chalk loamy sands in the area of West Row shading off into peaty soils of the fen edge (Trist 1971, 16). The thin calcareous sands of the Breckland are frequently alkaline, although showing all the characteristics of heathland. Typical is the Breckland around West Stow where the remarkable survival of bone in the archaeological deposits led to an unusually detailed interpretation of the site. By contrast some of the black to dark grey-brown sands are very acid. The underlying chalk is by no means even; crevices and hollows in the chalk were filled with drift deposits creating contrasting and highly localised soil types. The Breckland soils were clearly attractive to prehistoric settlers, but then they may have been more stable. It was not until the thirteenth century that over-cultivation and minor climatic changes caused them to break down into unstable wind-blown sands (West 1985, 9).

Where small streams run off the clayland on to the sandy gravels of the east coast abrupt slopes are found. Similarly along the clay edge overlooking the Waveney valley there are dramatic views of the rich marshlands of the Norfolk–Suffolk border; and again along the Stour Valley where good views are gained this way into Essex.

The Suffolk Sandling region of the east coast is marked by dry sandy heaths. So acid are the soils in the area east of Woodbridge that very little bone at all survived for archaeologists to study at Sutton Hoo, in marked contrast to the West Suffolk sands. The Sandling is deeply intersected by estuaries of the rivers Deben, Alde and Blyth; here contrasting habitats of salt marsh, shingle, sandy cliffs and open tracts of gorse and heather make one of the most attractive landscapes in England, much of which is now devoted to bird reserves, and Heritage coast. The southern Sandling, from Aldeburgh to Felixstowe, is characterised by the Red Crag. In fact the gravels here vary in colour from the buff Coraline Crag to the red and orange of the Red Crag; indeed, there is a great variety of soil textures throughout the Sandling region (Trist 1971, 18). Powdery wind-blown sands and markedly grey podzolised heathland soils are typical, but there are areas of pebble and shingle gravel which outcrop, most notably at Westleton and Dunwich heath.

The popular misconception that Suffolk is not a mineral-rich county is far from the truth; indeed there are few geological features found in the county that have not been exploited at one time or another. Clay, the most common sub-soil so characteristic of the Suffolk landscape, has been extensively dug and fired into tile and brick since Roman times. Roman kilns at Wattisfield lie close to the present Watson's pottery, still a successful commercial concern. Between 1844 and 1937 there were at least 250 brick kilns recorded in trade directories on the Suffolk claylands (Pankhirst 1988). The range of bricks produced was impressive and the variety of colours is largely dependent on the different types of clay found in the county.

Chalk is found at varying depths over large areas of Suffolk. Although it makes a poor building material, 'clunch' or the harder chalk rock, was used in some medieval church building. Most of the clunch found in West Suffolk churches probably came from Reach, the small port and decayed market town at the northern end of the Devil's Dyke, just outside the county. Chalk was burnt extensively for lime; the kilns and chalk quarries can still be seen at Coddenham. Extensive deep chalk pits are still visible at Brandon. Chalk was also used for marl, but some chalk for marl and lime burning was imported from Kent in the early eighteenth century (Defoe 1991). As late as 1939, Oldershaw and Dunnett were advocating 5–10 tons of chalk marl to the acre for reclaimed Sandling soils between the Orwell and the Deben (Oldershaw & Dunnett 1939, 60).

Flint, derived from silica and fossil sponges, is exposed in the Upper Middle Chalk of West Suffolk (see below) and has been mined since Neolithic times at Grimes Graves in Norfolk. Close by at Brandon in Suffolk, flint of the highest quality was made into gun-flints until very recent times. More significantly, flint was used widely as a decorative building stone for facing most of the medieval churches in the county. Pure black flints are usually quarried from tabular layers 12–30 feet below the surface where they escaped fracture and frosting in glacial times. Flint flush-work on some medieval churches is the result of carefully matching different shades of flint, contrasted sometimes with brown pebble flint quarried from the gravels of the Crag.

Clay marl was also used on most of the light soils. In the early nineteenth century it was said that between ? and 100 cart loads of about 32 bushels each to the acre was considered a suitable dressing for the lighter Suffolk soils (Marshall 1818, 132–3). 'Claying' or marling is well documented in medieval times and many of the pits found in the corners of clayland fields near lighter land may be of considerable age. A marl pit still surviving opposite Thorington church is mentioned in a charter of 1340 and others may be much earlier (Prince 1964; Warner 1982). The most successful marl was undoubtedly the 'coraline' or shelly Crag, dug to a depth of 15–20 feet from the area between Orford and Aldeburgh; it was particularly beneficial for the exploitation of heathland soils although the effect was, it seems, short lived (Marshall 1818, 433).

The crags of the Sandling region of Suffolk also produce high quality sands and gravels. The upper crags, particularly the Westleton Beds now quarried in the area of Reydon and Wangford, provide valuable pebble shingle for mixing concrete. Valuable sands from Henham, Wenhaston and Holton, in the Blyth valley, are used for casting. In the Deben valley at least one sand pit was providing ballast for schooners in the nineteenth century to be sold by the cart load in northern ports (Simper 1972, 69). Countless sand pits are also to be found wherever outcrops appear in the river valleys on the edge of the claylands where small streams drain off the clay plateau and expose the underlying crags. Sand and gravel galls also appear as the result of late glacial activity on the clay plateau.

Coprolites are said to have been discovered by the polymath Professor Henslow while on holiday at Felixstowe in 1843 (Russell-Gebbett 1977, 95). These fossiliferous nodules, with a high phosphate content, are found between the lower Red Crag and the London Clay of south-east Suffolk, particularly in the Shotley peninsula where there was a coprolite 'Gold Rush' between 1845 and 1893 (Trist 1971, 7–8). There was extensive surface digging over much of the Red Crag area, while pits over 20 feet deep, such as those at Waldringfield, allowed ships to transport coprolite to processing plants at Bramford and Kings Lynn. Surface digging of coprolite could be found at any point where the junction of the chalk and gault clay was exposed near the surface, but was dug more extensively over the border into Cambridgeshire (Grove 1976). There can be little doubt that this activity is associated with many archaeological discoveries in the coprolite areas on opposite sides of the county.

Peat was once dug and dried for fuel from most of the drowned valleys of the Suffolk coast and from the fenland west of Mildenhall. Charters from the Blythburgh Priory Cartulary describe peat-workings (turbaries) in the Blyth valley in the twelfth century. The pattern of meadows at Blyford, which once belonged to Blythburgh Priory, reflects the ancient pattern of narrow turbary plots. Elsewhere in the Waveney valley at Ellingham and in the Deben valley at North Meadow, Bromeswell, the same pattern can be seen. These turbaries seem to have gone out of use at an early date in the Middle Ages when the marshes were embanked and converted into more valuable grazing.

In Norfolk it has been established that the Broads were created through inundation of medieval peat-workings in the fourteenth century (Lambert *et al.* 1960). But there is no indication that the smaller broads found along the Suffolk coast, at Benacre, Covehithe, Easton, and Minsmere, were the result of similar turbaries. Little research has been done on these delightful smaller broads and they could yet prove to have a similar origin to their Norfolk counterparts.

Given the mineral resources of the county it is not surprising to find that in almost every parish there are pits, ponds and quarries revealing the underlying geology. This diversity is also reflected in the variety of soil types and landscapes that may be found throughout the county. Mineral extraction, well-digging and the many boreholes that have been sunk in recent years provide the necessary evidence to interpret the underlying geology of Suffolk.

Underlying geology

The geology of the region divides into two types, the drift geology resulting from successive phases of glaciation in recent geological time, and the underlying more ancient solid geology, laid down over many millions of years (Figure 1.7).

Chalk underlies most of the county of Suffolk and forms a substantial foundation under all other deposits; at Lowestoft its base is over 1,000 feet below the surface. The chalk is of ancient marine origin formed from minute shells, plankton and algae deposited over thousands of centuries, sometime between 144 and 65 million years ago. There are recognisable divisions in the chalk forming Lower, Middle and Upper layers. In subsequent millennia, and before the full impact of glaciation, the chalk strata tilted on its eastern side under the present North Sea. A western scarp was thus formed and eventually became the rim of the fenland basin running through Cambridgeshire, West Suffolk and West Norfolk. With erosion and glaciation the chalk along this western rim was planed

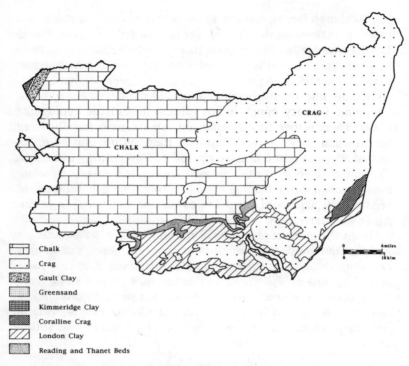

Chalk
Crag
Gault Clay
Greensand
Kimmeridge Clay
Coralline Crag
London Clay
Reading and Thanet Beds

1.7 Suffolk: solid underlying geology (from Chatwin 1961; Wymer 1988)

away to reveal the harder Lower Chalk along the line of the scarp and the Middle Chalk, containing flint, was exposed in West Suffolk and Norfolk. In East Suffolk the Upper Chalk is concealed by Eocene and much later glacial drift material as it lies deep beneath the coast.

In the area between Sudbury and the coast some Eocene deposits are exposed where they overlie the chalk. These appear in three divisions: the Reading and Thanet Beds and the London Clay. The lower Reading and Thanet Beds represent a shallow and turbulent sea with mixed deposits of clayey sands and different coloured stratified clays. They seem to contain no fossils, but weathered out of them appear large blocks of angular sandstone or sarsen 'greywethers', some of which became significant landmarks in prehistoric and later times (Dutt 1926). The London Clay represents a more tranquil sub-tropical sea with fossils of mammals and sharks' teeth from its lower layers. London Clay can be seen underlying the Crag where it is exposed in the Stour, Gipping and Deben river valleys and at the base of the cliffs along the coast at Felixstowe and Bawdsey.

After the end of the Eocene, about 38 million years ago, the succeeding Tertiary epoch is not represented in the geology of Suffolk. There is therefore a significant gap in time before the Crag (the principal shelly gravel deposit of East Suffolk and Norfolk) was laid down over the Eocene clays. The lower 'Coralline' Crag, composed of finely broken shells from a warm sea, derives from the later Pliocene period, from about 3 million years ago. Subsequent Crag deposits date from about 2 million years ago, from the beginning of the Pleistocene and represent a gradually cooling sea and eventually the onset of glaciation. The Red Crag is most notable for large numbers of fossil sea shells (Chatwin 1961, 48). The Norwich Crag can be seen exposed as sand and gravel beds with thin laminated clays in the cliffs north of Aldeburgh for 40 miles along the Suffolk coast. At its base are the stone beds which produce fossil bones of extinct mammals such as mastodon, giant beaver, hyaena and leopard (Chatwin 1961, 51). Successive phases of inundation and shifts from estuarine conditions to open sea, affected also by slight depressions of the land mass and rising sea levels, gave rise to different Crag deposits. The Chillesford Beds of micaceous sand and the Weybourne Crag of mixed clay, sand and pebbles, suggest, from fossil shell remains, an increasingly colder climate.

Overlying drift geology

With the onset of glaciation the upper levels of the preceding geological strata become contorted and affected by severe frosts and brief thaws. These thaws represent intervals between longer periods of glaciation that in turn bring with them geological debris and clays borne along by the ice sheets. Sparks and West admit that the number of glacial advances is not easy to decipher, but at Corton cliff near Lowestoft two layers of glacial till are recognisable, separated by stratified sands (Sparks & West 1972, 146). The upper of the two tills is the distinctive blue-grey chalky boulder clay known as the Lowestoft till, widespread over the claylands of Suffolk and south Norfolk. It is the most commonly found of all the

East Anglian tills and represents the first phase of severe glaciation. The Lowestoft till contains many chalky inclusions and Jurassic erratics picked up to the west of East Anglia. The stone orientation also suggests a west to east movement associated with the Anglian Glaciation. The chalky boulder clay can vary considerably in thickness; a depth of 150 feet is not uncommon in East Suffolk where it is intersected by small streams, while in the highest parts of Suffolk, south-west of Bury St Edmunds, the clay can go down to 230 feet (Chatwin 1961, 66).

The lower of the two tills, the North Sea Drift, consists of two types: a bluish Cromer till, similar to the Lowestoft till, under a more weathered till, the Norwich brick-earth. Although the North Sea Drift contains erratics of Scandinavian origin, they are both thought to belong to the same period of glacial advance, because their stone orientations are similar (Sparks & West 1972, 146–7). The North Sea Drift is represented in Suffolk by the Westleton Beds. These extend from Mundesley in Norfolk to Westleton, where they are clearly visible as the pebbly gravel which forms the basis of the dry heathlands in that part of Suffolk. Originally they formed a pebble beach or shore line of an advancing sea which lay in front of ice sheets moving down from the area north of Scandinavia.

Sub-glacial channels, ground ice depressions and other irregularities in the upper layers of the Lowestoft till are filled with interglacial deposits and material weathered out of the boulder clay, mostly from the Hoxnian temperate interglacial period (Prince 1964). The succeeding glacial period, the Wolstonian, is difficult to interpret, but seems to have left traces in the form of the Gipping till, which is only exposed in the area of Mildenhall and the upper Waveney valley. Stone orientation again suggests movement from the north. The final Ipswichian interglacial and succeeding glaciation have left relatively superficial terraces and alluvial deposits in the river valleys of East Suffolk.

The main rivers are relics of a much earlier and larger river system extending south-east towards the Thames and North Sea basin, all tributaries of the Rhine river system (Straw & Clayton 1979). With the rise in sea-levels in the post-glacial period these tributaries became detached as separate rivers, their once deep gravel valleys becoming infilled with peat and alluvium. In the Waveney valley, which is one of the oldest and deepest, three phases of alluvium are detectable, a lower Flandrian fresh-water peat, a middle Flandrian estuarine silt or clay and an upper Flandrian fresh-water peat overlain by estuarine silts. A similar pattern has been detected in other east coast valleys. In some areas peat is still accumulating in spite of drainage and lowering water-tables. The open salt marshes and great tracts of reed-swamp interspersed with low sand cliffs which are such a feature of the Suffolk coastline continue to be affected by coastal erosion; many acres of land have been lost at Covehithe, Dunwich and Thorpeness.

2

Boudica and beyond

Prehistoric settlement

Archaeological evidence for the prehistoric settlement of East Anglia is now substantial, thanks largely to the work of the Norfolk and Suffolk archaeological units over a twenty-year period and the publications of the Scole Archaeological Committee. Wisely, the archaeologists appreciate that in remote periods of prehistory the division between the two counties is of little consequence; we must always bear in mind the wider picture of the region as a whole. In the later Iron Age and early Roman period East Anglia was a political entity dominated by the Icenian tribe. Their indomitable leader, Queen Boudica, who led them in rebellion against the Romans in AD 60, has become a national figure, as any child who has experienced the rigours of the new National Curriculum will tell you. That the Iceni were a force to be reckoned with is borne out not only by classical writers such as Tacitus and Cassius Dio, but also through the archaeological record where we have evidence for fine metalwork, pottery and coins, not to mention spectacular hoards of gold and silver torcs discovered at Ipswich and Snettisham.

So when does it all begin? When can we first perceive enduring patterns of settlement and consistent foci of wealth and power in the Suffolk landscape? Most striking and consistent is the concentration of archaeological material on the Breckland sands of West Suffolk, and on the light Sandling soils of the coast. These became the core areas for settlement and ritual activity in the region, separated by the claylands which by comparison produce no more than a thin scatter of material throughout prehistory. This imbalance can be seen as far back as the Upper Palaeolithic in East Anglia (Wymer 1984), and, with some minor variations, is continually reaffirmed from the late Neolithic onwards (Dymond & Martin 1988).

These core areas of Suffolk are segments which fit into a wider distribution pattern of archaeological material; the Breckland of West Suffolk and Norfolk, focused on Thetford, extends up to the north Norfolk coast, and following the line of the Icknield Way reaches south to the Chilterns. The Sandling area of East Suffolk, particularly the area just north of Ipswich around Martlesham and Foxhall, is part of a core area extending either side of the Stour into Essex, and south towards Colchester and the Thames valley. Both areas are characterised now by arid heathland soils. In prehistory they were probably more fertile, but just how fertile remains uncertain. Their main deficiencies are the coarse sandy texture of the soil and its natural instability combined with low moisture content caused principally by low rainfall (Murphy 1985, 105). While there may have been minor changes in rainfall at different periods, it is unlikely that there would have been sufficient increase in moisture to counter these main soil deficiencies; indeed, an increase in rainfall might result in increased leaching and loss of nutrients. While their present soil nutrient deficiencies may in part be the result of over-cultivation, this too may have been a problem in the past, particularly in certain periods of prehistory.

More important is the fact that they were districts where communications were good and where populations were concentrated in river valleys. The rivers in turn provided easy ingress for coastal and long-distance trade. They are in marked contrast to the clayland areas where settlement has always been dispersed and communications difficult. The Suffolk clayland plateau also has a marked absence of navigable rivers, except the Waveney and Stour which mark its periphery and the Gipping and the Brett penetrating the clayland from the south. These core areas of settlement on the lighter soils persisted into post-Roman times, for although Roman roads opened up the claylands for settlement, in the post-Roman period the distribution of pagan Anglo-Saxon cemeteries

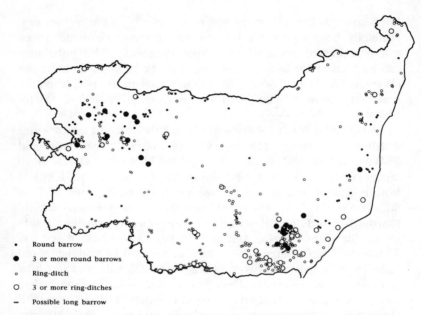

Round barrow
● 3 or more round barrows
○ Ring-ditch
◯ 3 or more ring-ditches
— Possible long barrow

2.1 Suffolk: distribution of barrows and ring-ditches of all periods (from Martin 1981)

and settlements reverts to the old prehistoric model (Figures 3.1 and 4.1).

This model of prehistoric settlement is most marked in the distribution of round barrows and ring-ditches in Suffolk (Figure 2.1), and indeed for East Anglia as a whole (Lawson *et al.* 1981). The barrows and ring-ditches (the latter are generally considered to be barrows that have been ploughed flat) represent the ancient ritual burial grounds of the region. There are a few possible Neolithic long barrows, but most are round barrows which originated in the early Bronze Age. Indeed, from the early Bronze Age in these core areas we begin to see the appearance of a few 'rich' graves containing prestige objects which clearly indicate a differentiated society, where power was focused on certain groups or individuals whose conspicuous wealth was demonstrated in a distinctive burial rite under earth mounds or barrows.

However, many barrows have secondary burials; urned cremations were added in the middle and late Bronze Age, two at

Rougham are Roman, while some, such as the mounds at Sutton Hoo, are as late as the pagan Anglo-Saxon period. At Snape there is evidence for the re-use of a Bronze Age barrow cemetery in the Anglo-Saxon period. The focus of human ritual on these two core areas can be traced back to the early Neolithic: we have evidence from aerial photographs of three causewayed enclosures, one at Fornham All Saints on the southern edge of the Breckland, which is crossed by a linear ditch feature or cursus (Plate 3), another at Freston overlooking the Orwell, with a second cursus a few miles to the south in the Stour valley at Stratford St Mary (Martin 1988), and a third at Kedington near Haverhill. The two cursuses at Fornham and Freston are associated with hengiform concentric ring-ditches although no certain henges have been identified as yet in Suffolk (Martin 1982). The appearance of Grooved ware and imported stone axes suggests the early development of 'a prestige goods economy' and a community that was interacting with its neighbours in systems of trade or exchange (Bradley 1984).

The impression given is that the claylands presented a physical barrier to both the development of settlement and the creation of wealth. There are obvious dangers in this argument. First, there are a number of prehistoric sites on the claylands, including round barrows, and also evidence of earlier Neolithic activity, particularly the distribution of local polished flint axes as opposed to imported stone types which are concentrated in the core areas. True, the clayland barrows are mostly found concentrated in the middle reaches of the river valleys, notably the Stour, Brett and Gipping valleys at the junction of the southern Sandling and clay edge. These valleys may have functioned as overland routes or arteries of interaction linking the Breckland and Sandling areas. There is no doubt that in later prehistory there were also important settlements within the clayland belt running from central Essex through Suffolk and south Norfolk. The distribution of isolated finds, particularly of late Bronze Age metalwork such as socketed axes, suggests a more dispersed pattern of distribution over the claylands (Lawson 1984). A similar pattern for the later Bronze Age appears in Essex (Couchman 1980).

Second, archaeologists are keenly aware that the work of their predecessors was not without regional bias. The Ipswich and District Field-Club, founded in 1903, has a lot to answer for in gathering material in the Gipping valley. Its distinguished members, which included national figures such as James Reid Moir and Nina Layard, ransacked the archaeology of the southern Sandling to the great benefit of Ipswich Museum. The equally distinguished and enthusiastic members of the Bury and West Suffolk Archaeological Institute, founded in March 1848 (later to become the Suffolk Institute of Archaeology in 1853), focused their attentions on the west of the county and the Breckland in particular (Dow 1947). Much of this material went to form the splendid collections in the Moyses Hall Museum at Bury St Edmunds. To a certain extent this east–west bias in the archaeology reflects the administrative divisions of the county with its intellectual focus on the two county towns of Ipswich and Bury. Compounding this problem, these areas have now become the hunting grounds of metal-detector users. The claylands are not only less productive but they are also much more difficult to field-walk and metal-detect. The result has been an ever-increasing imbalance of evidence emphasising the clayland hiatus and focusing attention on the extraordinary finds of gold hoards such as those found by metal-detector users at Snettisham and Thetford.

Third, it cannot be assumed that because archaeological material is concentrated in apparently wealthy core areas that other less well-off adjoining areas have not contributed to this apparent imbalance. Indeed, it is argued that such an imbalance could only be achieved where one area benefited at the expense of another; in the immediate pre-Roman period the imbalance becomes marked in south-east England as the result of imported prestige goods from the expanding Roman Empire (Haselgrove 1982). There can be no doubt that prehistoric communities in the Breckland benefited from their proximity to the resources of the fenland, indeed many of the Bronze Age sites of West Suffolk are on the fen edge. What appear to be the ritual deposition of large numbers of late Bronze Age artefacts in the fen merely highlights the importance of the fenland and the conspicuous expendable wealth of its neighbours. All the products of the fen – fish, eels, peat and wildfowl – would have been acquired and consumed at the focus of population in the adjoining Breckland (Figure 2.2).

So too, the waterways of the fenland may have brought in long-distance trade, particularly stone querns and axes as well as metals and high-status objects such as jet and amber (Shenman 1982). It is the folk of the Breckland who would have profited by trading-on

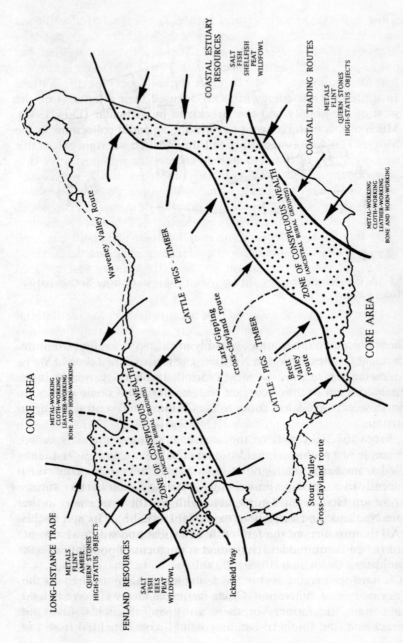

2.2 Suffolk: zones of interaction between core and peripheral areas

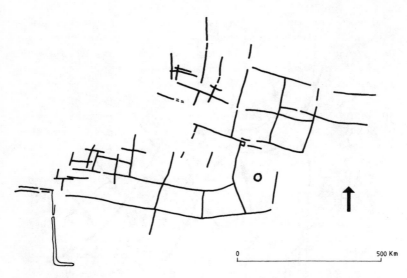

0   500 Km

2.3   A late Neolithic/early Bronze Age field system from Sutton parish (from Copp 1989)

these objects to other areas, possibly in exchange for flint from the mines at Grimes Graves in Norfolk. The route of the Icknield Way, following the line of the west Norfolk chalk ridge, would have enabled them to make contact with more distant communities in north-west Norfolk and south to the Chilterns and central southern Britain.

From the light soils of the Sandling we have the only dated example of a prehistoric field system in Suffolk (Copp 1989). Identified from aerial photography, the ditches have been confirmed recently by excavation underlying the Anglo-Saxon burial mounds at Sutton Hoo and are contiguous with a settlement dated to the late Neolithic and early Bronze Age (Figure 2.3). The soil in this area is now the most extreme acid heathland and can only be cultivated using modern fertilisers and irrigation systems. These prehistoric fields indicate significant soil and climatic change, yet it is hard to imagine such fields being anything more than on the very margin of cultivation. Other resources may well have helped to sustain the farmers of these early Suffolk fields. Like the Breckland, the southern Sandling would have benefited from the products of its adjoining estuaries and sea-shore as well as long-distance coastal trade. Imported stones, metals and prestige goods are evident in the local economy and clearly indicate a similar interaction between neighbouring communities. In this case there is some evidence for overland trade across the clay interior along the valleys of the Stour, Brett and Gipping linking up with the Breckland. Like the fenland and the coastal estuaries, the clayland must have made its contribution to the wealth of these core Breckland and Sandling communities (Figure 2.2).

It is the resources of the clayland, its timber, horses, pigs and cattle, that would have had wider importance. Cattle, wheat and pigs in particular were consumed in large quantities in feasts on or near ritual sites in neighbouring core communities elsewhere in Britain (Bradley 1984, 64). There can be no doubt that the adjoining peripheral areas of fen and clayland were exploited in prehistoric times, but their resources probably contributed to the development of neighbouring communities not towards the peripheral areas themselves. Perhaps they may also have contributed through a shift of human resources as no doubt people were drawn away from the peripheral areas in the time-honoured way to the core areas which were centres of wealth and human interest.

Bradley has commented that, 'the areas with significant concentrations of exotic axes are among the most fertile parts of England' (Bradley 1984, 63). It is difficult to judge the degree to which there have been significant changes in soil types over the region and to what extent this may have affected patterns of settlement. Certainly the Breckland soils suffered a severe deterioration in the early Middle Ages (West 1985, 9), while there is evidence to suggest that drainage and careful deep cultivation have made significant improvements to the clayland soils in the post-medieval period (Trist 1971). We cannot therefore judge by present appearances; the light soils of the Breckland and Sandling may have been easy to cultivate, but they were not without their problems of moisture deficiency and coarse granular texture. It is very doubtful as to whether they were significantly more productive than the clay loams. It is likely that interaction and trade with neighbouring communities were at least equally important for wealth creation as the productivity of the soil, indeed the deficiencies of the lighter soils may have been a stimulus to trade whereby to supply their wants from neighbouring areas.

As we move into the late Iron Age and into the Roman and post-Roman periods there seems to be more and more evidence for conspicuous wealth in these same core areas, in particular the burying of hoards of coins and bullion. We understand little of the motivation for this hoard burying. Some of the recent Snettisham finds suggest a ritual element, deposited perhaps as part of a religious or royal treasury (Stead 1991, 463). Other hoards seem to represent a loss of wealth by individuals at a time of risk. These hoards imply discontinuity and a few individuals who took knowledge of their hoards to the grave. The core areas in which they are found represent not only places advantageous for the acquisition of wealth, but also areas of the greatest risk and political instability, contrasting again with the peripheral fenland and clayland areas.

Thus the prehistoric settlement model for Suffolk with its core and peripheral areas represents a timeless human dilemma: whether to live in a quiet, impoverished backwater in some sleepy clayland community untroubled by the outside world, or to move to the Breckland or Sandling where fortunes were won, lost or buried, where there was the possibility of meeting people and traders from more distant communities and where the rich and powerful might be found acting out their lives and deaths. In graphic terms the clayland and fenland in prehistory represent the slow-lane of security, poverty and boredom, while the Breckland and Sandling represent the fast-lane of insecurity, riches and excitement.

In Roman times the development of the clayland coincides with the appearance of towns and improved communications. The towns, with their market economies, craft and industrial centres, tend to detract from the ancient prehistoric model of settlement and wealth creation. The Roman network of roads cutting across the clayland ameliorated the imbalance of settlement (Figure 3.1). However, the Roman towns and roads were artificial implants on the prehistoric landscape and with the decline of the Roman colonial economy there is a reversion to the old prehistoric model of wealth creation. This reversion coincides with Anglo-Saxon settlement drawn into the old depleted core areas from overseas up the river system of the fenland basin and the estuaries of the Suffolk coast. So the Anglo-Saxons took over the economic and political hot-spots which naturally reasserted their importance as the artificial Roman infrastructure got into economic difficulties and declined. The emergence of towns in the Late Saxon period coincided with a rising tide of population and a need to cultivate more lands at a time when soil exhaustion was beginning to affect the lighter soils. Now the urban infrastructure was the result of natural economic growth and was not in any sense artificial. Eventually the claylands benefited from the development of urban markets and overtook their heathland neighbours in economic importance once and for all.

The Iceni and their origins

The origins of the Iceni are shrouded in mystery. Their weapons and Celtic art-style suggest that they derived from the mainstream of European Iron Age culture (Collis 1984). The old idea of Marnian invasion from France in the third century BC, supported by Rainbird Clarke in 1960, has long since been discredited. However, for some of the southern British Iron Age tribes a continental origin is accepted. The distribution of Gallo-Belgic coins combined with distinctive wheel-made pottery and a cremation burial rite, points towards a strong Belgic presence in the Catuvellaunian and Trinovantian areas north of London, in Hertfordshire and Essex, extending to both sides of the Stour valley and into south Suffolk.

If the Iceni had a continental origin, they must have migrated significantly earlier than the immediate pre-Roman period. Although British derivatives of Gallo-Belgic coins are not uncommon in East Anglia, as they are elsewhere south of the Trent, it is the Icenian coinage which dominates in Norfolk and north Suffolk and is rarely found outside the area and nowhere on the continent. Likewise it is the local hand-made pottery with its long tradition in East Anglian prehistory which predominates. Some scholars have attempted to suggest continental origins for the Iceni on the basis of the name itself. Links have been suggested with the Cenomanni who gave their name to Le Mans, of the Départment de Sarthe in France, but there is nothing apart from a similarity of name to suggest that the Iceni came from this area. This and other suggestions for continental origins are on the whole unconvincing (Rivet & Smith 1979, 374–5).

It is accepted that the Iceni were among the five tribes that submitted to Caesar in 54 BC. The *Cenomagni* as they were then called implies a grouping of tribes, *Iceni magni* indicating a 'stronger' or 'greater' Iceni. We know that Iron Age settlement in East Anglia was split into three principal areas: the Breckland of west Norfolk, the Sandling of East Suffolk and the area of north-west Norfolk. This coming together and recognition perhaps of a common ethnicity between these areas may have been prompted by the threat of invasion from Rome. There are also three different tribal sections of the Iceni identifiable from their coins, a pattern similar to other tribes such as the Dobunni and the Coritani (Nash 1987). It has been suggested that these represent federated group-ings, probably without a single overlord in the first instance, but representing a 'progressive steepening of the political hierarchy' which eventually resulted in kingdoms being established (Nash 1987, 141).

Unfortunately the distribution of different Icenian coin types does not correlate with the three main areas of archaeological material. But the tribal name itself clearly had political implications for it appears on the coins variously as ECEN, ECENI, ECN, ECE and CEN, while some have the names of rulers on the obverse (Allen 1970). The use of dual names in this way follows the pattern of Coritannian coins and those of Cunobelinus of the Trinovantes, neighbours of the Iceni (Martin 1993). Unusual also is the use of ICINOS, the tribal name on its own for the Roman provincial capital at Caistor St Edmond (near Norwich), as it appears in the Antonine Itinerary, while the Ravenna Cosmography uses *Venta Cenomum* (Rivet & Smith 1979, 374).

So a local origin for the Iceni is suggested in East Anglia formed from the political unification of three or more distinct concentra-tions of Iron Age populations. These groups, which seem to share a very similar material culture, and by implication perhaps a com-mon ethnicity, combined sometime before 54 BC and then went from strength to strength until their complete conquest by the Romans following the Boudican revolt of AD 60. Their hand-made pottery is unremarkable and suggests a long local tradition of pre-historic pottery making. This tradition dominates in the face of fine wheel-thrown Belgic techniques that are such a feature of Catuvellaunian and Trinovantian areas to the south and west in the immediate pre-Roman period (Figure 2.4).

Belgic pottery appears in the upper Stour valley where there are two Belgic cremation cemeteries at Boxford (Rainbird Clarke 1960, 52; Moore *et al.* 1988). Some Belgic penetration is also evident in West Suffolk, at Lakenheath and Elveden where in 1888–9 Sir Arthur Evans noted the discovery of pottery similar to the classic Aylesford wheel-made Belgic pottery. Here the pottery was associated with a bronze tankard in late La Tène style datable to the immediate pre-Roman period (Rainbird Clarke 1939, 55). However, these were associated with inhumation burials rather than the Belgic style of cremation.

The tribal territory

The Icenian territory was bordered by the sea on the east and north, and by the fenlands of the Wash basin on the west, but to the south there was no fixed geographical boundary and it is here that we have some difficulty in determining the Icenian frontier. Some writers have indicated that the whole of the Sandling area of East Suffolk lay in Trinovantian hands (Phillips & River 1962). Others, such as Webster, see the Stour as the dividing line (Webster 1978). But given recent finds of Icenian coins in the area of the Gipping valley near Ipswich and the excavations at Burgh-by-Woodbridge by the Suffolk Archaeological Unit in 1975, the southern Icenian boundary needs a more careful explanation.

The distribution of Iron Age coins in East Anglia, when combined with finds of distinctive late Iron Age horse trappings and metalwork, provide clues about social grouping and tribal boundaries (Figure 2.4) (Gregory 1977; Cunliffe 1981; Martin 1989a). Descriptions given to us by Roman writers, particularly Tacitus's account of the Boudican revolt in AD 60, make it clear that the Iceni were bordered on the south-east by the Trinovantes, on the south-west by the Catuvellauni and on the north-west by the Coritani. As such the Iceni lay between the more romanised tribes of southern England and the more barbarian tribes of the north (Nash 1987, 141; Millett 1990). However, these tribal territories are unlikely to have been very stable and the distribution of coins and hoards of metalwork are not entirely coincidental (Martin 1989a). We must therefore accept a degree of fluidity, particularly on the southern and western boundaries of the Icenian tribal territory.

The metalwork on its own is not a wholly reliable indicator of Icenian territory. The distribution of horse trappings and in particular the fine bronze chariot fittings or terret rings decorated in champlevé red enamel in late La Tène style may be deceptive.

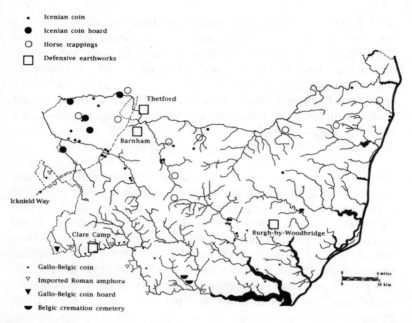

Icenian coin

Icenian coin hoard

Horse trappings

Defensive earthworks

Thetford

Barnham

Icknield Way

Clare Camp

Burgh-by-Woodbridge

Gallo-Belgic coin

Imported Roman amphora

Gallo-Belgic coin hoard

Belgic cremation cemetery

6 miles

10 klm

2.4 Suffolk: distribution of Iron Age sites and finds (from Gregory 1977; Cunliffe 1981; Martin 1989a)

Some of these objects, such as one found in a garden in Weybread, have come to light recently (Martin 1978), while others have been known about for many years, such as the complete set of eight terrets of three different sizes (Figure 2.4), discovered at Westhall in 1855 (Rainbird Clarke 1939; Spratling 1972) (Plate 4). The Westhall terrets were found among a mass of Roman pottery and a coin of Faustina (*c.* AD 125); other Roman metalwork, including a number of bronze bowls and a bronze lamp, has an uncertain association with this hoard, but a mid-Roman context seems highly likely. Although a significant number of these terrets are found in Icenian areas, others are widely scattered, with examples from Scotland, Somerset and Germany (Spratling 1972). It would be dangerous, therefore, to use this material as an indicator of the extent of Icenian territory.

The distribution of defensive sites, or 'lowland hill-forts' for want of a better term in East Anglia, is just as important as the distribution of coins when coming to terms with this territory (Figure 2.4). There are few natural defensive sites in East Anglia comparable to those found on the limestone hills of the West Midlands. Every inch of the Iron Age forts of our region had to be dug out by hand. It is not surprising, therefore, to find that most are small and on or near potential boundaries. Until recently it was thought that Tasburgh in south Norfolk was a central Iron Age citadel of 6.2 hectares. Excavations in 1979 produced only 43 Iron Age pot-sherds, no evidence of Romano-British occupation and no Early Saxon finds; instead there were large quantities of Late Saxon Thetford ware in and around the ditches which effectively proved that it was built in the tenth century AD (Davies *et al.* 1992, 31). It is now considered that the impressive site at Gallow Hill, Thetford, is central to the late Iron Age of the Breckland, but whether it was a defensive site or a temple remains uncertain (Gregory 1981). Recent excavations at Barnham, a small double-ditched rectangular enclosure of just 1 hectare, suggest that this might have preceded Thetford as an Icenian stronghold, but no internal buildings were found, nor are there any internal features visible on aerial photographs (Martin 1993).

Wandlebury, in Cambridgeshire, was probably in Catuvellaunian territory and seems to have guarded the line of the Icknield Way from Icenian attack. Clare Camp, on Clare Common, guarded the upper reaches of the River Stour. Its impressive earthworks are described as being Iron Age (Rainbird Clarke 1939, 48). Their location on the Icenian side of the Stour might suggest that the earthworks defended Icenian territory. Although Iron Age pottery and at least one Trinovantian coin has been found at Clare, the earthworks of Clare Camp remain essentially undated (Martin 1989b, 60). Recent excavations at Sudbury suggest that there was a triple ditched enclosure in the late Iron Age, corresponding with the circuit of the Middle Saxon town defences, looking south over the Stour valley. Certainly this was a high-status site, but more excavation is need to determine its full extent and its tribal affiliation (Newman 1990).

Burgh is well placed near Woodbridge to guard the northern Sandling of East Suffolk (Figure 2.4). Excavations at Burgh suggest that this was a major defensive site of 7 hectares, possibly a minor *oppida*, large enough to be a defended regional centre in its own right (Plate 5). Part of the site continued in use into the Roman period with a substantial villa constructed in one corner. Remarkably, it produced no Iron Age coins, but this reinforces its function as a defensive site rather than a market centre (Martin 1988). The initial phase of construction at Burgh produced only hand-made native pottery, without any indication of influence from Belgic tribes to the south. Following a destruction phase, Belgic pottery of the Camulodunum type makes its appearance, during which time the ditch was silting up and out of use. Dating evidence from this phase suggests a period contemporary with Catuvellaunian expansion under Cunobelinus in about AD 15–25. At or about the time of Roman conquest a smaller fort of just 1 hectare was constructed in the north-west corner, but the ditch was not of Roman military type. It was suggested by the excavator that this may have represented 'a reassertion of original tribal territory following the downfall of the Catuvellaunian and Trinovantian empire at the hands of the Romans in AD 43' (Martin 1988, 73).

The implications of these excavations are that the southern Icenian boundary was essentially unstable and contested on more than one occasion. The fort at Burgh was probably first built as an Icenian outpost in the face of combined Trinovantian and Catuvellaunian aggression. It was subsequently lost when the Icenian boundary must have moved substantially further north, perhaps to a line nearer the Alde, as suggested by some writers (Phillips & River 1962). Clare Camp may also have been lost at this time although there is insufficient archaeological evidence to be certain. A strong Belgic presence is evident in the Stour and Brett valleys with a significant number of Gallo-Belgic coins and two Belgic cemeteries at Boxford. With the Roman conquest of tribes to the south and the establishment of the Icenian client kingdom of Prasutagus, Burgh may have been restored to the Iceni. But after a minor revolt in AD 48 they were no longer allowed to bear arms and, to judge from the very few coins with PRASTO or SUBIPRASTO inscriptions, Prasutagus was no longer allowed to mint his own coins in the years leading up to AD 60 (Webster 1978, 48).

The Boudican revolt

On the death of Prasutagus in AD 60 and following brutalities committed by the Romans against Queen Boudica and her daughters, the Iceni rose in revolt rather than submit to colonisation. The causes of the revolt are complex and the outrages committed by Roman troops against the Icenian royal family were merely the sparks that ignited a general conflagration. The Iceni joined forces with their old enemies, the Trinovantes, and set about the systematic destruction of the new Roman towns of Colchester, London and Verulamium. This was widely recognised as one of the most serious revolts ever experienced in a new Roman province (Webster 1978).

Under the inept government of Nero, corruption and misappropriation of public and private property had got out of hand. One contemporary Roman official commented cynically that he needed to make three fortunes, one to pay his way, another for bribes and a third to retire on (Webster 1978, 88). We hear of heavy taxes being imposed in order to build the temple of Claudius at Camulodunum and with it the appropriation of Trinovantian lands to provide for retired soldiers in the new colonial town. Attempts to disarm all the tribes east of the Trent and Severn in AD 48 had met with limited success. The outright hostility of the Iceni at this time suggests that any such policy was ineffective in areas controlled by this extensive client kingdom. Tribal land was probably regarded by the British as inalienable and the whole idea of client kingdom status may have meant two entirely different things to both parties. Certainly the Iceni were not expecting to lose all their land as well as their independence on the death of their king. Conversely, it was probably regarded as normal practice by the Romans for all the lands and estates of a client ruler to fall into a provincial governor's hands on the death of the incumbent. Under the lax government of Nero this may have given licence for a free-for-all among local Roman officials.

Prasutagus had no male heir. In the northern Celtic world, particularly in Britain, female tribal rulers were not uncommon and like the northern Picts, the process of inheritance may have followed the matrilineal line of succession. But the very notion of women holding high office was unacceptable to southern Classical society. To get around this problem Prasutagus had nominated the Emperor Nero as co-heir with his two daughters. This was clearly anomalous. It seems that Boudica tried to intervene, but with disastrous results. The Romans not only underestimated the power of a woman scorned but also her personal qualities of leadership. There may also have been a religious dimension. To what extent the royal family was itself the subject of veneration we shall never know, but it has been suggested that the revolt was timed to coincide with the attack by Suetonius Paulinus on the Druidic enclave of Anglesey. Unfortunately we know nothing about the religious beliefs of the Iceni (Webster 1978).

The ferocity and violence of the revolt took the Romans by surprise, and with the destruction of emerging urban centres at Colchester, London and Verulamium the province of Britain itself seemed threatened. Casualties were high. If we accept the round figures given by Tacitus, there were 70,000 dead on the Roman side following the destruction of the three provincial centres and 80,000 tribespeople killed in the final battle, most of whom were probably Iceni; the basis of these figures is probably accurate (Webster 1978, 99). Cassius Dio mentions horrific atrocities committed by the rebels, but these were more than matched by Roman brutalities as the Icenian and Trinovantian territories fell to the vengeance of Suetonius Paulinus. Such was the scale of destruction that Roman troops had to be kept under canvas until the following year. Tacitus reports how the region was laid waste and famine overtook the land (Webster 1978).

After AD 60 the Iceni lost their client kingdom status, but not their identity. It became clear that Suetonius Paulinus was not without blame for the outbreak of the Boudican revolt, although it was accepted that he had shown considerable bravery and coolness of head in winning the final battle against overwhelming odds. The new Procurator Fiscal, Julius Classicianus (his predecessor had fled in an undignified manner to Gaul), perceived that the resulting devastation was not good for tax collection and that a new policy was needed. A concerted effort was then made to rehabilitate the Iceni and to establish a long-term policy of reconciliation. More subtle policies of exploitation were initiated with the development of a colonial Roman economy, based on urban growth and involvement of the natives in administration. It was normal practice for the Roman authorities to utilise the pre-existing tribal hierarchy and incorporate it within the local colonial administrative system. Thus the tribal territory became the *territorium* administered from a smart new Roman town, *Venta Icenorum*, itself the tribal and provincial capital. A few generations after the Boudican revolt we can imagine tribal elders presiding in the *ordo* or town council in the basilica at the heart of the new provincial town. Integration proved

36

so popular that, as Tacitus comments: 'the population was gradually led into the demoralizing temptations of arcades, baths, and sumptuous banquets. The unsuspecting Britons spoke of such novelties as "civilization", when in fact they were only a feature of their enslavement' (Agricola 21).

There are some startling archaeological finds from Suffolk which may well be legacies of the Boudican revolt. A bronze head of the Emperor Claudius, probably from an equestrian statue, found in 1907 in the mud of the River Alde at Rendham, is one of the great treasures from Suffolk to be seen in Colchester Museum. Just life size, it may be too small to have come from the great temple of Claudius at Camulodunum. This symbol of oppression was hacked violently from its body as the metal indicates. The glass eyes were gouged out and it was bashed vigorously on the back of the head. Was this some trophy of the Icenian rebels, flung into the river on their retreat when the threat of Roman retribution was at hand and the plunder became too hot to handle, or was it an offering to the gods?

Other material, which may be loot from the sack of Camulodunum, is contained in the Hockwold Treasure from Norfolk. This badly damaged hoard of finely-decorated Roman silver table-ware consists of five double-handled wine cups and two bowls (Toynbee 1964, 302–3). It was almost certainly deposited at about this time. More relevant to Suffolk is the Hawkedon Helmet. This massive object of tinned bronze, weighing over five and a half pounds, was ploughed up in 1965. It is the type of helmet used by gladiators when practising for the arena. As such it can only have come from a large town such as Camulodunum where there must have been a gladiatorial school (Painter 1967). It is suggested that the rebels won on to their side slaves and gladiators from the towns they overran, some of whom seized this opportunity to taste freedom, however briefly, regardless of the terrible consequences (Webster 1978, 125–6).

3

Roman Suffolk

Roads, forts and towns

Roman settlement in East Anglia followed in the aftermath of the Boudican revolt. The framework of military roads was probably laid down in the years immediately following AD 60 (Figure 3.1). Military marching camps have been identified from the air at Horstead-with-Stanningfield, Norfolk, at Stuston near Diss on the Norfolk–Suffolk border and at Baylham House, Coddenham, where two forts have been identified as superimposed cropmarks (Moore *et al.* 1988, 22). The main Roman road from Colchester to Venta Icenorum was found to overlie the smaller of these two forts and a date of *c.* AD 70 was established for the building of the road (West 1956). At Pakenham near Ixworth an early military site with a triple ditch enclosure seems in later years to have developed into a small town (Plate 6). Preliminary results from excavation in advance of the Ixworth by-pass indicate that this, too, was a post-Boudican campaign fort, which was not long occupied by the army before being rapidly developed as a market centre (Plouviez 1986). The early Roman settlement at Coddenham, on the main road (Iter IX) from Colchester to Venta Icenorum, may have been a military staging post (Margary 1973). Likewise at Scole, where the line of the same Roman road, still in use as the A140 from Ipswich to Norwich, crosses the Waveney, a bridge-head settlement was established, probably on a military base. At Bungay there is evidence of Roman and Iron Age settlement close to the Wainford, where

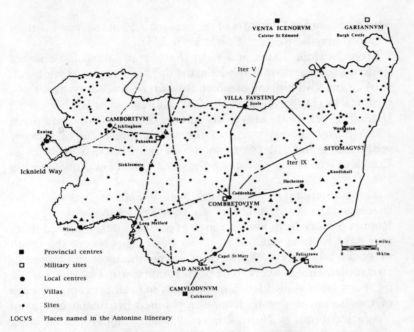

3.1 Suffolk: distribution of Roman sites and finds in relation to known Roman roads and places named in the Antonine Itinerary (from Moore *et al.* 1988)

Stone Street crosses the Waveney near Bungay (Margary 1973, No. 36).

The continued use of the pre-Roman Icknield Way and the development of *Camboritum* (Icklingham) which was clearly dependent upon it is particularly interesting. It has been suggested by Scarfe that place-names such as Icklingham and Ixworth may have some etymological link with the Iceni, but more recent work has cast doubt on this theory (Scarfe 1976; Warner 1988). Other less well-attested trackways may also be of pre-Roman origin such as the road known in the Middle Ages as 'Pilgrims Way' or 'Peddarisway' (not to be confused with the Peddars Way of west Norfolk), which runs from Beccles towards the coast south of Dunwich (Figure 3.6). This route appears to pre-date an early medieval network of roads radiating out of Dunwich and indeed it seems also to pre-date coastal erosion further south (Warner 1982).

Scarfe has argued that parts of the present A12 in the area north of Yoxford may be Roman (Scarfe 1986, 143).

From Norfolk, Essex and Kent there is an increasing body of evidence to suggest that the Romans utilised the pre-existing network of trackways many of which still survive as country lanes and farm tracks (Drury & Rodwell 1980; Williamson & Bellamy 1987; Higham 1992). There also exists a network of trackways and roads which bridge the clayland interfluves and link areas of primary settlement in the valleys running down to the coast. Some such as Cookley Green Lane give an impression of great antiquity (Warner 1982).

The Roman development of Suffolk is well attested in the archaeological record; there is no shortage of mid-first century Roman pottery from a wide range of Suffolk sites. Many of these may have become established under Prasutagus before the revolt of AD 60, but the establishment of towns, the most romanised of civil settlements, is likely to be post-Boudica. The fact that Suffolk lacks any large walled Roman town may in itself be a consequence of the Boudican revolt. Even the planned provincial capital of Venta Icenorum in Norfolk is small when compared with other *Civitas* capitals (Wacher 1974, 229; 1978, 74). This is surprising given its extremely large and agriculturally rich market catchment area, which was in effect the whole of the old Icenian tribal territory. Nevertheless, enough centres can be identified to suggest a fairly even distribution of market towns and villages over the county (Moore *et al.* 1988, 57). Not surprisingly the main centres, which have a number of well appointed villas in their vicinity, lie close to, if not on, the arterial roads. Scole, Coddenham and Capel St Mary in the centre of the county lay on Iter IX, and Pakenham, Sicklesmere and Long Melford to the west of the county lay on Margary's route 33a, with Icklingham on the north-west lying on the Icknield Way (Figure 3.1). To the east large centres are thinner on the ground, but those at Wenhaston and Knodishall have only recently been discovered and a number of coins from Thorpeness and Covehithe may indicate that substantial settlements there were lost through coastal erosion. Another, as yet unlocated, centre is implied at the convergence of Roman roads in the area of Sibton and Peasenhall (Figure 3.2). Recent work on the configuration of parish boundaries and trackways combined with field-name evidence from medieval sources in this area, points strongly towards

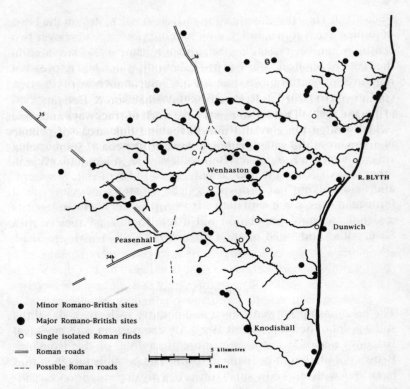

3.2 The Blyth valley: distribution of Roman sites and roads (from Warner 1982)

the presence at Peasenhall of another minor Roman town (Warner 1982, fig. 35).

The main arterial roads with their major named centres seem clear enough, but the minor Roman road pattern, particularly in East Suffolk, lacks logic; short lengths of road seem to have no purpose in that they lead nowhere, while others converge on apparently blank areas of the map (Figure 3.1). These simply reflect our ignorance of the Roman landscape. Apart from field surveys focused on specific areas and excavations by the Suffolk Archaeological Unit in advance of road building, there has been remarkably little systematic work done on Roman settlement for the county. There has been no major excavation of a villa in Suffolk since 1959. Thus the classification of Roman villa sites on the basis of limited excavations, isolated finds and reports accruing over two centuries can be misleading. Sites such as the 'villa' excavated in the 1930s at Stanton, near Bury St Edmunds, which had a spread of buildings and bath-houses over 300 feet long and where occupation continued from AD 130 to the 390s, might equally well be classified as part of a small urban complex (Moore *et al.* 1988, 51).

There are also concentrations of highly romanised settlements in some areas, for example north-west of Ipswich in the Gipping valley and in the Kennet and Lark valleys near Mildenhall, while in other areas, such as the middle Waveney and Blyth valleys systematic field-walking has brought to light a pattern of many small farmstead sites, some with native Iron Age pottery, which suggests a significant rural population but a less romanised society with fewer villas and small towns (Warner 1982, 48–57; Moore *et al.* 1988, 56–9).

Town and country

The relationship between town and country in Roman Britain is still a point of debate (Millett 1990). By comparison with medieval Britain we should not expect more than 15% of the Romano-British population to be living in towns, and possibly less than that in an area with markedly small towns heavily dependent on agriculture such as East Anglia. However, our understanding of the scale of rural settlement in Roman Britain has been transformed in recent years and nowhere is this more evident than in Suffolk. Due to a combination of aerial photography and field-walking, large numbers of small Romano-British farmstead sites and villages have come to light – part of what has been described as a quantitative explosion in archaeological knowledge (Taylor 1983). Added to this is the popular sport of metal-detecting, which has itself resulted in the honest discovery of many important Roman sites in the county, but also, alas, the illegal plundering of other listed Roman monuments and the scattering of unprovenanced material onto the international antiquities market.

The rate of discovery has been remarkable. In 1960, when Rainbird Clarke published his distribution map of Roman East Anglia (Rainbird Clarke 1960, fig. 29) only three minor settlements were noted in the Blyth valley and few others in East Suffolk as a whole. By 1982 this figure had risen to nearly fifty (Figure 3.2). In those places where the full pattern can be recovered, small Romano-British farmstead sites are to be found at intervals of 1 kilometre along the gravel soils of the valley sides in prominent positions overlooking the meadows, while on the heavier clayland soils above the valleys in the interfluves, the farms lie in more isolated positions. In parts of Suffolk where detailed surveys have been carried out, at Flixton and Mendham in the Waveney valley and in the Deben and Blyth valleys, we can perceive a fully developed landscape, one which has its origins in the late Iron Age and which was significantly expanded in the first and second centuries AD. In some respects it was a landscape very comparable to the late Middle Ages or early Tudor period (Warner 1982; Newman 1988; Hardy 1989a & b).

The quality of material life evident on these small rural sites in the first and second centuries seems very acceptable. Wheelmade, locally produced, utilitarian grey-ware pottery is abundant; fragments of roof tiles and the occasional box-flue tile, presumably for chimney flues, are also common. A few sherds of imported Samian ware can be expected on all but the very smallest farmstead sites. Iron tools, coins and small pieces of fine bronze metalwork such as fibula brooches abound, suggesting a strong local market economy which must surely have been urban based. Small-scale metalworking sites are known to have existed at Hacheston, Beck Row, Mildenhall, and Ixworth (Plouviez 1986; Moore *et al.* 1988).

As yet it is not possible to establish the market catchment areas, although from a scientific analysis of the clay used in the locally-made pottery, this must be possible. Certainly there were large-scale pottery production centres around Wattisfield, at Rickinghall and Hinderclay. Others on West Stow heath and at Pakenham served the west of the county while kilns at Coddenham, Hacheston and Homersfield served the East Suffolk markets. No doubt other production centres have yet to be found. Along the coastal belt salt production must have been as significant as it was in medieval times and presumably was traded well inland. Salt-pans have been found at Trimley, Snape, Iken and Blythburgh (Moore *et al.* 1988, 60–8). In the first and second centuries we can build up a picture of a prosperous, populated landscape, filled up with farms and villages surrounded by well tilled fields. But there remain many blank areas of the map where more systematic field surveys would certainly reap dividends.

Layering in the landscape

The Romans took over a landscape which was already very old and in East Anglia it is possible to see Roman roads overlying earlier field systems, where in some cases both roads and fields have remained in continuous use. Williamson's work suggests that the coaxial field systems found either side of the Waveney valley and which are crossed diagonally by the Pye Road (the Roman road from Colchester to Venta Icenorum), essentially belong to a pre-Roman landscape extending over many square miles, similar perhaps to the reaves of Dartmoor, dated by Fleming to between 1500 and 1200 BC (Fleming 1988; Williamson 1993, fig. 2.1). Williamson has also identified coaxial field patterns in Suffolk at Yaxley where modern fields can clearly be seen crossed diagonally by the Roman road (Figure 3.3).

The dating of these fields in Suffolk and Norfolk is still problematic and not all of them may be as old as has been suggested, but the best parallel from modern archaeology is the small group of prehistoric fields discovered and dated recently as part of the Sutton Hoo project and illustrated in Chapter 2 (Figure 2.3). The ditches extending away from the site, which were noticed on aerial photographs, were found to underlie the Anglo-Saxon burial mounds and were clearly associated with a settlement of the late Neolithic and early Bronze Age (Copp 1989). Williamson has identified other coaxial field systems in the Stonham–Crowfield area (Figure 3.6, area B) (Williamson 1989), while others at South Elmham and Ilketshall, either side of the Stone Street Roman road, it is argued, may be of early Roman date (Figure 3.4) (Bigmore 1973; Warner 1982).

This work is of far-reaching importance for it suggests that the essential underlying pattern of modern lanes and field boundaries on the south Norfolk and north Suffolk clayland landscape may be of prehistoric or early Roman origin. Williamson's argument is based on ideas first put forward by Flinders Petrie in the nineteenth century: the concept of 'unconformable or conformable juxtapositions' in the landscape (Drury & Rodwell 1980, 59). The fact that the Roman road at Yaxley does not conform to the field pattern,

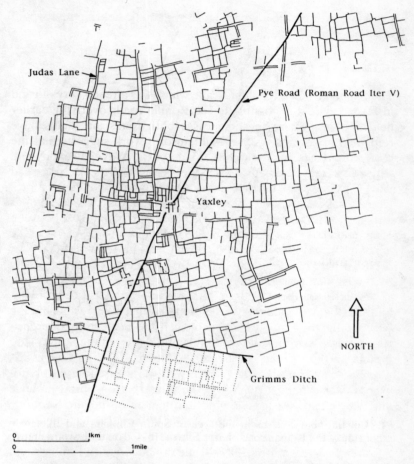

Judas Lane

Pye Road (Roman Road Iter V)

Yaxley

NORTH

Grimms Ditch

0 ————— 1km
0 ———————————— 1mile

3.3 Nonconformity demonstrated at Yaxley, Suffolk, where the Roman Pye Road overlies earlier rectangular field systems (from Williamson & Bellamy 1987). The Roman Pye Road (modern A140) cuts through an organised coaxial field system around Yaxley. The Grimms Ditch is a possible late Roman or early Anglo-Saxon linear earthwork with field systems to the south aligned upon it (after Scarfe 1986)

but is diagonal to it, indicates that the road is later than the field boundaries (Figure 3.3). Here the Roman road almost certainly dates to the period immediately after AD 60, but can the clayland coaxial field patterns all be as old as the fragmentary example from

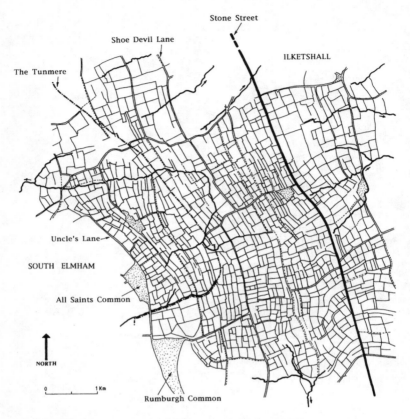

3.4 Coaxial field systems in the area of South Elmham and Ilketshall either side of the Roman road of Stone Street (based on tithe award maps)

the parish of Sutton, where they have long since disappeared under the light Sandling soil?

The examples put forward by Williamson are of late surviving rectilinear coaxial field systems, found on the flat clay tablelands of Norfolk and Suffolk. They extend well away from the lighter, more accessible soils of the river valleys and must represent areas of secondary colonisation. Other examples, which may be just as old, have curvilinear boundaries. These are particularly noticeable at breaks in surviving Roman roads, where they cross minor river valleys which intersect the clay plateau (Warner 1987). For exam-

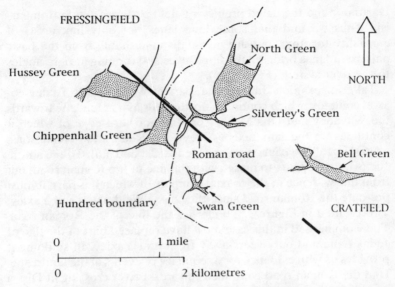

3.5 Nonconformity demonstrated at Fressingfield, Suffolk, where the Roman road (Margary 35) overlies earlier curvilinear boundaries (from Warner 1987)

ple, at Fressingfield a minor Roman road overlies a curvilinear pattern of greens and commons (Figure 3.5).

These field systems seem to be extreme examples, which appear at first sight in isolation atypical of the Suffolk landscape as a whole, but this is not necessarily the case. By no means all the Suffolk landscape is flat and covered by regular field systems of this type, yet Williamson's theories, which have now received wide acceptance, may well focus on the exceptions which prove a rule. These coaxial field systems fit into a much wider pattern of trackways and boundaries which can be seen extending over large parts of the region. Distinctive elements of Williamson's coaxial field systems are the long lanes and drifts that extend for many miles beyond the areas he selected for study. The essence of the coaxial pattern is not so much the grid pattern of fields, but the linear pattern of boundaries running in parallel, roughly north–south, with shorter east–west divisions bridging the longer north–south boundaries. This basic pattern is true also for the reaves of

Dartmoor and the dated prehistoric field pattern from Sutton parish. Thus we find that some long lanes not only link areas of coaxiality together, but are also indistinguishable from the basic pattern of lanes bridging the interfluves and running at right angles to the river system (Figure 3.6).

Take for example Judas Lane, part of Williamson's Yaxley coaxial complex, which continues northwards as a green lane towards the Waveney and Diss Mere, from the northern edge of which it continues on the same axis as Heywood Road into Williamson's south Norfolk coaxial complex (Figures 3.3 and 3.6). To the south, Judas Lane appears to merge with the line of the Roman road, but from the evidence of the coaxial complex of which it is part, it must pre-date the Roman road since the coaxial field pattern at Yaxley, as presented in Figure 3.3, underlies the line of the Roman road. The Roman road in this case must have replaced part of the line of Judas Lane and only veers away from it at Yaxley. In so doing it provides us with evidence for a sequence of events in the landscape. Had the Roman road continued towards a river crossing at Diss a very different interpretation might have been placed on the Yaxley coaxial field complex, for it would have aligned with the Roman road and would have appeared to be contemporary with it. Roman roads which replace or duplicate pre-existing trackways have been demonstrated in other counties including Kent, Warwickshire and Essex (Phythian-Adams 1978; Drury & Rodwell 1980; Everitt 1986; Higham 1992).

The long lanes of Norfolk and Suffolk are one of the regions' most charming and enigmatic features. Some of them survive as modern roads and tracks, while others tail off into field boundaries and footpaths, or are continued in the line of parish and hundredal boundaries. Some are several miles long while others are relatively short; many conform to a coaxial pattern of the type highlighted by Williamson, but others run at right angles to the dominant coaxial pattern, sometimes acting as a terminus to a group of coaxial lanes. This is strikingly similar to the pattern, observed by Fleming, in the reaves of Dartmoor and by Drury and Rodwell in Essex, and it is also discernible on a smaller scale in the Neolithic and early Bronze Age field system from Sutton parish (Drury & Rodwell 1980; Fleming 1988; Copp 1989).

In Figure 3.6 an impression is given of the general pattern of coaxial lanes, trackways and boundaries over a large area of north-east Suffolk and south Norfolk, taking in those areas of coaxial field complexes already illustrated in Figures 3.3–3.5. It has to be said that few of these lanes and boundaries are of known date, but each one conforms to a linear pattern of boundaries running in parallel, either related to a coaxial field pattern or to a pattern of lanes at right angles to the river system. Such a pattern of long lanes in parallel is similar to the 'droves' which cross the North Downs of Kent only a half-mile or so apart. Alan Everitt has linked these 'droves' to an ancient pattern of transhumance – a seasonal migration of pigs and swineherds which exploited the remote wood-pastures of the Weald of Kent (Everitt 1986, 36; Higham 1992, 130).

The relationship between these East Anglian coaxial long lanes and Roman roads and rivers is at first glance bewilderingly complicated, but it is none the less revealing. When attempting to describe the reaves of Dartmoor, Fleming used the word 'awesome'. The confines of this book fail utterly to reveal the true grandeur of these long East Anglian lanes and tracks. They are no less awesome than the Dartmoor reaves, for they too are relics of an ancient landscape, as they drift gently and timelessly over the land reminding us of a lost uncluttered world in which they were created.

What we see now is a tangled network of lines, appearing layer upon layer in a vast palimpsest of landscape history. There are marked differences in this network pattern from one area of Figure 3.6 to another. On the flat clayland interfluves either side of the Waveney valley, long irregular parallel lanes and boundaries dominate the landscape, while further south, where the landscape is interrupted by river systems, shorter lanes bridge the narrower interfluves at right angles to the rivers, also in parallel, but twisting and turning with the meander of the stream. This pattern can be seen clearly in the Gipping and Deben valleys. Both Waveney and Gipping/Deben systems are essentially the same; it is a difference of scale, with the width and flatness of the clayland interfluves accentuating the length of the lanes either side of the river valley. These are, of course, the areas of extreme regularity selected by Williamson and others.

It is as if a net were lowered gently over the landscape so that where it fell on flat ground the linear pattern of the net remains more or less unchanged, but where it fell on uneven ground the pattern of the net became deformed and distorted by the

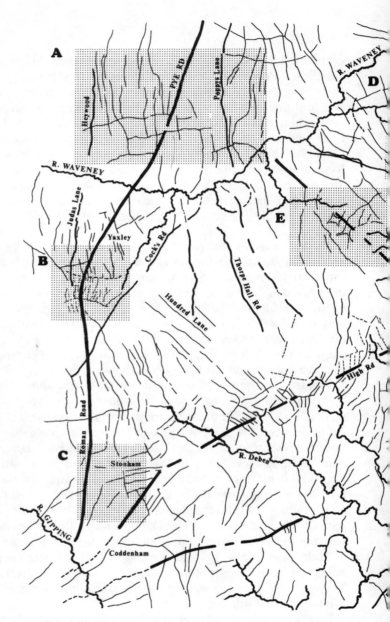

3.6 Coaxial roads, tracks and boundaries in north-east Suffolk and south Norfolk. A, B & C cover the areas of coaxial field systems identified by Williamson at Burstall, Yaxley (Figure 3.3) and Stonham. D and E relate to Figures 3.4 & 3.5, where field systems have been identified by Bigmore and Warner

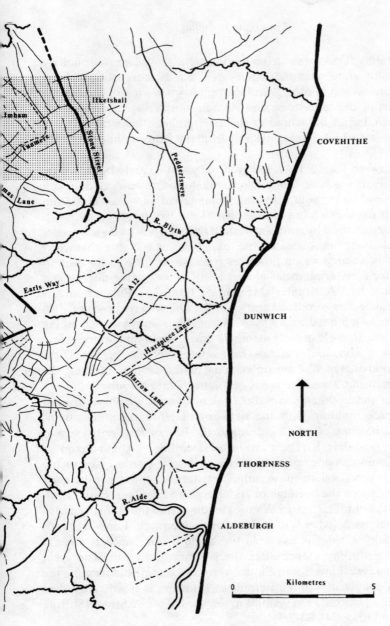

3.6 Continued

topography. Thus we see a basic principle of landscape morphology that holds good over the whole area, but is more noticeable in some areas than in others. In fact, in this small area of Suffolk we see part of the prehistoric and Roman morphological framework which underlies the whole of the East Anglian landscape. It is a framework which is also evident in many other counties (Lilley 1992, 11).

Central to Figure 3.6 is the great clayland triangle bordered by the Roman roads of Stone Street on the north-east, Badingham High Road on the south, and the Roman road, now the A140 from Ipswich to Norwich but also known as the Pye Road, to the west. Although crossed by trackways and long lanes this triangle appears as a relatively blank area on the map. But this is highly character-istic: it is an area which produces remarkably little in the way of prehistoric material, it has almost no barrows or ring-ditches and very little Iron Age material (Figures 2.1 and 2.5). Furthermore, it is dominated by woodland entries in the Domesday survey of 1086 (Figure 7.4), indeed, more than half of the county's woodland lay within this triangle in early medieval times. A similar pattern of late surviving woodland extends into south Norfolk in the Diss–Heywood area of Williamson's coaxial field system, reinforcing the statement that these are areas of relatively late colonisation.

Later developments are also evident in another phase of road and track building with the network of lanes radiating out of Dunwich, some of which cut across the line of *Pedderisweye* and clearly post-date it. These are almost certainly Anglo-Saxon as there is no convincing evidence for a Roman predecessor to the stricken medieval town. A similar pattern of roads can be seen converging on the borough of Aldeburgh and the late coastal town of Southwold. The 'Earl's Way', extending from the Roman road at Heveningham, where it is known as Dunwich Lane, towards Bramfield 'Castle' is likely to be Anglo-Saxon, since Bramfield was of little importance after the Norman Conquest. The great 'Tunmere' dividing South Elmham from Ilketshall and forming the hundredal division of the Ferding of Elmham, is clearly later than the grid of coaxial field systems in the area of Stone Street (Suffolk Record Office 741/B1/2/3).

In the case of the Roman road known as Stone Street, the coaxial field pattern appears to run in parallel with the road and this has led several writers to argue for a Roman or post-Roman date (Bigmore

1973; Williamson 1989). There is striking evidence to link this area with its neighbour in south Norfolk. Both the ancient parish boundary of Halesworth in Suffolk and the original boundary of Diss in Norfolk extended several miles north embracing large blocks of their respective field systems. Diss extends into the area of Heywood and Burstall, while Halesworth extended into Spexhall and Wissett with detached blocks of land corresponding with blocks of coaxial field systems (Figure 3.4). In the case of Halesworth there is good evidence to suggest these were areas of detached woodland, or wood-pasture, shared between parishes over a wide area. But this must have been wood-pasture which regenerated in the post-Roman period, for small abandoned Romano-British farmstead sites abound in the area (Warner 1982).

Some woodland regeneration took place on these claylands in the late or post-Roman period, but it was not sufficient to prevent the essential framework of field and property boundaries surviving into medieval and modern times (Warner 1982). Pollen analysis from the 14 metres of mud at the bottom of Diss Mere tends to support this hypothesis. There is evidence for wholesale woodland clearance in the late Iron Age in this part of the Waveney valley, which could be the time when some of these impressive field systems came into being (Sims 1978; Peglar *et al.* 1989). More environmental evidence of this type is needed to enable us to arrive at a sharply defined picture of the relationship between Roman and prehistoric landscapes. The evidence is certainly there waiting, trapped in the deep peat deposits of East Anglian rivers and estuaries.

A changing world

While the early Roman landscape of Suffolk incorporated within it many ancient pre-Roman features, some of which were to survive until modern times, the basis of the Roman agricultural economy was not static, neither was the pattern of settlement. Towards the end of the Roman period we begin to see the break-down of the rural economy, one which was essentially inherited from the Iron Age, and which had probably remained unchanged for several hundred years. The reason why it is possible to find so many small Romano-British farmstead sites is because the majority of them seem to have been deserted from the late third century onwards.

The phenomenon has been widely recognised not only throughout Britain but also over most of western Europe (Salway 1981). Its cause remains a mystery, but it must represent a major social and economic upheaval; it is hard to imagine the distress which is clearly implied in the evidence for desertion in the countryside at this time.

The economic and political misfortunes of the late third century are well known, but whether this was the cause or simply the effect of changes in the pattern of landholding we may never know. Population decline is also well attested in the late Western Empire, but whether this was the cause or result of recession it is impossible to determine. Significant climatic changes may be partly to blame. Higher rainfall and lower mean temperatures may have resulted in the construction of corn-drying ovens on some fen-edge estates. There is evidence for a major inundation of the fens in about AD 275, which caused the collapse of the Roman fenland drainage system (Rainbird Clarke 1960, 126; Salway 1970). From coastal sites, such as Caister-on-Sea (near Yarmouth), there is evidence of a rise in sea-levels or what has been described as a late Roman 'marine transgression' (Green 1961).

The desertion of many minor farmstead sites is not reflected in the larger estates and urban centres; these continue to produce evidence of a strong economy. The presence of carding combs or heckles and other items indicative of a thriving woollen cloth industry, particularly in the Breckland, suggests a move towards a more pastoral economy (Moore *et al.* 1988, 54). A shift to less labour-intensive agriculture could well be the consequence of sudden population decline, such as that which followed in the century after the Black Death of AD 1348–9 and resulted ultimately in the desertion of many minor settlements in Suffolk in the late Middle Ages. Some late Roman rural centres such as those recently discovered at Knodishall and Wenhaston may have benefited from an influx of rural population (Warner 1982). There is also evidence for substantial villa building, indicative of a polarisation of wealth at this time. But some of that wealth may have been brought in from outside the province by military personnel and aristocrats wishing to escape rampant inflation, political trauma and religious persecution that racked the Empire and the great cities of the East (Salway 1981).

This was a time not only of material and social change, but also of changing religious beliefs. If visitors to Roman Suffolk could not have found any large walled towns they would certainly have found a number of temples and other places of worship. Convincing archaeological evidence for a temple structure was lacking until, in the summer of 1994, one was excavated in advance of road building near Scole. Four large post-holes marked an inner *temenos*, or base to the temple, and a rough outer line of flints marked the precinct wall. Although it was roofed with Roman tiles, the plan suggests a Romano-British Celtic temple. Votive objects included a miniature axe and a miniature pottery cauldron, and there were also a number of coins and brooches (Flitcroft 1994). If few temples remain, there is no shortage of evidence for a variety of worship within the county. A small bronze figurine of Venus, found near Blyford bridge and subsequently stolen from Wenhaston church in the early years of this century, may be a household god (Clare 1903). Another Venus figurine comes from Hawkedon, and figurines of Mercury and Hercules come from Flempton and one of Mars comes from Bury St Edmunds and there are many more, including cult objects imported from the Near East in the later Roman period such as Cybele and Atys. A splendid inlaid statue of Nero may represent the Imperial cult near Barking, close to a major centre at Coddenham (Moore *et al*. 1988). A more local Celtic deity is represented in another figurine from Martlesham with a combined dedication to Mars-*Corotiacus* (Moore *et al*. 1988, 68).

A set of three bronze head-dresses, known as the 'Cavenham Crowns', probably come from a temple site at Lackford, and it is now thought that the Mildenhall treasure probably came from a temple, somewhere in the region, dedicated to Bacchus. Icklingham produced a mysterious array of artefacts, lifted by treasure hunters and sold on the international antiquities market. These subsequently appeared in an antiquities shop in the USA and, thanks to assiduous legal battles fought by the landowner, John Browning, will eventually find their way to the British Museum. These objects, which include several bronze cult heads and animal art, must have come from a temple site. Icklingham also has a very rare example of a late Roman church and cemetery (West 1976). Although only fragments of the foundations of a rectangular building remained (*c.* 7.5 by 4.5 metres), it was associated with a smaller plaster-lined apsidal structure, possibly a baptistry. Three large lead tanks or portable fonts are known from the site. One found *in situ* has raised Christian Chi-Rho monograms; certainly Christianity was well established in the west of the county by the end of the Roman period.

The end of Roman Suffolk

In the 280s, population decline, rising sea-levels and the contraction of village and urban sites were accompanied by pirate raiding along the coast; as if the rural population did not have enough troubles. In response, massive forts were built along the Saxon Shore (*Litus Saxonicum*) on both sides of the English Channel in a determined effort to protect the seaways that separated Britain from the Empire. The forts are thought to date from either the reign of Probus (AD 276–282), or from the time of Carausius, when he tried to establish a separate empire in Britain in AD 286 (Johnson 1976; Maxfield 1989). A fort at Brancaster (*Branodunum*) in north Norfolk controlled the entrance to the Wash, while Burgh Castle (*Gariannonum*), guarded the Yare and Bure river system, and at Walton, near Felixstowe, a fort protected the mouth of the River Deben (Plate 7).

These forts were probably constructed before the end of the third century, but not all at the same time, and not all to the same plan; there are slight differences in design and wall thickness (Maxfield 1989). Later, solid rubble-stone bastions were added to take large catapults. Walton was lost to coastal erosion in the eighteenth century, but Burgh survives as one of the best preserved of all the forts of the Saxon Shore. It is a testimony to the fact that the Suffolk coast in the late third century was a frontier in a way that it had not been a century earlier. From the *Notatia Dignitatum* we know that a detachment of the Stablensian Horse, *Equitates Stablensianorum*, was stationed at Burgh. Originating from Greece, they had previously served in Holland, where they must have gained experience of cavalry operations in marshy terrain (Johnson 1976; 1983). Cavalry at this period were the military elite and their presence reflects a determination on the part of the Roman authorities to come to grips with pirate raiding which was, no doubt, having a serious effect on the economy of the region.

With an influx of troops and fort building along the East Anglian coast in the years following AD 286, there comes evidence for economic recovery. Some of the finer villas inland from Walton at Whitton and Burgh may have been built or refurbished at this time by officers stationed along the coast (Moore 1948). Their presence seems to have deflected pirate attacks, for there follows a period of peace and prosperity in East Anglia lasting until the 360s, while fort building continues along the south coast of Britain into the 380s. Then in AD 367 a major disaster overwhelmed the whole of Britain; *Amiannus Marcellinus* tell us that Picts and Scots combined with others in a *barbarica conspiratio* and attempted to over-run the country. A Count or commander of the Saxon Shore, Nectaridus, was killed and serious disruption followed for two years before Britain was restored to order by Count Theodosius. The Mildenhall treasure is believed to have been hidden in the 360s possibly as a consequence of this disturbance (Bruce-Mitford 1955). By AD 368–9, Count Theodosius was able to set about reconstructing the frontiers, forts and military dispositions of Britain. He also strengthened many town walls, including those at Venta Icenorum, but the town was in decline by this date and its new fortifications excluded part of the southern street plan (Wacher 1974, 234). Signal stations were also constructed along the coast to link the shore forts with Hadrian's Wall. One has been identified as a 25 feet square structure at Corton, near Lowestoft; others have been suggested at Covehithe, Dunwich and Bawdsey, but an allowance must be made for loss through coastal erosion (Moore 1948, 176).

Following their refurbishment under Count Theodosius, both Burgh Castle and Walton shore forts continued to be occupied at least until the time when the usurper Constantine III took the last remaining Roman troops with him to fight on the continent in AD 407. This is attested not only from the coin series found at both sites, which continue into the reign of Honorius (AD 393–423), but also by Honorian coin hoards that turn up in the hinterland of Walton in the upper reaches of the Deben valley (Figure 6.3). Both forts were probably abandoned sometime between AD 406 and 410. The hoards indicate discontinuity; clearly there was an intention to return, but a failure to do so. Notable coin hoards of this date have also been found in other parts of Suffolk. At Eye 650 gold coins, which concluded with the reign of Honorius, were found in the eighteenth century, but do not survive. Substantial Honorian hoards have also been found at Icklingham and Mildenhall (Moore 1948, 174–5). Better known are the outstanding gold and silver hoards found recently at Thetford and Hoxne.

The Thetford treasure is sadly incomplete. Although found in Norfolk, it needs to be considered in relation to the far more spectacular find in 1992 at Hoxne. Both hoards contained large numbers of gold and silver coins. The 200 or more silver *siliquae* rumoured to have been part of the Thetford treasure were never recovered and if they ever existed seem modest by comparison with the 14,171 silver *siliquae* and half *siliquae* all dating from the fourth and very early fifth century found at Hoxne (Bland & Johns 1993). Both hoards contained gold and silver jewellery of breathtaking quality and a large number of silver spoons with straight and swan-neck handles, some with Latin inscriptions. The Hoxne treasure was carefully buried in a wooden chest well away from any Roman buildings.

The latest coins in the Hoxne hoard are of the usurper Constantine III and date to AD 407–8, while the Thetford treasure is also believed to have been deposited in the early 400s. Both hoards contain collections of jewellery as well as coins which suggests that they may have been the contents of single wealthy households. The earliest coins in the Hoxne hoard date from the period after currency reforms in AD 365–8 and most date from the period AD 394 to 405 (Bland & Johns 1993, 4). In other words the bulk had been acquired over the ten years prior to deposition and none pre-date the arrival of troops under Count Theodosius following the Barbarian Conspiracy of AD 367. It is tempting, therefore, to suggest that the Hoxne hoard belonged to a wealthy military family that arrived in Britain with Count Theodosius in AD 368–9 and departed with Constantine III in AD 407. So who were they? The name JULIANE, prefixed by *domina*, meaning the lady Juliane, appears on one of the bracelets, while the name AURURSICINI, *Aur[elius] Ursicinus* appears ten times on a set of spoons. Other names, *Peregrinus*, *Faustinus* and a feminine name *Silvicola* appear on other spoons (Bland & Johns 1993, 29). As yet the key male surname of *Ursicinus* cannot be linked with any historical personage of that name. But was it a husband and wife, *Aurelius* and *Juliane* with their three children, two boys *Peregrinus* and *Faustinus*, and a daughter *Silvicola*? No such family link is implied with the loose association of these names in a hoard of this type.

Early newspaper reports based on inscriptions from the hoard made links with the *Faustini* family, on the basis of just one inscription, and hence with the as yet unlocated site of the *Villa Faustini*, mentioned in the Antonine Itinerary (Keys 1992). This seemed very plausible at the time, but the weight of inscriptions point to *Ursicinus* as the owner of the hoard, while the name *Faustinus* is very common and may be no more than coincidence. The *Villa Faustini* (Iter V) was clearly a sufficient landmark for it to be mentioned in the Itinerary. It lay somewhere on the line of the present A140 and is usually associated with known Roman sites at either Scole or Stonham. Hoxne lies 4.8 kilometres (3 miles) east of Scole and as a result of the discovery and excavation of this hoard it may eventually be possible to locate a substantial villa in this area and perhaps link it archaeologically with the hoard.

The deposition of such wealth and the presence of so many hoards in this area at this time suggests disorder and discontinuity in the final years of Roman occupation. If leading families failed to return and collect what must have represented a very sizeable proportion of their family fortune, the complete collapse of the Roman colonial infrastructure which followed in the generation after AD 410 seems wholly understandable. *Zozimus* and the Gallic Chronicle tell us that Britain was devastated by the Saxons some time between AD 408 and 410 (Frere 1974). In the absence of military protection for those with the means to leave, the decision to get out carrying the minimum of valuables may have been an easy one. Contrary to expectation, returning was clearly the problem, for thereafter followed the period of Anglo-Saxon settlement and the loss of Britain as an outpost of the Roman Empire.

4

Anglian Suffolk

The Angles and their origins

It is possible that the Romans employed Germanic mercenaries to
supplement dwindling numbers of troops in the towns of Roman
Britain and in the forts of the Saxon Shore, particularly in the
period after military reorganisation under Count Theodosius in AD
368–9. Their presence is attested in East Anglia by a few Germanic-
style belt buckles and cremation cemeteries in close association
with late Roman defended urban centres such as Caister-on-Sea
(near Yarmouth) and Venta Icenorum (near Norwich) (Hawkes
1949; Myres & Green 1973). This tenuous evidence for a late
Roman Germanic presence should not be confused with the idea of
foederati or *laeti* first proposed by Myres (Myres 1969; Scull 1992).
In recent years there has been a tendency for historians to argue for
an earlier *Adventus Saxonum* than the archaeological evidence in
eastern England can sustain, in consequence the status, significance
and chronology of the earliest Anglo-Saxon settlements remain a
matter of debate (Welch 1992; Higham 1994). The earliest Germanic metalwork comes from late Roman sites and is significantly
earlier than the material found in the first Anglo-Saxon rural sites
and cemeteries. Early Germanic metalwork has been found in
Suffolk at Lakenheath, Icklingham and Ixworth, all of which were
important late Roman urban centres in the west of the county, and
at Brent Eleigh, near to the Roman road leading from Long

Melford to Coddenham, and at Felixstowe, close to the late Roman shore fort at Walton (Moore *et al.* 1988).

The almost total collapse of the Roman colonial urban infrastructure, including the regional pottery industry and coinage system, in the ten to fifteen years after AD 407 must mean that the overlap between the residual urban population and the Anglo-Saxon migrants was brief in the extreme. The popular view of destruction by fire and sword, elaborated upon many years after the event by Bede, cannot be supported by archaeological evidence. Because of a lack of new coins coming into the province after AD 410 it is very difficult to date the upper levels of abandoned villa sites, but the overall impression is of slow decay and the presence of squatters. At Stanton and Castle Hill villas, fires were lit on the open floors in the final years of occupation, sometime in the fourth century or later. There is no evidence of violent attack (Moore *et al.* 1988, 81–4).

By the middle of the fifth century the first settlers had filtered into the fenland basin up the Wash river system becoming established in the Lark, Blackbourn and Ouse valleys, areas which had been densely settled and highly urbanised in Roman times (Figure 4.1). They cremated their dead and buried the ashes in hand-made pots with distinctive decoration. These urns are almost identical to ones found in much larger cemeteries in the Elbe–Weser area, south of Hamburg, in northern Germany. The earliest migrants seem to be of mixed Anglian, Saxon and Frisian stock. Bede, in the *Ecclesiastical History of the English People* (hereafter HE), written in the early eighth century, tells us that the Angles came from Angulus in the lower Schleswig-Holstein peninsula, in what is now Denmark, and that from them were descended the 'East Angles, the Middle Angles, the Mercians, and all the Northumbrian race (that is those people who dwell north of the river Humber), as well as the other Anglian tribes.'

He says that the Saxons came from 'Old Saxony', the area of what is now northern Germany, from whom 'came the East Saxons, the South Saxons and the West Saxons', the kingdoms of Essex, Sussex and Wessex (HE, I, 15). In essence, Bede's statement is borne out by the archaeological evidence, but the process of migration had resulted in ethnically mixed groups and later Bede himself mentions the diverse character of the old Germanic races, which included Danes and Frisians, from whom the Anglo-Saxon settlers

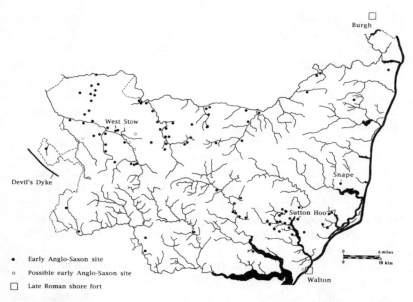

4.1 Suffolk: distribution of early Anglo-Saxon cemeteries and settlements (from West 1988)

of Britain were also believed to have been descended (HE, V, 9). Recent work by Hines has pointed to a link with south-west Norway, again reinforcing a Scandinavian origin for some Anglian groups (Hines 1984; 1992).

West Stow epitomises early Anglo-Saxon settlement in the Lark valley. However, it was unusual in one respect in that the site was largely confined to a low sandy knoll well out into the valley floodplain overlooking the River Lark (Figure 4.2). Such central river valley sites are rare and may have a specialist function. Although West Stow is unique in being so early, there are comparable sites in Suffolk which are much later, such as the Middle Saxon site at Staunch Meadow, Brandon, on the Little Ouse, and the twelfth-century site of Mendham Priory and the church of Syleham with its round tower both in the Waveney valley; late medieval pottery from the churchyard of Syleham might suggest that it was a landing-place and market. At West Stow the buildings are more clustered than is normally found in rural early Anglo-Saxon villages; this may be due to the confined nature of the knoll, but there is also

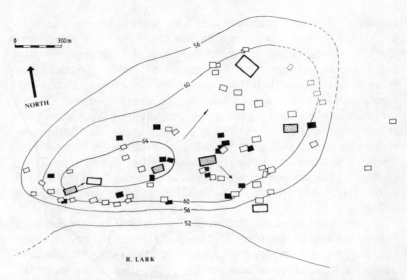

4.2 West Stow: the Anglo-Saxon settlement of timbered halls and sunken-featured buildings on a low sandy knoll beside the River Lark dates from the mid-fourth to late sixth or early seventh century. The black rectangles represent buildings known to have been occupied in the fifth century. The larger shaded rectangles represent the earliest halls with arrows to indicate subsequent developments on the site (from West 1985)

evidence for many craft skills being practised and large numbers of late Roman coins, indicating that the community was not wholly dependent on agriculture. Whatever its significance, this unusual concentration of material enabled large-scale open-area excavation which was undertaken seasonally by Stanley West from 1965 to 1972. More than one hundred post-hole clusters including seven recognisable halls and 69 sunken-featured buildings (*Grubenhäuser*) were revealed, with many thousands of associated artefacts (Figure 4.2). West Stow remains one of the most important excavated Anglo-Saxon settlement sites in Britain. Reconstruction of some of the key buildings began in 1972 and now it is possible to visit the site and gain a real appreciation of life in the formative years of East Anglia's history (Plate 8).

The buildings are on the whole smaller and less sophisticated than their continental counterparts from sites such as Wijster and Warendorf (West 1985, 168). West comments that the physical migration from the continent acted as 'a great leveller'; there is evidence not only of a cultural mix in the West Stow community but also of a reduction in overall scale in both building and settlement size as a consequence of migration. From the outset there seem to be no more than three main groups of buildings each with a hall and attendant sunken-featured buildings (Figure 4.2). This arrangement seems to have been perpetuated with successive rebuildings throughout the life of the settlement. The little community of timber buildings flourished as a centre for pottery production, woollen cloth weaving and leather-working until the seventh century when groups moved away from the knoll by the River Lark to establish farmstead sites in open country (West 1985).

In the fifth century, settlements were also appearing near Felixstowe and in the lower Deben at Waldringfield and near the late Roman industrialised settlement of Hacheston, but the evidence for these is sparse and the size of the cemeteries uncertain. By the sixth century settlement had expanded to the upper Deben, Orwell and Alde river systems (Figure 4.1). To the east of the county there are significant gaps from the Alde to the Waveney and along most of the Stour valley. Settlement along the Waveney seems to have developed from the west of the county and peters out towards Bungay although there is a cluster of cemeteries on the north side of the river in Norfolk at this point (Penn 1993). There is also evidence for two important cemeteries, both noted in the eighteenth century, one at Lound which produced a *francisca* throwing axe and a 'Kentish' buckle and another at Bloodmoor Hill, Carlton Colville, which produced a mounted Visigothic coin (Bruce-Mitford 1975, 663; Warner 1982, 60). It could be that the shore fort at Burgh Castle inhibited the Waveney being used as an artery of settlement from the east, but then the Walton shore fort did not seem to prevent settlement in the Deben valley. Such arguments cannot account for the blank areas, particularly in the Blyth valley and in the central clayland triangle (as discussed in the previous chapter), where a high density of woodland is recorded at the end of the Anglo-Saxon period at the time of the Domesday survey. In the latter area the evidence for pre-Roman settlement is also thin. Although the Romans penetrated the claylands and early Roman farmsteads abound, late Roman coins and pottery are harder to find and there are clear indications from the abandonment of sites that there was a retreat from the claylands long before the Anglo-Saxons arrived.

The patchiness of the settlement and cemetery evidence is noticeable elsewhere in East Anglia, indeed it should be regarded as one of its distinguishing features (Davis & Vierck 1974; Warner 1988, 34). It has been argued that the blank areas of the map could represent enclaves of residual Romano-British population who had effectively prevented Anglo-Saxon settlement in these areas. But such areas are archaeologically 'invisible'; they produce no evidence of any settlement, neither Anglo-Saxon, nor Romano-British, neither cemeteries nor settlements of any kind; neither do they produce late Roman hoards. It is fashionable now to argue for integration and it is also suggested that graves in Anglo-Saxon cemeteries, which produce no grave goods, could be the remnants of the Romano-British population. Both arguments lack the conviction of real evidence.

West has pointed to the exceptionally large cremation cemetery at Lackford in the Lark valley, close to the important late Roman religious site of Icklingham, in an area which produces predominantly Anglo-Saxon inhumation cemeteries. Its size suggests that it contains bodies from outside the area. His tentative suggestion is that we might regard some cremation burials as representing elements of the Romano-British population. This is more convincing perhaps than some of the other arguments based on negative evidence (West 1985). Perhaps one day, with the development of DNA sampling in archaeology, we will be able to answer this question once and for all. However, the post-Roman reversion to pre-Roman sites, the abandonment of towns for the countryside, the return to prehistoric settlement patterns – all this might logically be followed by a return to traditional Belgic burial practices of urned cremation. If West is right about the unusual nature of the Icklingham cemetery, it argues for some degree of separation between the two communities, at least in the first century of migration and settlement.

Late Roman hoards also abound in areas favoured by Anglo-Saxon settlement. If the hoards represent discontinuity, as they surely must, then the evidence would seem to indicate a degree of ethnic separation between areas once wealthy and highly romanised, but now settled by Anglo-Saxons, and areas less well romanised, where there is little or no evidence for Saxon settle-

ment and where we can only presume some of the residual population survived. This period marks a reversion to an essentially
pre-Roman, or prehistoric settlement pattern, with concentrations
on the lighter soils of Breckland and Sandling. As already discussed
(Chapter 3), the resources of the clayland were to some extent
being exploited in prehistoric times and this must also be true for
the Anglo-Saxon period. The presence of mayweed seeds on the
site of the Anglo-Saxon village of West Stow has been used to
suggest the importation of wheat from clayland areas to supplement the rye, barley and oats grown on the Breckland sands
(Murphy 1985). As in prehistoric times the Breckland and Sandling
became again the core areas for the control of prestige goods and
resources. They returned also to their function as ancestral burial
grounds. But then, power, wealth and control in these core areas
fell into the hands of a new elite, the Anglo-Saxons, while a depleted residual population supplied their needs from the peripheral
clayland, fenland and estuary areas (Figure 2.2).

We must not forget that these barbarian settlers, before migration, were relatively unaffected by Roman civilisation. They retained their traditional style of dress and weapons, they spoke a
different language and had a different religion and art-style. Their
social customs and life-style were at odds with a Roman province
softened by 400 years of colonial rule. The first Anglo-Saxon migrants may have been deliberately settled by the Romans on the
edges of larger estates in areas where there were villas and small
towns. At some point after AD 410 the villa owners, the old provincial elite, buried their valuables and decided to leave in a hurry,
moving either westwards to areas unaffected by Anglo-Saxon
settlement or fled to the continent in the wake of final troop with-
drawals. Their intention to return and recover their buried valuables was frustrated by a turn of events consequent on the fall of
Constantine III and his subsequent execution.

As more Anglo-Saxon migrants moved in, so these core areas,
once the focus of Roman settlement, fell under the control of the
Anglo-Saxons. In consequence the core areas may have become
less acceptable places to live for the residual Romano-British population. A degree of ethnic separation must have developed, but
it was the more aggressive and resourceful migrants who, through
a protracted internal power struggle, achieved ascendancy, until
by the sixth century larger and larger kingdoms were formed

which eventually controlled areas similar to the old Roman *territoria*. The new imported institution of kingship then effectively replaced the function of the urban *civitas* capitals which had once been the administrative centres of these same *territoria* (Bassett 1989).

Because of their archaeological 'invisibility' we cannot identify the remaining Romano-British population. However, in the cemeteries at West Stow, excavated in the nineteenth century, and from Spong Hill in Norfolk, there survive a number of annular and penannular brooches that may derive from a late Romano-British style of dress. Perhaps there was some inter-marriage between the two groups and ultimately, following the re-establishment of Christianity in East Anglia in the years after AD 630, the two populations may have become indistinguishable.

A struggle for power

Nothing highlights more clearly the struggle for power and the dislocation of East Anglia from the rest of Britain in the post-Roman period than the great Cambridgeshire dykes. These colossal earthworks truncate the chalk downland corridor and the ancient path of the Icknield Way which led into the heartland of the region. The sheer size of the Devil's Dyke – $7\frac{1}{2}$ miles long and over 40 feet wide – betokens territorial organisation on a vast scale and a commitment to defend what must have been a cohesive and well-organised population (Plate 2).

There are archaeological problems in dating the dykes accurately, but they were probably constructed sometime following the Barbarian Conspiracy of AD 365-7 and before the early seventh century. The lesser Cambridgeshire dykes, the Fleam, Hadon and Brent dykes, which all form part of this same system of defence in depth along the East Anglian frontier remain essentially undated. So also do the enigmatic 'Black Ditches' which run across Cavenham and Risby Poor's heath and bar the western approaches to Icklingham (West 1985, 170). Recent work on the Launditch of west Norfolk suggests that it may be Iron Age and a similar date for some of these smaller Suffolk and Cambridgeshire dykes cannot be ruled out (Scull 1992, 15).

What then was the function of these extraordinary earthworks? Before modern farming and the development of horse-racing stables, the chalk downland of Newmarket heath provided a wide open stretch of countryside bordered by fens to the north and the wooded claylands to the south. For raiders on horseback this was an open invitation, for it provided a natural corridor into the agriculturally rich heartlands of West Suffolk and Norfolk. The dykes confronted raiding parties approaching from the south-west; all have ditches on their western side and high banks to the east. They were therefore built by folk determined to defend East Anglian territory at inestimable cost in terms of construction-hours and hard labour. Indeed, the size and length of the Devil's Dyke poses questions about how many warriors would be needed to defend it, or even if it could be defended at all. This may not be a problem if its principal function was to prevent cattle-rustling and to check small raiding parties. The dykes may thus have provided an early warning system through which western raiders could only pass with difficulty. They might also have provided a useful artificial barrier – a killing ground – to pin down raiders on horseback, if they could be encircled by the defenders.

The dykes served another function, as a political frontier. By blocking the path of the Icknield Way they may also have confined the normal traffic across the frontier and thus served as a checkpoint – an East Anglian customs post. The numbers of individuals needed to patrol the dykes may not have been great in order to fulfil this purpose. But such mundane functions cannot detract from the immeasurable effort and sophisticated planning needed in their construction. We are dealing with a highly organised society capable of solving problems on a gigantic scale. Who were the organisers and why does there seem to be such a contrast between the sophistication of the dyke-builders and the scattered remains of Anglo-Saxon cemeteries and settlements in the Anglian region?

These are difficult questions to answer and in no way is it possible to unravel entirely the mystery of the dykes. However, it can be observed that the pattern of settlement and distribution of Anglo-Saxon settlement is riverine, running up the small streams radiating out of the fenland basin (Figure 4.1). As such the pattern of settlement runs parallel to the line of the dykes. Also there is no inherent distinction to be made between the settlements and cemeteries on either side of the dykes. Indeed, from the workshop of the Illington/Lackford potter, based at West Stow where the antler pottery stamps were found, pots were finding their way across the frontier and being used in cemeteries as far west as Cambridge and as far north as Wretham in Norfolk (Green *et al.* 1981). Clearly there was economic and social interchange across this frontier and whatever the threat which caused the dykes to be built, it was not the threat of Anglo-Saxon settlement.

Until the archaeologists are able to give us a more precise date for the construction of the Devil's Dyke, we can only speculate about when and why it was built. If a late date is accepted then it must come at a period well after the formation of the Anglo-Saxon kingdom of East Anglia, perhaps during the period of Mercian aggression under King Penda *c*. AD 654. But even then one wonders whether the East Anglian dynasty was capable of organising construction work on such a scale. If, on the other hand, an earlier date is accepted then it may well come in the period preceding the main influx of Anglo-Saxon settlement. Like the Bockerly Dyke, near Chichester, it may ultimately prove to belong to the period of defensive works associated with Count Theodosius in AD 368–9, following the Barbarian Conspiracy. Certainly the size, scale and straightness of the Devil's Dyke suggest late Roman defensive engineering. It is very similar in size to the bank and ditch surrounding Venta Icenorum, which was almost certainly strengthened as part of the Theodosian campaign to re-fortify the towns and cities of Britain.

The struggle for power in the late Roman and early Anglo-Saxon period continued within the framework of boundaries established in late Iron Age and early Roman times. The Cambridgeshire dykes clearly delineate a western frontier for East Anglia, one that was not only vulnerable to attack, but also capable of being vigorously defended. A sophisticated regional organisation must have existed in the late Roman period, but sadly we know very little about late Roman provincial rural administration. However, a Roman provincial elite is clearly indicated in the hoards of jewellery, coins and silver table-ware deposited in the late fourth and early fifth centuries at Mildenhall, Icklingham, Thetford and Hoxne. By the late sixth century a new but equally sophisticated political order was emerging and struggling to control the same territory, but this time as a separate kingdom, the kingdom of East Anglia.

The Wuffinga dynasty

All that is known about the history of the East Anglian kings stems principally from two sources. The first is a somewhat laconic genealogy, or regnal list, dating from the 790s (known to historians as *Cotton Vespasian B vi*), which traces their ancestry most dubiously from the god Woden, son of Frealaf, to Ælfwald, who we know died in AD 749. At some point in this list there is a transition from dynastic origin-myth to fact. The second document may be more reliable but is dependent on similar sources, namely the Venerable Bede, who wrote his *Ecclesiastical History of the English People* (HE) in the 720s and in it included many anecdotes about royal families, including the East Anglian kings. Bede's work has been described as an exemplary history for kings, and of course for their offspring who played a central part in the conversion of the English to Christianity in the seventh century. The *Anglo-Saxon Chronicle* also gives supporting information to Bede's account. It is Bede who tells us about *Wuffa*, 'from whom the kings of the East Angles are called Wuffings' (HE, II, 15).

Taken literally the dynastic name *Wuffings* means 'the kin of Wuffa', but what were the origins of the *Wuffings*? One important documentary clue comes from Procopius's Gothic War (IV, 20), which mentions Radiger, a prince of the *Warni* who lived *c.* AD 545–80, betrothed to the sister of the 'King of the Angli' in Britain. A war was subsequently fought on the continent, between the Angles and their ancestral neighbours, the *Warni*. Procopius dates this event to the period following the death of Theodebert, king of the Franks, in AD 548. It has been suggested that *Wuffa* was the brother of the bride in question and that he was 'King of the Angli', in East Anglia, as early as AD 548–51. His predecessor, *Wehha*, is mentioned in the *Historia Brittonum* as the father of *Wuffa* and the first to reign in Britain over the *Gens Estanglorum* (Bruce-Mitford 1975, 694). Such sparse information, interesting in itself, does not get us much further in answering our initial question: who were the Wuffings?

When we turn to the archaeology we find more clues, but fewer answers. Central to the Wuffings question is the undoubted royal dynastic cemetery at Sutton Hoo (Figure 4.3). It has been accepted for some time, on the basis of the coin evidence, that the ship-burial from Mound 1 at Sutton Hoo is the memorial to Rædwald,

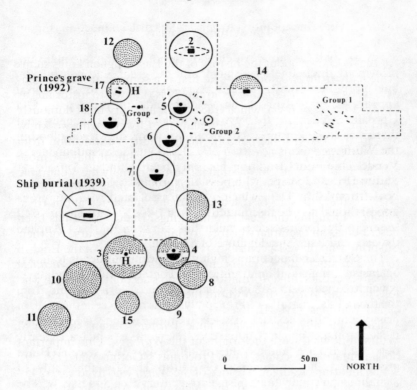

4.3 Sutton Hoo: plan of the Wuffinga cemetery. Shaded circles indicate those barrows not yet excavated but believed to have been robbed in antiquity

bretwalda or high-king of East Anglia, whose *imperium* extended over neighbouring kingdoms south of the Humber and who died in *c.* AD 625. He is described by Bede as the son of *Tytil* whose father was *Wuffa* (HE, II, 15), two names which accord with the regnal list in *Cotton Vespasian B vi* from which Rædwald is absent. The Sutton Hoo material from Mound 1 contains a vast array of princely material from many different sources, but among them are vital clues pointing towards a Swedish connection (Figure 4.4).

Several objects show evidence of Swedish-style craftsmanship, principally the helmet and shield, and the great gold belt-buckle, but more importantly the funerary assemblage of ship-burial appears as an outlier of the Vendel tradition, centred on Old Uppsala, Sweden. At the very least it would seem to suggest that there was some kinship relationship if not Swedish royal blood in the Wuffings' veins (Newton 1993, 113). Outside Scandinavia, the Vendel ship-burial tradition has only been found in Suffolk, at Sutton Hoo and Snape, with possible variants at Caister-on-Sea; a boat from Ashby Dell, which was not associated with any grave goods, should now be discounted (Green 1963, 57–63). This in itself seems to reinforce some peculiar link between the East Anglian dynasty and the Vendel culture of Sweden.

The Swedish connection is highly significant but needs to be set against a long-standing tradition of contacts with Scandinavia which are evident in Anglian cemeteries in eastern England from the time of the migrations. Principally this is manifest in the form of art-style on brooches and wrist-clasps, items which suggest a composite form of Anglian national dress, elements of which are clearly borrowed from Scandinavian traditions. For this reason, Hines argues that the prominence of Sutton Hoo in the study of Scandinavian connections in seventh-century England may well be misleading. The point being that by the time of Rædwald there was an 'established line of communication and trade' between Anglian Suffolk and Scandinavia, reaching back well over a hundred years (Hines 1992, 326).

Developments at Sutton Hoo need to be seen against the wider world of political change taking place, not just in south-eastern England, but over northern Europe. To some extent the development of *Bretwaldae* in England reflect these changes. Bede tells us that the *primus imperium* was Ælle, king of the South Saxons, second was Cælin, king of the West Saxons, then came Æthelberht of Kent, fourthly came Rædwald, followed by Edwin of Northumbria (HE, II, 5). This progressive shift of power from the south coast, through Kent to East Anglia and Northumbria is undoubtedly significant. In the sixth century, the pagan kingdoms south of the Thames, particularly Kent, were clearly benefiting from close trade contacts with Christian Merovingian Gaul. These contacts

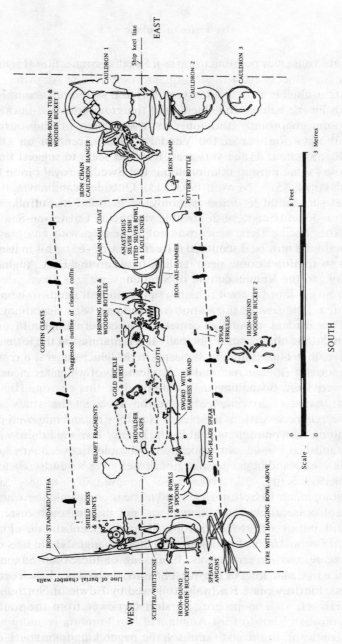

4.4 Sutton Hoo: plan of burial chamber in the Mound 1 ship. The outline of the body, the coffin and its alignment are speculative (from Bruce-Mitford 1975; Evison 1979; Evans 1986)

EAST

CAULDRON 1

Ship keel line

CAULDRON 2

CAULDRON 3

IRON-BOUND TUB &
WOODEN BUCKET 1

IRON CHAIN
CAULDRON HANGER

POTTERY BOTTLE

ANASTASIUS
SILVER DISH
FLUTED SILVER BOWL
& LADLE UNDER

CHAIN-MAIL COAT

IRON AXE-HAMMER

COFFIN CLEATS

Suggested outline of cleated coffin

NORTH

DRINKING HORNS &
WOODEN BOTTLES

SPEAR
FERRULES

IRON-BOUND
WOODEN BUCKET 2

GOLD BUCKLE
& PURSE

CLOTH

HELMET FRAGMENTS

SWORD WITH
HARNESS & WAND

SHOULDER
CLASPS

LONG-BLADE SPEAR

SHIELD BOSS
& MOUNTS

SILVER BOWLS
& SPOONS

LYRE WITH HANGING BOWL ABOVE

IRON STANDARD/TUFFA

Line of burial chamber walls

SCEPTRE/WHETSTONE

IRON-BOUND
WOODEN BUCKET 3

SPEARS &
ANGONS

WEST

SOUTH

Scale

0

8 Feet

0

3 Metres

reached a climax with the marriage of Æthelberht to a Merovingian Christian princess and the subsequent mission of St Augustine in AD 597. Æthelberht then attempted to force the conversion on to his sub-kingdoms and with it presumably his Gaulish alliance; there were some baptisms, including that of Rædwald, but ultimately Æthelberht's policy failed (Brooks 1984, 63; Wallace-Hadrill 1988, 59). Rædwald did not establish a diocese on his return from Kent and soon was attempting to combine old and new religious practices (HE, II, 15).

When Rædwald returned to the old religion he also turned his back on Kent. But Kent controlled the traffic of prestige goods from the continent and was probably the principal source of iron. Mercia could not be relied upon for such supplies and Rædwald was at war with Northumbria, therefore East Anglia had to look overseas to the Rhineland and to Scandinavia where Sweden was the principal source of iron. This was an easy matter, for as we have seen, from the time of the migration there had been cultural links with Scandinavia which are evident in art-style, metalwork and national dress. It was at this period, in the first half of the seventh century, that Dorestad near Utrecht, at the junction of the rivers Rhine and Lek, became a major trading partner with Ipswich (Verwers 1988; Wade 1988).

Furthermore the Vendel culture of Sweden was at its zenith and this corresponds with a significant shift northward in economic growth on the continent with the appearance of mints in northern Gaul and the spread of unmounted gold coins into eastern and northern England in the period after AD 625 (Arnold 1988, 56). (At this period, some gold coins were mounted in jewellery and had gone out of circulation.) The political geography favoured Rædwald's ascendancy, which marks a significant shift of power to Anglian areas north of the Thames. The maritime character of the site at Sutton Hoo, overlooking the Deben, and the ship-burial itself point towards an economy burgeoning on coastal and long-distance trade (Kirby 1991, 66). The East Anglian kingdom reaped inestimable benefits from this enforced change of foreign policy and we clearly see some of the material gains in the Sutton Hoo assemblage.

Recently, Pearson and others have argued that Sutton Hoo might be considered as a royal cemetery for the kingdom of Essex rather than East Anglia (Filmer-Sankey 1992; Pearson et al. 1993).

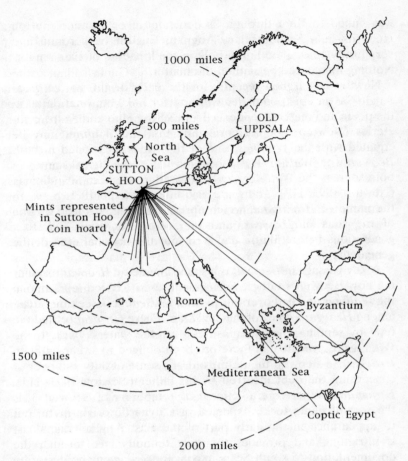

4.5 Sutton Hoo: the suggested provenance of objects from the ship-burial (Mound 1) (from Carver 1986; Hooper, after Bruce-Mitford 1975, 1978, 1983)

Even if we allow for the fact that the 'Coptic' bowl is more likely to have come from the Rhineland or Italy than from Coptic Egypt (Welch 1992, 116–19), so cosmopolitan is the material from Sutton Hoo that it is possible to make links with most countries in northern and central Europe if not further afield (Figure 4.5). In this respect, Essex does not stand out from the crowd and when pitched against the argument outlined above it has no place at all, for Essex was linked to Kent through its dependence on London. Sutton Hoo sits in a Scandinavian, Anglian, English background and very firmly among the South Folk in the kingdom of East Anglia. Nothing more need be said on the matter.

Newton has argued recently for the early origins of the great Anglo-Saxon epic poem *Beowulf* and for links between detail in the poem and material evidence from Sutton Hoo and Snape cemeteries (Newton 1993). He suggests that the *Wuffings* may be equated with the *Wulfings*, one of the tribes mentioned in both *Beowulf* and *Widsith*. By association with other tribal names in both sources the *Wulfings* can be located in southern Scandinavia (Newton 1993, 117). There are also interesting parallels between the name of *Hroðmund*, which appears both in *Beowulf* as one of the sons of *Hroðgar*, and in *Cotton Vespasian Bvi*, four generations before *Wuffa* and well into the fictional area of the genealogy.

A key passage in *Beowulf* is a speech made by *Hroðgar* explaining how Beowulf's father, *Ecgtheow*, caused a blood-feud among the *Wulfings* and fled overseas to the *Suð-Dena folk* seeking refuge among *Hroðgar's* court of the *Scyldings*. There *Hroðgar* settled the feud by sending ancient treasures over the waters' back to the *Wulfings*. *Ecgtheow* had therefore been obliged to swear oaths to *Hroðgar*. So Beowulf then came out of a sense of duty and honour concerning the debt incurred by his father (Newton 1993, 114). *Hroðmund* is therefore a fictional contemporary of Beowulf. It is the sort of name to be expected in a dynastic origin-myth, but its appearance in the early part of the East Anglian regnal list is intriguing and provides the only tenuous link through the documentation to south Scandinavia. Indeed, even the desire by later East Anglian kings to make this link through the dynastic origin-myth would be interesting enough.

The text of *Beowulf* cannot be any earlier than the eighth century, but like other great epic poems, such as the Celtic Irish myths and the Homeric tales of ancient Greece, it was composed in an oral tradition which extends back into the remote past. *Beowulf* therefore contains episodes of factual material from different points in time and different locations juxtaposed and embroidered with poetic ingenuity. The reality of the ship-burial at Sutton Hoo falls somewhere midstream in the formation of this oral tradition, but before the composition of the final *Beowulf*. We therefore find ourselves in a circular argument; was the poem created in recollection of a magnificent heroic past such as is encapsulated in Mound 1 at Sutton Hoo and other Vendel sites? Or is the ship-burial itself a re-enactment of the fantasy developed by epic poetry? The function of such poetry was, of course, to enhance the mystique of warrior kingship; the function of elaborate and costly funerary rites, such as Sutton Hoo Mound 1 was, indeed, precisely the same. There is much therefore that is theatrical and false in both poem and grave assemblage; much that is of the nature of propaganda, flummery and protocol, to be expected at any royal court. We are in the realms of partial-reality, of fact and fantasy inextricably intertwined. Yet both articulate the same message about the mystique of lordship in an idealised world of valour and conspicuous wealth: the preoccupation of kings vainly searching for fame and immortality. Such were the Wuffings.

We must bear in mind that as well as a Swedish/*Beowulf* connection at Sutton Hoo, there are Celtic, Byzantine and Merovingian connections, although no one is seriously suggesting that the Wuffings were of Byzantine origin. This was a world of cosmopolitan kingship – an essential ingredient in the medieval world of northern Europe. Indeed, has there ever been a later English monarch who could claim a wholly English pedigree? German, Scots, Welsh, French, Norman, Danish, yes; anything but English. The same could be said for other European monarchies; indeed, it would seem to be a requirement of later medieval monarchy that it should have an ancestry linked to a wider world beyond its established territory. Diplomatic marriages were an essential part of this process, as attested from the time of Wuffa himself from the evidence of Procopius. Bede likewise gives the consequential example of Æthelberht of Kent marrying Bertha, a Merovingian Christian princess. We should therefore expect to find more than Swedish and Anglian blood in the Wuffings's veins. The idea of kingship, with its distant Germanic traditions, was borrowed from the continent at this period, it was not invented on arrival in Britain (Wallace-Hadrill 1971). So although Sutton Hoo provides us with some of the earliest evidence about the formative character of Anglo-Saxon monarchy, it is itself just one scene from the great epic of northern European kingship which recedes from our own day back into darkest prehistory.

A chamber horizon

The excavation of the Sutton Hoo ship-burial in 1939 has been described as one of the most dramatic archaeological discoveries of the twentieth century (Evans 1986). Until this extraordinary material came to light it was not thought possible that a provincial king of East Anglia could command the sort of wealth and prestige which is represented by the cosmopolitan array of artefacts placed in the Sutton Hoo ship (Figure 4.4). Ship-burials, although not unusual in Scandinavia, are very rare in Britain: indications of another were discovered by Basil Brown, the original excavator, on the same site in 1938 and more fully excavated by Martin Carver in 1985–92, while the only other excavated example comes from Snape, discovered in 1862 by Septimus Davidson. All of these appear as outliers of the Scandinavian Vendel burial tradition from Sweden (Bruce-Mitford 1975; Evans 1986, 113; Filmer-Sankey 1992).

Other princely graves containing comparable objects, but in fewer quantities, have been found at Taplow, Buckinghamshire, in the nineteenth century, and at Broomfield, near Colchester. The helmet from Bentley Grange in Yorkshire may also represent another princely grave, while finds of garnet and gold jewellery from Cuddesdon-upon-Thames and Sarre in Kent are of comparable quality and status (Bruce-Mitford 1975). It is the size and quantity of the Sutton Hoo material that makes it stand out head and shoulders above all other princely graves known in the British archaeological record. Recent discoveries at Sutton Hoo, the result of the excavation project initiated in 1983, have revealed other rich graves with comparable objects, but none with the quantity of material represented by the excavations of 1939.

Excavations by Carver at Sutton Hoo and by Filmer-Sankey at Snape have shed important new light on the character of these two cemeteries. No longer can the ship-burials from these two sites be seen in isolation, but as part of a developing tradition of regional burial practice. On the one hand Sutton Hoo appears to be a cemetery reserved for an aristocratic elite and dates from the mid-sixth century – this date is tentative since at the time of writing carbon 14 dates have yet to be published. On the other hand the cemetery at Snape is significantly earlier, beginning perhaps as early as the fifth century. It is estimated to contain a large number of cremations and clearly began as a 'folk' cemetery sited on a pre-existing Bronze Age barrow (Carver 1992, 365; Filmer-Sankey 1992, 47). The Snape boat-burial appears to be the 'founder's' grave for a phase of inhumation, beginning in the second half of the sixth century. This may just pre-date the foundation of the 'royal' cemetery at Sutton Hoo, or there may be some degree of overlap, given that in both cases significant areas remain unexcavated.

Among the inhumation graves at Snape there appears an extraordinary variety of burial rite, but linking them are certain common strands, principally the use of wooden coffins or containers in six of the twenty-one inhumations excavated. These vary from structures with posts set in the grave itself to rectangular coffins, one with pointed ends like a boat. What we see is a developing tradition of burial in timber containers which culminates in large timber chambers reserved for the wealthiest individuals. Timber burial chambers are known elsewhere in the county. Three come from mounds 2, 14 and 17 at Sutton Hoo itself, and one from the Boss Hall Industrial Estate, Ipswich, where in 1990 a large chambered grave was discovered under a small barrow in an extensive cremation and inhumation cemetery. This cemetery also contained a remarkable female grave with a silver manicure set and a breathtaking collection of jewellery, which included four gold pendants and a circular garnet-encrusted brooch with four gold triangular panels in cruciform design. This high-status female grave cannot be earlier than AD 690 on the basis of one of two coins found in a bag with the jewellery (Newman 1992a; Webster & Backhouse 1991).

The Boss Hall male chamber grave contained three spearheads and a shield boss. Evidence was found for timber planking around the edge of this chamber which was nearly twice the width of any of the other graves. The site was excavated under far from ideal conditions, but the chamber grave appeared to pre-date the cremations set around the rim of its small barrow (Newman 1991a, 269–71). Two chamber graves were excavated at Spong Hill in Norfolk (Hills 1984) and at Broomfield in Essex, Taplow in Buckinghamshire, and Dover and Lyminge in Kent, all of which contained high-status individuals (Bruce-Mitford 1983). There is sufficient evidence now to suggest a 'chamber horizon' appearing in some south-eastern Anglo-Saxon cemeteries in the second half of the sixth century. They represent the upper echelons of a more steeply-ranked society, which is matched by a significant decrease in the number and quality of grave goods among the lower echelons. These chamber graves therefore seem to represent an upwardly mobile aristocratic elite whose rise to power appears to be at the expense of others and coincidental with the emergence of early kingdoms and the formation of the Heptarchy (Arnold 1982; Carver 1989, 143).

The work of the Sutton Hoo research project, although as yet incomplete, has begun to unravel the complexities of the site. So far, Carver has tentatively identified four main phases, taking account of what little stratigraphy the site offers and those carbon 14 dates that are available (Carver 1992, 365). The first phase is marked by one of the most important intact graves to be excavated so far in East Anglia, found at the very end of the project under Mound 17 (Figure 4.3). Under a low mound were two grave pits, one containing the complete skeleton of a horse, without grave goods other than some kind of organic furnishing, and the other a large cylindrical log coffin with curved iron cleats laid inside an even larger grave pit. Inside were the remains of a young male warrior complete with sword, pyramidal sword-studs and a garnet-inlaid buckle. By his head was a strike-a-light box.

The grave has subsequently become known as the 'Sutton Hoo Prince'. Beside his coffin on the north was a two-sided comb, an iron-bound bucket and a cauldron with a pottery vessel inside. At the east end of the grave was a group comprising a bronze drinking bowl resting on some animal ribs – a joint of meat of some kind. Other organic material may have been present in this area. At the western end lay a mass of metalwork which was subsequently lifted *en bloc* and excavated in the British Museum. At the time of writing it has just been placed on display and comprises: a bridle with an iron snaffle bit and gilt-bronze axe-shaped pendants; two exquisitely decorated circular gilt-bronze strap-distributors, and a number of small copper-bronze pendants or horse brasses. The bridle may have been placed in or below a circular wooden tub. Beneath the log-shaped coffin lay two spears and a shield. Carver suggests that an analysis of the metalwork may result in a mid to late sixth-century date for the Sutton Hoo Prince (Carver 1992). Clustering of objects both inside and outside the coffin is highly characteristic of this type of chamber grave, only exceeded in magnitude by Mound 1.

A second phase of barrow burial at Sutton Hoo is implicated by Mound 5. Here the mound occupies a central position in relation to the cemetery and is axial to Mounds 6 and 7. Like them it shares the same distinctive burial rite of cremation, wrapped in cloth and placed in a bronze bowl (Figure 4.3). Mound 5, which also contained a comb, shears and gaming pieces, appears to be stratigraphically earlier than Mound 6. What distinguishes Mound 5 is the presence of 16 bodies scattered in an irregular pattern around the south-eastern rim of the mound (Group 2). Although the body forms were indicated by nothing more than stains in the sub-soil, these, like others found on the eastern edge of the cemetery (Group 1), show evidence of trauma, of binding, hanging and beheading. They have all the appearance of sacrificial victims; indeed human sacrifice, which is well documented in the Scandinavian world, seems to be the only likely interpretation (Ellis Davidson 1992).

Carver has argued on the basis of this evidence that Mound 5 represents a 'founder's' grave for this second phase of cremation burial on the site and has even tentatively suggested that this might be Wuffa, the founder of the Wuffinga dynasty himself (Carver 1992, 366). Mound 4, the third barrow excavated by Basil Brown in 1938, must belong to phase 2 for it also contained the cremated bones of a young adult male wrapped in fine cloth and placed in a bronze bowl. With it were the cremated remains of a horse and a smaller animal, possibly a dog. There were indications of a feather pillow, small fragments of sheet bronze and a burnt bone or ivory gaming piece. Mound 3 is less characteristic of phase 2 in that two heaps of cremated bone, an adult male and another horse, lay on a wooden 'tray' about 1.70 by 0.56 metres. This was the first mound excavated by Brown in 1938 and one that was extremely confused by earlier grave robbers. Again, there are just enough pieces to indicate that this was once another rich grave. Fragments of a carved bone casket were also found and a piece of a stone plaque with a delicately carved winged victory of late Roman or Byzantine style. Brown also found a bronze lid with two links of chain which must once have attached it to a ewer of Mediterranean origin. Away from the western end of the wooden tray was the iron head of a *francisca* throwing axe.

A third phase is represented by coffin burials, particularly for adolescents and children. The only certain female chamber grave under Mound 14 may also belong to this phase although study of the artefacts which include a small silver buckle, a silver chain and a chatelaine, is as yet incomplete. The final phase, phase 4, includes those most 'extravagant and defiant' non-Christian gestures, the two ship-burials contained under Mounds 1 and 2 (Figure 4.3). Mound 1 will be discussed in the next two sections, but Mound 2 is equally deserving of attention, although like most of the mounds it had been robbed several times in antiquity. This was the second of the three mounds opened by Basil Brown in 1938. He recorded a random scatter of iron clench-nails and, after finding the bottom of the burial chamber with indications of timber staining, saw what he felt sure were the tapering bows of a small boat. One problem with this theory was his interpretation of the stern which appeared to have a very unconvincing timber transom; as far as we know, tran-soms – the squared-off stern of a boat – did not exist at this period in northern European waters.

Once again Brown had collected enough material to indicate that there had once been a spectacular grave assemblage. This was the only Sutton Hoo grave to produce a glass vessel and there are other clues making it directly comparable to Mound 1. Not only were there indications that it contained a ship with large numbers of iron rivets, but there was an iron-bound wooden tub, similar to that found in Mound 1. There was the tip of a pattern-welded sword, a 'scramasax' or single-edged battle knife, a silver buckle, a bronze ring with its attachment plate, presumably from a hanging bowl, two separate iron knives and a pair of opposed sheathed knife blades, fragments of a blue glass jar, two gilt bronze mounts, poss-ibly from a shield, and a silver gilt triangular mount from a drinking vessel.

One of the tantalising objectives of the Sutton Hoo project was to sort out the confusion over Mound 2 and try to place these objects in a more accurate context. By an extraordinary chance, the original plans of Basil Brown's excavation of Mound 2, drawn by Guy Maynard, were discovered by the author following a tip-off by Elizabeth Owles, in a Lowestoft antique shop at the very time when the mound was reopened. It was a rare experience to stand on the top of Mound 2 with Martin Carver as we unrolled these yellowing scrolls and observed the outline of the trenches. But Mound 2 proved to be a real Anglo-Saxon riddle, for as excavation pro-ceeded the random scatter of clench nails, nearly 500 in all, and confused state of the interior of the mound baffled the excavators. It took several seasons, meticulous recording of another 140 scraps of gold, silver, bronze and other materials, and total excavation of the mound and burial chamber before the riddle was finally cracked (Carver 1992, 355).

What transpired was a timber-lined burial chamber, 3.8 by 1.5 metres, with its base set 2 metres below the original ground surface. From stains in the sand at the bottom of the chamber it was possible to detect the outline of an adult male lying in a crouched position at the western end. Further stains and fragments clearly confirmed the presence of the iron-bound tub, the sword, the cauldron, the blue glass vessel, the drinking horns and other objects which Brown's excavations had indicated. But where was the boat? Brown had supposed, as had the modern excavators, that the burial chamber would be in the boat, but clearly this was not the case.

Repeated grave robbing and excavation had removed the pattern of rivets in the central area of the mound, but by exploring the whole of the mound, Carver's team was able to pick up some indication of the original arrangement of rivets inside the eastern and western slopes of the mound. Contrary to expectation the ship had been placed at ground level to form a lid over the underground burial chamber. The barrow had then been constructed over the ship, possibly leaving the prows protruding either side of the mound. Carver has noted a comparable example of this type of burial rite from Haithabu in southern Denmark (Carver 1992, 355). This ingenuity is so characteristic of the Anglo-Saxons. From their art and their literature, from their belief in 'weird', a concept poorly translated by the word 'fate', we know they regarded life and death as the greatest of all riddles. One cannot help wondering if there is not some Anglo-Saxon warrior, a Wuffinga no doubt, laughing into his drinking horn as he looks down on the archaeologists from somewhere in Valhalla.

Rædwald and Sutton Hoo

In 1939, Sutton Hoo Mound 1 produced material of international importance which transformed our understanding of early English kingship, yet so remarkable is it that it is difficult to place it in a national context, let alone the local context of the county in which it was found. Central to this is our understanding of whom it represents: there has never been any biological confirmation of the presence of a body in Mound 1, yet a body there must have been. Recent work by Carver suggests that all trace of flesh, bone and teeth would have been lost through the extreme acid soil environment within the treasure chamber, yet there is a strange absence of personal objects such as fibulae and finger-rings. However, this mystery does not detract from the main issue, the date of deposition, which hinges on the *terminus post quem* for the 37 Merovingian tremisses contained in the purse.

This issue has given rise to debate ever since the coins saw light of day in 1939. For many years numismatists pointed to a date in the middle of the seventh century until, in 1960, Lafaurie brought the terminal date back to AD 625 based on a study of the Escharen hoard. In a detailed analysis commissioned by Bruce-Mitford for the British Museum, Kent reaffirmed a date of AD 620–5, with the possible exception of coins 14 and 34, which could be as late as the early 630s (Bruce-Mitford 1975, 582). In 1982, Brown warned again about a possibility of a date as late as AD 626–9, and in 1991 Kirby warned about the uncertainty surrounding the assumed date of Rædwald's death (Brown 1982; Kirby 1991, 66, 77).

Given these uncertainties, the balance of probability still falls on a terminal date of approximately AD 625. This is crucial, for it narrows the field down to four possible contenders from the Wuffinga dynasty who reigned between AD 599 and 637: Rædwald, Earpwald, Sigeberht and Ecgric. Bede tells us that both Ecgric and Sigeberht were killed together in battle against King Penda of Mercia in AD 636/7. Both were ardent Christians – Sigeberht was in fact in religious orders at the time of his death, and he is believed to have been buried at *Bedericsworth*, the later site of Bury St Edmunds, and was most unlikely to have been given a pagan burial by King Anna, his Christian successor. We know very little about the brief reign of Earpwald, other than that he was converted to Christianity by Edwin, king of Northumbria, before being murdered by the pagan Ricbert. Earpwald does not seem to be a very likely candidate for celebration on the scale of Sutton Hoo Mound 1, although he may be represented by one of the smaller mounds.

Rædwald alone has all the right qualities; he was the greatest of all the pagan Wuffings, the fourth *bretwalda*, or high king, and he enjoyed a long and successful reign. Amongst other things, Bede tells us that Rædwald fought a successful campaign against Æthelfrid of Northumbria, raising a great army which defeated and killed Æthelfrid in Mercian territory (HE, II, 12). Bede also tells us that Rædwald had:

> long before been initiated into the mysteries of the Christian faith in Kent, but in vain; for on his return home, he was seduced by his wife and by certain evil teachers and perverted from the sincerity of his faith, so that his last state was worse than his first. After the manner of the ancient Samaritans, he seemed to be serving both Christ and the gods whom he had previously served; in the same temple he had one altar for the Christian sacrifice and another small altar on which to offer victims to devils. (HE, II, 15)

This extract is often quoted to account for the presence of objects charged with Christian symbolism in Mound 1. In particular the ten silver bowls with cruciform decoration and the matching pair of silver spoons inscribed with the names of Saul and Paul in letters of the Greek alphabet and small equal-armed crosses (Plate 11). The spoons in particular are suggestive of conversion and may have been baptismal gifts from Æthelberht of Kent. However, these objects are subordinate to the ship-burial ritual which is itself a wholly pagan rite. It is, in many respects, the final statement symbolising the power of the old pagan religion, now under threat from Christianity. Rædwald was the last pagan *bretwalda* and the antique quality of much of the Sutton Hoo treasure together with the style of burial reflects a powerful, pagan, reactionary court.

Bede explains the circumstances of the Northumbrian exile Edwin, effectively Rædwald's captive in East Anglia. Æthelfrid, king of Northumbria, tried to bribe Rædwald into releasing Edwin:

> he sent messengers offering Rædwald large sums of money to put Edwin to death. But it had no effect. He sent a second and third time, offering even larger gifts of silver and further threatening to make war on him if Rædwald despised his offer. The king, being either weakened by his threats or corrupted by his bribes, yielded to his request and promised either to slay Edwin or to give him up to the messengers . . .
>
> When he secretly told the queen of his plan . . . she dissuaded him from it, warning him that it was in no way fitting for so great a king to sell his best friend for gold when he was in such trouble, still less to sacrifice his own honour, which is more precious than any ornament, for the love of money. (HE, II, 12)

Scarfe has argued effectively that this statement, with its reference to bribes, silver and money, could indicate that the exceptional material in Mound 1 includes objects sent from Northumbria which were regarded by Rædwald's queen as in some way tainted – being blood-money given to betray a friend – and therefore consigned to the grave, where it could do no more evil (Scarfe 1980). This idea is intriguing, since there is a northern and Celtic element in the Sutton Hoo material with the whetstone and the three hanging bowls (Figure 4.4). But the main elements of the treasure, the gold and garnet regalia, which are almost certainly from an East Anglian workshop, and the Byzantine silver and the Merovingian coins, do not, in the view of this writer fit into a Northumbrian background, and it is these that Scarfe has suggested might be the objects of Æthelfrid's bribe. Sadly we do not know the name of Rædwald's ardently pagan and persuasive queen; she sounds an interesting character. Neither can we be certain that she out-lived Rædwald, or that she was responsible for his funeral arrangements.

Symbolism, mystique and protocol

The contents of the great ship-burial can only be regarded as symbolic, but symbolic of what? If the objects are symbolic of kingship at this period, then surely they must have been carefully chosen to represent different aspects and functions of early Anglo-Saxon kingship. The clustering and positioning of the objects must also have been significant, for just as the alignment of the ship with its bows to the east and stern to the west was a deliberate act, so each object lay in relation to that same orientation and had a spatial relationship to the whole assemblage. Although there was no material evidence for a human corpse, Evison has argued convincingly for the presence of a body in relation to a coffin on the basis of the iron cleats found in the central area of the burial deposit (Evison 1979).

These cleats are all slightly curved and may indicate a cylindrical log-shaped coffin, although it has to be said that the rate of curve on the surviving iron cleats illustrated by Bruce-Mitford varies in radius from 36 cm to 60 cm, when the distance between cleats across the burial chamber might suggest a radius of 75 cm. However, the cleats are contorted by corrosion and the coffin may not have been perfectly cylindrical, but may have had curving sides. Similar cleats have been found recently in relation to a cylindrical coffin in Mound 17, the 'Prince's' grave at Sutton Hoo, and are known elsewhere from princely graves at Broomfield, Taplow, Lyminge, Dover and possibly Saare, while a single example is recorded from Boat Grave XI at Vendel, in Sweden (Bruce-Mitford 1983, 913–23; Carver 1992, 362).

In fact the cleats were aligned at a slight angle (4–5°) to the keel, suggesting that this was a large coffin, separate and movable, within a fixed tent-like timber chamber constructed inside the boat (Figure 4.4). It is argued that although no trace of a body was found, simply concentrations of phosphate in the area of the sword, shield and Anastasius dish, a body there must have been. Central to the body's waist line must also have been the great gold belt-buckle and, logically, the shoulder-clasps must have been on or very close to the shoulders. Evison suggests that the helmet (Plate 10), which appeared crushed like an empty shell, would have been placed beside the head as there was no indication of a skull inside it (Evison 1979). Thus if we accept the outline of a body as postulated by Evison, but allow for a slight angle of 4–5° to the keel to take into account the true alignment of the coffin cleats, the arrangement of different elements of the ship-burial become apparent (Figure 4.4).

First, there are those objects placed within the central coffin; presumably these were most intimate to their late owner. Second, a group of objects, including the standard, sceptre and shield, was placed between the head of the coffin and the chamber wall at the western end. Third, a bundle of spears and angons with an iron-bound bucket were on the south side; the tips of the angons were linked to the 'Coptic' bowl and its contents. And a fourth group of objects was outside the foot of the coffin, between it and the eastern chamber wall. These four groups are also distinguished by their decreasing intrinsic value and functional status. The highest status objects, including all the solid gold and garnet jewellery, and all the silver and objects of personal apparel were contained neatly within the inner coffin. Outside the coffin at the head end were less personal objects, more ceremonial and symbolic of emergent statehood, such as the standard, the shield, the lyre and whetstone or sceptre; these objects appear to be of less intrinsic value – only the shield and lyre have gold upon them but it is applied gold leaf on copper-bronze alloy, not solid gold.

The bundle of spears and angons lay on the south side and slightly under the curving side of the coffin, but were clearly linked to the group at the western end by three of the angons which were carefully passed through one of the drop-handles of the 'Coptic' hanging bowl (Evans 1986, 430). A similar arrangement may have linked the butts of the spears to the iron-bound bucket placed in the middle of the south side of the coffin, where the spear ferrules were also found (Figure 4.4). At the eastern end lay the third and most utilitarian group, the three cauldrons and the cauldron hanger and other objects of a more domestic and culinary nature. Thus the assemblage had a 'high' and a 'low' end, rather like the contents of an Anglo-Saxon feasting hall. The body lay in such a position that if it sat upright it would look towards the bows of the ship and the 'low' service end of the 'hall' assemblage. Behind it were piled all the ceremonial trappings of kingship, stacked as if they were behind the king lying in state.

To what extent does the Sutton Hoo material reflect not only the functions of kingship, but also the duties of functionaries within the royal household? Anglo-Saxon and medieval kings had retinues; the greater the king the greater the retinue (Brooke 1963). At this period we may be talking more about Scandinavian or Germanic warbands rather than a dignified court retinue of the later Middle Ages (Hedeager 1992). However, even at this early date service in the king's hall would have brought with it power and influence. Positions in the royal household were key posts in later Anglo-Saxon and medieval government; such *domestici* also acted as *ministri* in a king's private council (Stenton 1958; Campbell 1987, 211). Indeed, we might well expect to find such positions being held by junior members of the royal family, by Wuffings themselves; possibly some of those *gesiths* and king's *thegns* – members of the king's body guard – that might be represented in other princely graves at Sutton Hoo (Loyn 1992).

So the four groups of material in the Sutton Hoo ship-burial may well be associated with divisions of status within the royal household – each group of objects is clearly both symbolic and functional within a hierarchical structure. Each in its different way represents a buttress to the mystique of kingship and is a propaganda statement about the power and influence of this man; a statement designed to resound in the halls of Valhalla just as much as it had done on earth. Let us speculate further about these groups and subgroups. A distinction can be made between those objects which relate directly to the personal and primary functions of kingship, and others which from their grouping seem to be symbolic of secondary functions and may perhaps have been placed in the ship by functionaries in the king's court in a way designed to reflect their individual honorific duties.

Thus the helmet, shield, sword and sword harness, and the gold mounted wand or pointing stick were personal to the king. No doubt they were fitting to his status as monarch, and his function as law-maker and supreme judge. However, at least one pre-Viking East Anglian king had a sword bearer; St Edmund's armour bearer was supposedly the key witness to his lord's martyrdom (Whitelock 1969). The cluster of drinking vessels, on the other hand, including the two great drinking horns and the six maplewood bottles, all carefully placed on piles of folded cloth, might represent the role of master-brewer or master of ceremonies (Figure 4.4). Brewing and drinking ceremonies were central to court life in the *Beowulf* epic and central also to what we know about later Scandinavian funerary customs where up to a third of the dead man's wealth might be spent on ale for the wake (Ellis Davidson 1992, 335).

At the feet of the king, inside his coffin and under the great Anastasius dish, was a complex of personal items arranged on a wooden 'trough'. These items lay in, under and around the small and medium sized hanging bowls and included two pairs of stitched leather shoes with silver buckles and straps, a leather tunic, a leather down-filled pillow, a wooden bowl or scoop and a horn cup. There was also a set of gaming pieces, possibly in a leather bag. Inside the fluted silver bowl, also under the Anastasius dish, but above the mail shirt and leather tunic, was a separate group of items including a silver ladle handle and bowl, some burr-wood cups, four bone-handled knives, some textiles, an otter-skin cap and three fine bone combs. Although many of these objects were small they were piled high in a great heap with the chain-mail shirt and axe-hammer at the bottom and the Anastasius dish balanced on top. In fact the objects may have been supported from toppling over by being stacked at the lower end of the coffin, indeed, the wooden 'trough' below all the objects may well have been the hollowed-out eastern end of the coffin (Bruce-Mitford 1983, 835).

Inside the coffin there were two separate distinctive clusters of silver-ware. The first cluster, inside the eastern end of the coffin, included the great Anastasius dish with its pile of cremated matter and the ladle and fluted silver bowl under it. The cremated matter may represent a burnt offering of some kind with the ladle used for the pouring of libations, while the knives and cups may have been used at sacrificial feasts. Beside this group was a small pottery bottle, which once contained a viscous liquid, perhaps an oil or unguent of some kind, and an iron lamp; the latter and possibly also the former may have been placed on top of the coffin. This group suggests a religious function and might have been placed by a pagan high priest at the feet of the dead man. That there were such priests in positions of power in the pagan royal courts is not in doubt; Bede relates the story of Coifi, Edwin's high priest, who burnt the temple at Goodmanham, so aiding the Christian conversion of Northumbria (HE, II, 13). The second cluster, which comprised a nest of ten silver bowls and two spoons with their obvious Christian emblems, may have been placed by a royal chaplain. We know that Rædwald was baptised into Christianity when visiting Kent, only to apostatise on his return; the two clusters of silver vessels may therefore formally recognise the dualities of belief which caused him to set up an altar to Christ beside one to pagan gods (HE, II, 15).

Underneath the great silver dish lay the hauberk of chain-mail and the iron axe-hammer, both masterpieces of the ironsmith's craft. Were these placed in the coffin by some Wayland or armourer attached to the court? Hung on the belt attached to the waist, rather like a sporran, was the purse with its carefully selected collection of 37 tiny gold tremisses, each one from a different mint in Merovingian Gaul, three matching gold blanks and two small gold billets. These, it is suggested, were intended as payment for forty oarsmen and a ship's captain (Evans 1986, 88–9). The purse itself may well have been placed by a royal treasurer or a similar functionary with power to pick and choose coins out of the royal treasury.

Such arguments are, of course, purely speculation and lie outside the area of normal archaeological interpretation, but clearly the groups of objects relate to different social and economic functions of kingship and the social hierarchy which supported the institution of kingship, such as it was at this early date. There can be no doubt that we are dealing with an increasingly complex society, where kingship had progressed to a level where it could only be sustained by large numbers of privileged functionaries whose own position and status was dependent on ensuring the continued power, prestige and good will of their monarch; failure in this obligation might bring disgrace, ruin, exile or even death. It is therefore not unreasonable to suggest that the clusters of objects in the coffin could well relate to an inner circle of highly trusted advisers and privileged functionaries in the king's household, possibly even members of a royal council.

In similar fashion we can speculate on the functional symbolism and relationships of other objects and clusters within the western group, lying between the head of the coffin and the burial chamber wall. The whole character of this group is one of ceremonial and complex symbolism. The great iron standard or 'tuffa' could only have been carried by a burly standard bearer or marshal; it lay beside the whetstone or sceptre, the function of which remains obscure, but the two may have been the responsibility of the same royal appointment. The shield is so fine and decorative that it can only be ceremonial; a shield of state perhaps carried by a shield-bearer or personal bodyguard. In the middle of this group lay a small bronze bell, probably of late Roman workmanship. Of all the objects in this group, the bell most clearly indicates the ordering of ceremonies.

The lyre, in its beaver-skin bag, carefully placed inside the bronze 'Coptic' bowl must surely represent the royal bard, laid to rest by some grateful *Deor*, or Saxon bard, of the East Anglian court. However, we must recognise that kings themselves may have been skilled in the musical arts and this could have been the king's own lyre. The function of corporate entertainment is very evident in many of the objects in the assemblage, but like all entertainment at this level it no doubt had a purpose; we must not forget that the great epics like *Beowulf* enshrined within them a blend of historical fact and genealogical propaganda. They were a significant buttress to the mystique of kingship and it was the bard who orchestrated and praised the dynasty's historical achievements.

The 'Coptic' bowl itself could also have been part of the lyrist's deposition, but for the fact that the three angons, in the same bundle as the five spears, had been passed through one of its drop-handles. The eight spears and angons might be symbolic of a small household guard, but they seem inadequate to the scale of the burial. If on the other hand they were the spears of the king's huntsmen they would fit into the entertainment role so evident in other aspects of the assemblage. Hunting was certainly the entertainment of kings in the later Anglo-Saxon period and by the time of Henry I the king's hunting staff formed the largest department of the royal household (Brooke 1963, 71).

At the eastern end were clustered one large and three smaller cauldrons and an iron pot-hanger, an iron-bound tub and a wooden bucket. These are of a culinary function, but their size and weight are clearly designed to impress. The height of the pot-hanger (3.45 metres) is often quoted as indicative of the height of a cross-beam in the king's hall (Evans 1986, 79), but the size of the cauldron and the iron-bound tub, both of which would hold about 100 litres, may also be indicative of the size of the king's retinue (Evans 1986, 77).

Three groups can therefore be recognised outside the coffin; a western ceremonial group, a southern spearman group and an eastern culinary group. The only objects which are common to all three of these groups are the three iron-bound stave-wood buckets. These vary somewhat in style of decoration, but are essentially functional objects. There is no evidence as to what they contained. They also vary in size; bucket 1 was the smallest with a rim diameter of 22 cm and was placed inside the tub with the culinary objects at the eastern end. Bucket 2 was placed well out from the coffin in the middle of the south side close to the spear ferrules; it had a rim diameter of 25 cm. The largest, bucket 3, made of yew wood, had a rim diameter of 33 cm and was placed with the ceremonial group at the western end. This grading of size has to be significant for it equates with the intrinsic value and status of the groups concerned. There is little point in speculating about the contents of these buckets. Stave buckets are made by the cooper's craft and are designed to hold liquid, but we can be sure in this case that it was not water – a strong beverage suitable perhaps for three thirsty groups of household retainers and royal officials.

Thus we have a vision of the royal court and household of the Wuffinga dynasty. A king on his own is no king at all. We are not looking at an isolated figure; Rædwald was certainly no Lear. He undoubtedly commanded a great retinue, a troop of followers and a household of servants. Like the kings of later centuries, an office in the king's household and a place in the king's hall brought with it honour, prestige, wealth and dignity (Stenton 1958). At Sutton Hoo we do not just see the cenotaph of a provincial king of the East Angles; we see a whole system of government by powerful dignitaries who inhabited a splendid court surrounded by protocol and complex diplomacy, every detail of which was probably determined by precedent and a long established tradition of kingship both in East Anglia and the continental homelands.

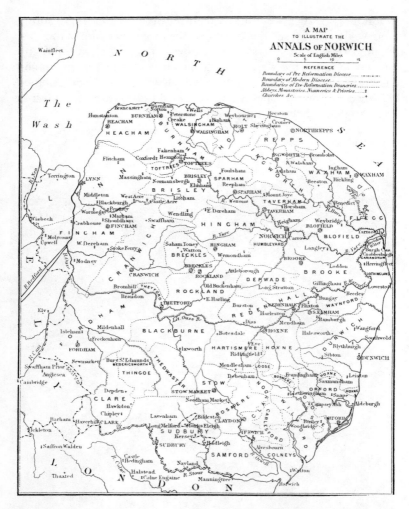

Plate 1   The medieval diocese of Norwich: the old East Anglian diocese included both counties of Norfolk and Suffolk and extended westwards to the line of the Devil's Dyke and the Isle of Ely; its boundary derives from the frontiers of the old Anglo-Saxon kingdom of East Anglia

Plate 2 The Devil's Dyke: a late Roman or early Anglo-Saxon frontier to the territory which later became the kingdom of East Anglia

Plate 3 Crop-marks of the Fornham cursus and interrupted ditch systems. The narrow parallel lines receding from view in the centre of the picture mark the cursus, while the curving dotted lines in the foreground represent two interrupted ditch systems. Both the ditch systems and the cursus indicate a focus of ritual activity during the early and late Neolithic respectively

Plate 4 Westhall terrets: found on a small early Roman site in 1854 when new ditches were being dug near the line of the East Suffolk railway. These bronze enamelled terrets represent the best of late Icenian metalwork intended for a decorative chariot or wheeled vehicle

Plate 5 Burgh-by-Woodbridge: although ploughed almost flat the lighter colour of the rectangular banked and ditched enclosure can be clearly seen. The church of Burgh stands in the trees near the centre. This major Iron Age fortification later served as the site of a Roman villa

Plate 6 Roman fort and later Roman settlement at Pakenham, near Bury St Edmunds. The site is now crossed by the Ixworth by-pass

Walton Castle, Suffolk.

Plate 7 Ruins of the Roman shore fort at Walton, near Felixstowe, as they appeared in 1786. Coastal erosion has left blocks of masonry stranded on the sea-shore, while larger sections of wall appear to have toppled over the cliff. Coin series indicate a substantial Roman presence here in the fourth century

Plate 8 The reconstructed buildings of the early Anglo-Saxon village at West Stow Country Park

Plate 9 Brandon. Staunch Meadow: the excavated remains of a timber Middle Saxon church, the only one of its kind to have been found in Suffolk

Plate 10 The Sutton Hoo helmet: this, the most evocative symbol of power and prestige, was worn by a senior member of the Wuffings, the early Anglo-Saxon dynasty that ruled over seventh-century East Anglia. Its design owes much to the late Roman world, but its workmanship derives ultimately from the Vendel culture of Sweden

Plate 11 The Sutton Hoo silver spoons: these symbolise the uncertain
transition to Christianity in seventh-century East Anglia. They are late
Roman, a matching pair, marked SAULOS and PAULOS in rather irregular
and malformed Greek characters in two different hands. The reference
must be to baptism, but few in the seventh-century East Anglian court
could have understood their subtle message. Consigned to a pagan burial
they further highlight the difficulties faced by the Christian mission at this
time

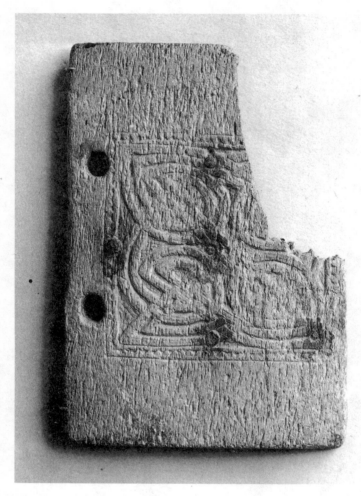

Plate 12 The Blythburgh writing tablet: 9.4 by 6.3 cm.
Found in 1902 with three *styli* on the land of Blythburgh Priory. The tablet
is of bone recessed for wax on the inside and decorated on the outside
(seen here) with an incised quadripartite knot design of the eighth century.
Copper-alloy rivets indicate some later attachment or clasp. There are
traces of a runic inscription in Latin on the inside

Plate 13 The Old Minster, South Elmham St Cross: in the foreground lies the wooded square of the banked and ditched enclosure which contains the ruins of the Old Minster. The farm at the top of the picture marks the moated site of the later medieval episcopal palace

Plate 14 Brandon gold plaque inlaid with niello: 3.5 by 3.3 cm. Found in 1978 near the excavated Middle Saxon timber church at Staunch Meadow. The symbolism and the inscription relate to St John the Evangelist and indicate that it was one of four attached to a book cover or the arms of an altar cross

Plate 15 View of Iken and the Alde estuary from the south-west: St Botolph established a monastery near here in AD 654 at a place called *Icanhoh*

5

The early Church

Conversion of the Angles

The early days of Christianity in East Anglia were troubled indeed. We have seen how Rædwald was baptised in Kent at the behest of his *bretwalda*, King Æthelberht, only to apostatise from the true faith and then serve both Christ and the ancient gods. Thus, says Bede, his last state was worse than his first (HE, II, 15). As far as is known, Rædwald made no attempt to establish a diocese in his kingdom, but his son, Earpwald, accepted Christianity and some attempt was made to convert the province during his brief reign (*c.* AD 625–27). However, he was soon deposed and murdered by a pagan named Ricbert and for three years East Anglia lapsed into heathenism (HE, II, 15). During this time Sigeberht, a brother of Earpwald, was educated and converted to Christianity while exiled in Gaul; indeed the name, Sigeberht, is of Frankish origin. It was not uncommon for opposition parties to find themselves exiled, either to other English courts, as in the case of Edwin of Northumbria exiled to pagan East Anglia, or to the continent and the Christian courts of Merovingia. These periods of exile were formative in the education of young princes and a major stimulus to the spread of new ideas between the kingdoms of northern Europe.

Links between East Anglia and Gaul are noticeable before the conversion proper with the presence of Merovingian tremisses in the Sutton Hoo purse and one or two other isolated finds, such as the gold coin of Sigebert III (AD 634–56) found recently in a rich female grave at Boss Hall, Ipswich (Newman 1991a). By the second half of the seventh century contacts have become formalised:

> because there were not yet many monasteries founded in England, numbers of people from Britain used to enter the monasteries of the Franks or Gauls to practise the monastic life; they also sent their daughters to be wedded to the heavenly bridegroom. They mostly went to the monasteries at Brie, Chelles, and Andelys-sur-Seine; among these was Sæthryd, step-daughter of Anna, king of East Anglia . . . and Æthelberga, his own daughter. Both of these though foreigners were, by the merit of their virtues, made abbesses of Brie. (HE, III, 8)

Chelles was also the chosen place for retreat when Hilda of Whitby renounced the secular life in about AD 647, 'Her sister Hereswith, mother of Ealdwulf, king of the East Angles, was at that time living in the monastery under the discipline of the Rule and awaiting her heavenly crown' (HE, IV, 23). Links between this area of northern Gaul and women of Anglo-Saxon royal background persisted down to the time of the Norman Conquest, when Githa, the mother of Harold, led the women-folk who had lost husbands and lands after the Battle of Hastings to Saint-Omer (Garmonsway 1972, 202).

In AD 630, when Sigeberht came to the East Anglian throne after his exile in Gaul the process of conversion began in earnest.

> [Sigeberht] was a devout Christian and a very learned man in all respects. . . . As soon as he began to reign he made it his business to see that the whole kingdom shared his faith. Bishop Felix most nobly supported his efforts. This bishop, who had been born and consecrated in Burgundy, came to Archbishop Honorius, to whom he expressed his longings; so the archbishop sent him to preach the word of life to this nation of the Angles. . . . He received the seat of his bishopric in the city of Dommoc [Dunwich]. (HE, II, 15)
>
> Sigeberht was a good and religious man . . . when he returned to his own land to become king, he at once sought to imitate some of the excellent institutions which he had seen in Gaul, and established a school where boys could be taught letters with the help of Bishop Felix, who had come to him from Kent and who provided him with masters and teachers as in the Kentish school. (HE, III, 18)

The process of education combined with Christian teaching formed the bed-rock upon which the conversion was based. The Augustinian mission, begun in AD 597, was directed at the Kentish court and the upper echelons of society in the belief that Christian teaching would then spread down the social scale. In fact it took more than ninety years to convert all the English courts and Christian teaching may not have reached the *pagi*, the grass-roots of rural society, until the time of Edgar in the late tenth century.

Unfortunately, Sigeberht's enthusiasm for the new faith undermined the ancient principles of Anglo-Saxon kingship and the need for a visible and determined leader:

> So greatly did he love the kingdom of heaven that at last he resigned his kingly office and entrusted it to his kinsman Ecgric, who had previously ruled over part of the kingdom. He thereupon entered a monastery which he himself had founded. He received the tonsure and made it his business to fight instead for the heavenly kingdom. (HE, III, 18)

Bede often begs more questions than he answers. Later tradition suggests that the monastery concerned was *Bedericsworth*, the predecessor to Bury St Edmunds, where Sigeberht is believed to have been buried (Blake 1962, 11). That part of East Anglia ruled by Ecgric must remain forever obscure. It does however confirm the existence of sub-kingdoms, shires or *regios* within the territory, some of which are clearly recognisable in the pattern of later administrative boundaries in Suffolk (Figure 5.1) and will be discussed in the next chapter.

Felix, we are told, died peacefully in office after a ministry of seventeen years, yet his life must have been anything but peaceful. Throughout this period East Anglia was at war with Mercia and four of its kings died on the battlefield. The backdrop to the conversion of the East Anglians was a three-cornered power struggle between East Anglia, Mercia and Northumbria. Christian ideology was charged with political significance, for it introduced new concepts of kingship and weakened a social structure unified by the prime function of kingship, the wageing of war. About five or six years after Sigeberht came to the throne:

> When he had been in the monastery for some considerable time, it happened that the East Anglians were attacked by the Mercians under their king Penda. As the East Anglians realised that they were no match for their enemies, they asked Sigeberht to go into fight with them in order to inspire the army with confidence. He was unwilling and refused, so they dragged him to the fight from the monastery, in

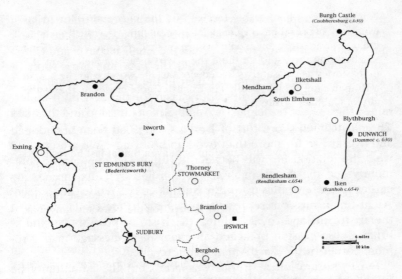

5.1 Suffolk: *villa regia* and ecclesiastical centres mentioned in early sources

the hope that the soldiers would be less afraid and less ready to flee if they had with them one who was once their most vigorous and distinguished leader. But remembering his profession and surrounded though he was by a splendid army, he refused to carry anything but a staff in his hand. He was killed together with King Ecgric, and the whole army was either slain or scattered by the heathen (HE, III, 18).

The date and site of this battle is unknown (Stenton & Clemoes 1959; Colgrave & Mynors 1969, 268). The refusal to bear arms when in religious orders was not something to bother abbots and monks in the later Middle Ages, but at this period it might have been a hang-over from the pagan past, for Bede tells us elsewhere that the pagan high-priest of Northumbria was normally forbidden to carry weapons or to ride anything but a mare (HE, II, 13).

During Sigeberht's reign, in about AD 633:

there came a holy man from Ireland called Fursey; he was renowned in word and deed and remarkable for his singular virtues. He was anxious to live the life of a pilgrim for the Lord's sake, wherever opportunity offered. When he came to the kingdom of the East

Angles, he was honourably received by the king and followed his usual task of preaching the Gospel. . . . he set himself with all speed to build a monastery on a site which he had received from King Sigeberht and to establish there the observance of a Rule. Now the monastery was pleasantly situated close to the woods and the sea, in a Roman camp which is called in English Cnobheresburg, that is the city of Cnobhere [Burgh Castle]. (HE, III, 19)

The old Roman shore fort of Burgh Castle had been abandoned and overgrown for more than two hundred years. We are not told what the relationship was between this new Celtic monastic community and the Augustinian see established by Felix three years earlier just a few miles down the Suffolk coast. While the 'official' Augustinian mission, represented by Felix, directed its efforts at the aristocrats and royal families, the Irish, or possibly Northumbrian–Celtic mission preached an evangelical message in this remote corner of the East Anglian countryside.

Fursey's duration at Burgh was brief, but the community he established may have survived, for it was further endowed by King Anna, the Christian successor to Sigeberht and the son of Eni, with finer buildings and gifts.

Then Fursey:

leaving his brother Foillán in charge of the monastery and its souls and also the priests Gobán and Dícuill and, being free from all worldly cares, he resolved to end his life as a hermit. . . . Then seeing that the kingdom was disturbed by heathen invasions and that the monasteries were also threatened with danger, he left things in order and sailed for Gaul, where he was honorably entertained by Clovis, king of the Franks, and by the patrician Eorcenwold. He built a monastery in a place called Lagny [Lagny sur Marne], where, not long afterwards he was taken ill and died. (HE, III, 19)

It is possible that this enclave of Irish missionary activity directed its efforts inland up the Waveney valley. Fursey's disciples being entrusted with the care of souls implies the presence of several congregations. Bede specifically mentions the effectiveness of Fursey's teaching and the practice of some kind of monastic Rule, although it is hard to imagine that this Irish aristocrat and his followers brought with them anything resembling the Rule of St Benedict. The priest *Dícuill* may possibly have given his name to Dickleburgh in south Norfolk (Scarfe 1972, 119).

Such associations between place-names and the names of early saints is highly attractive, but otherwise unsubstantiated by any other evidence, either archaeological or documentary. The same can be said for place-names such as Chediston, Chedburgh and Chadacre which have been linked to the name of Bishop Cedd of Essex and his brother Chad, more commonly associated with the site of Bradwell-on-Sea (HE, III, 22). Bede states that Cedd baptised Swithhelm, king of Essex, at Rendlesham, where King Æthelwold of East Anglia acted as his sponsor, but there is nothing else to link Cedd with Suffolk place-names beginning with Ched-, none of which are recorded until the time of the Domesday survey, 400 years later (HE, III, 22; Scarfe 1986, 21). Chad, we are told, 'had come with Queen Æthelthryth [Etheldreda] from the kingdom of the East Angles, being the chief of her officers and the head of her household (*primus ministrorum et princeps domus*)' (HE, IV, 3). He eventually renounced the world and established a monastery at Lastingham in Mercia and for three years was the bishop of York (HE, V, 19).

The presence of pre-Conquest monastic sites in the Waveney, Yare and Bure river systems, at Mendham, South Elmham and St Benet's Abbey, Holme, begs a question as to whether they might not have their origins in this early conversion period – a question which only excavation might answer. It is unlikely however that the influence of the monastery at Burgh Castle was of any duration. Fursey's stay at Burgh Castle was curtailed in part by the threat of war and Scarfe has noted that in early hagiographic sources for Foillan, who was Fursey's half-brother, written within six years of his death, *Cnobheresburg* was sacked after Fursey's departure. Foillan was only saved by the approach of King Anna and he subsequently rescued books and valuables and took them to France (West *et al.* 1984, 294).

In AD 654, King Anna and his son were killed at Bulcamp, near Blythburgh, by Penda at the head of another pagan Mercian army, and from this time onwards East Anglia seems to be subordinate to the rising power of Mercia. However, in the following year, Anna's brother and successor, Ethelhere, was killed at the Battle of Winwead with all his thegns and followers. He was fighting on the side of Penda, perhaps as a puppet king, although Bede says that he was responsible for the war (HE, III, 24; Garmonsway 1972, 29). How could Christianity survive in such political turmoil? Yet the implication of Bede is that much missionary activity continued during this period. In the year before the Battle of Bulcamp, 'Botolph began to build a monastery at Icanhoh' (Garmonsway 1972, 28-9), in the Alde estuary. Botolph or Botwulf is an otherwise obscure saint, and his life, written in the eleventh century by Bishop Folcard of Thorney, is not to be trusted. He is commonly associated with the town of Boston in Lincolnshire (Farmer 1985). However, his cult gave rise to the dedication of more than 64 churches, many of them near town gateways, as he later became recognised as the patron saint of travellers.

For many years there was doubt about Botolph's popular association with Iken in Suffolk, but in 1977, Stanley West discovered the lower section of a carved late ninth/early tenth-century stone cross-shaft built into the base of Iken church tower (West et al. 1984). The stone was exposed partly as a result of a fire which destroyed the thatched roof of the church in 1968. Prior to restoration, excavation took place under the floor of the old church and the cross-shaft was extracted from the tower wall. Although the church fabric proved to be of Norman origin, a Middle Saxon phase of activity on the site was evidenced by three sherds of Ipswich ware. It was suggested by Rosemary Cramp that the stone cross-shaft was commemorative and may have been positioned when the bones of St Botolph were dispersed on the orders of Bishop Æthelwold in the tenth century with other relics being recovered from monastic sites destroyed by the Danes (West et al. 1984, 298–9).

This new archaeological work, although not conclusive, greatly strengthens the argument for associating Botolph with the parish of Iken in Suffolk (Plate 15). In addition, work by Fenwick and others on Burrow Hill in Butley, overlooking the Ore estuary, 8 kilometres (5 miles) to the south, has revealed an extensive site and cemetery of mid to late eighth-century date. There was some evidence for an Ipswich-'type' ware and other imported pottery from northern France. Although no buildings were found there was some window glass; locks, keys and writing implements are also recorded, suggestive of an early monastic site. The hill-top site appears to have been enclosed by three boundary ditches although these may have been Iron Age in origin. Dating evidence rests on a single radiocarbon date, nevertheless this is another important

Middle to Late Saxon site which may not be unconnected with Botolph's monastery at *Icanhoh* (Fenwick 1984).

Thus, between AD 630 and 645, there is early documentary evidence for three key monastic sites being established on the Suffolk coast, at Dunwich, Burgh and Iken, and from which the process of conversion took place (Figure 5.1). There may well have been others for which there is only circumstantial evidence, such as Blythburgh, South Elmham, Mendham, Nayland and Hoxne, all of which appear to have been later Saxon 'minsters', some with 'communities' of monks (Blair 1985). There are also isolated finds of archaeological material, such as the seventh-century gold and garnet pectoral cross found in 1886 in a grave at Stanton, near Ixworth – it may have come from the same workshop as some of the Sutton Hoo jewellery and the Wilton cross from Norfolk (Webster & Backhouse 1991, 26–7). It has a more distant parallel in the pectoral cross found in the grave of St Cuthbert now at Durham Cathedral. We must not forget that the fenland abbeys outside the county at Thorney, Peterborough and Ely were if anything more influential, in particular Ely, founded in AD 672 by Etheldreda (the daughter of King Anna of East Anglia), as a direct result of royal patronage of the type initiated by Sigeberht.

Regios and minsters

The earliest and best documented royal estate is Rendlesham, the country seat of Rædwald. Bede mentions this *uico regio*, because it was the place where Swidhelm, son of Sexbald, a king of the East Saxons, was baptised by Cedd (HE, III, 22). This implies the presence of a church, but exactly where remains uncertain. The surviving church of St Gregory at Rendlesham gives away no clues about its age, although its dedication suggests an early date. This church is likely to be the one mentioned under Rendlesham in the Domesday survey with just 20 acres (DB ii, 326b). It was part of a small estate of one carucate held by Ulchetel before the Conquest and with it in Rendlesham were a number of other freemen and a freewoman with small acreages under different lordships; nothing to suggest the remains of a large estate (DB ii, 293b, 326, 343b, 388b, 443b). Recent work by Newman, surveying sites in the Deben valley, has detected an extensive pottery scatter to the north of St

Gregory's church. The whole site covers more than 15 hectares and appears to be multi-period producing prehistoric, Romano-British as well as Anglo-Saxon and later material. Quantities of Ipswich ware suggest a peak of occupation in the Middle Saxon period. Small-scale excavation in 1982 tended to confirm this Middle Saxon date, but a scrap of decorated copper-alloy sheet indicates the presence of some earlier sixth/seventh-century activity nearby (Newman 1992, 36–7). This site is therefore a strong candidate for the location of Rædwald's country seat, but there are other contenders.

Rendlesham lies near to the centre of the Wicklaw hundreds close to a small cluster of place-names containing Latin loan-words, which are believed by Gelling to indicate contact between Latin word-users and early Anglo-Saxon Germanic-speaking settlers (Gelling 1977). Campsey Ash contains the element *campus* meaning an open space or field and Wickam Market has the first element *wic*, which, with Wicklaw itself and the manor of Wicklows, may indicate a late surviving centre of Roman administration, possibly the late Roman site of Hacheston (Warner 1988, 15). From a study of parish boundaries and place-names in the area it is clear that the parish of Rendlesham was also once much larger and may have included the neighbouring parishes of Eyke and Bromeswell, together with another Domesday vill, Wilford.

First, the church of St Gregory's in Rendlesham is very close to the boundary with Eyke (Figure 5.2). Second, Bromeswell has a number of small entries in the Domesday survey to individual freemen holding small acreages and also mentions two churches, one with just 6 acres of land and the other with 16 acres (DB, ii, 293, 318, 319, 319b, 324, 324b, 387, 387b). The present church of Bromeswell is dedicated to St Edmund, a dedication which must be later than AD 870. One of the Domesday churches mentioned under Bromeswell could belong to Eyke, but the present parish of Bromeswell includes within it another Domesday vill, Wilford, which also had three small entries (DB ii, 318b, 325, 343b). The impression given by the Domesday survey is that Bromeswell is a relatively late parish with many small scattered holdings under different lordships. If there ever had been a large royal estate in the area of Rendlesham and Bromeswell in the seventh century, then by the time of the Domesday survey it had become so fragmented as to be indistinguishable from surrounding landholdings.

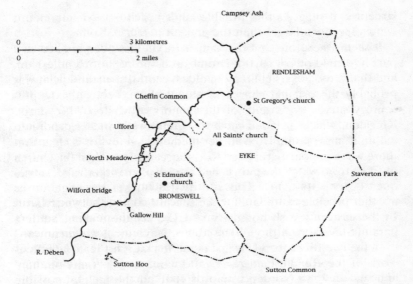

5.2 The *regio* of Rendlesham, including the parishes of Eyke and Bromeswell

Third, Eyke is a late place-name of Scandinavian origin, meaning oak, and does not appear in the Domesday survey, although it could be included under one or other of the many Bromeswell entries. Yet Eyke has for its parish church the fragmentary remains of what was once a large Saxo-Norman structure, of cruciform plan, with evidence for a central tower, north and south transepts and a south aisle – the sort of church that one would normally associate with a late minster church and an important Saxo-Norman estate, but no evidence for such an estate exists in Eyke parish. Furthermore, the east end of this church contains quantities of re-used stone which appear to have come from an earlier, much larger building. Its present dedication to All Saints may well be a re-dedication (Bond 1914). Eyke church would appear to be central to the Rendlesham *regio* complex (Figure 5.2). As it appears today, Eyke church has suffered from severe contraction over many centuries so that all that is left is the stump of its central tower, part of the nave and south aisle and chancel. This is typical of an ancient church which has lost revenue from tithes to maintain the original structure; it suggests that tithable lands which once maintained it were very much larger than the present parish.

It seems therefore that the name of Eyke has been applied to a parish formed out of part of Bromeswell and part of Rendlesham, and that it took as its church the oldest central structure, what was probably the original church of Rendlesham. From a sixteenth-century survey or 'extent' of the manors of Melton, Ufford and Kingston, which included most of Bromeswell, and incorporated within it information from earlier medieval surveys, it is clear that there was a major site referred to as the 'castle', north of the church of Eyke from which the pub, called the Elephant and Castle, subsequently took its name. This site invites further investigation as another possible candidate for the site of Rædwald's country seat. In the eastern parish boundary of Eyke lay the ancient hunting park of Staverton. Although the park at Staverton is not mentioned until the twelfth century it is just possible that it fits into the framework of the Rendlesham *regio*. The name of 'Cheffin Common' appears on John Norden's map of 1601 on the meadows of the River Deben below Eyke church near Reves Hall farm. The first place-name element of Cheffin may, like 'Chermoor' or 'Shermoor' in the Blyth valley, mean 'Shire-fen': an area of meadow which was common grazing for the shire, in this case the five and a half hundreds of Wicklaw (Suffolk Record Office V5/22/1; Warner 1982, 29).

The southern edge of the Rendlesham *regio* was marked by the burial mounds at Sutton Hoo (Figure 5.2) – a common enough feature on Anglo-Saxon charter bounds was the presence of 'heathen' burials which marked and protected ancient boundaries. South lay Sutton, the 'South-ton'; such cardinal place-names are highly characteristic of large estates which serve as a central place in relation to neighbouring smaller places. The boundary also took in the meeting-place of Wilford hundred with its place of execution on the hill-top above Wilford bridge. The gallows appears clearly marked on Norden's map of Bromeswell in 1601 (Figure 5.2). This was probably the earliest of the hundredal meeting-places among the Wicklaw hundreds, second only to Wicklaw itself. The site is associated with a possible heathen place-name, *harrough*, which may indicate the presence of a heathen temple site on or close to the place of execution (Warner 1988).

The link between early hundredal meeting-places, pagan place-names and places of execution has long been recognised and is evidenced in the names of Gallow hundred in Norfolk and Wodneslawe in Bedfordshire (Anderson 1934). Wilford itself was a separate vill at the time of the Domesday survey; the site of the village, which produces Middle Saxon pottery, has been located by Newman as part of his Deben valley survey (Newman 1992b). Within the parish of Bromeswell has been found an extraordinary fragment of decorated copper-alloy bucket of late Roman Mediterranean origin (Carver 1992, plate 1). The closest parallel for this object is a complete bucket, without provenance, now in the Ashmolean Museum, Oxford, while other parallels are known from the Chessel Down cemetery on the Isle of Wight (Bruce-Mitford 1983, 749–52). So within the area that once constituted the *regio* of Rendlesham there are a number of early Anglo-Saxon sites which may well owe their presence to the proximity of Rædwald's country seat.

From the work of Bede, the *Anglo-Saxon Chronicle* and early charters it is possible to identify important early religious centres, often linked to the presence of a royal estate. So rare are these references that the mere mention of a place at such an early date charges it with extraordinary significance. The mention of Exning in the *Liber Eliensis* as the birthplace of St Etheldreda, the famous foundress of Ely and daughter of King Anna of East Anglia, is a case in point (Blake 1962, 13). Exning is now Suffolk's most westerly parish and it lies centrally and most strategically behind the Devil's Dyke. A pagan Anglo-Saxon cemetery is known from Exning and excavations in 1973, in advance of road building, produced three sherds of Middle Saxon Ipswich ware and a quantity of Thetford ware with other imported pottery, suggesting that there was an important Saxon site somewhere in the vicinity, possibly under the existing village of Exning (Martin 1975). At the time of the Domesday survey the main manor of $13\frac{1}{2}$ hides lay in Cambridgeshire and was in the hands of the king having been the estate of Edith the Fair, mistress of King Harold (DB i, 189, 194; Barlow 1970, 192). It seems very likely that this was ancient royal demesne. The presence of a royal estate in this position needs no explanation, but we would dearly love to know more. Was it, for instance, a defended site? If it had a military function, was it designed as one with the Dyke and at what date? Such military dispositions on the frontiers of kingdoms were not uncommon. Mereton (meaning boundary -*tun*), in Wessex, was twice associated with bitter battles mentioned in the *Anglo-Saxon Chronicle*, once following the murder of King Cynewulf as he was visiting his mistress there in *c.* AD 757 and again in AD 867 with one of Alfred's Danish skirmishes (Garmonsway 1972, 47, 70).

Another likely *regio* is Blythburgh, believed to be the burial place of King Anna and his son following the Battle of Bulcamp, on the opposite side of the River Blyth, in AD 654. Bulcamp is derived in part from the Latin loan-word *campus* and like Campsey Ash near Rendlesham is believed by Gelling to be significantly early and indicative of some contact between Latin word-users and early Anglo-Saxon Germanic-speaking settlers (Gelling 1977). The *Liber Eliensis* claims that the body of King Anna was still being venerated at Blythburgh in the twelfth century, which suggests that there was continuity of Christian worship on the site through the period of Danish raiding (Blake 1962, 18). A later tradition says that his son, Iurminus, a figure otherwise undocumented, was buried with him there, but later translated to Bury St Edmunds (Whitelock 1972, 9). An obscure Norfolk cult practised by 'all mowers and sythe followers' was associated with Walstan of Bawburgh who, legend has it, was the son of a prince born at Blythburgh. He is supposed to have died about 1016 (Farmer 1985).

There is, therefore, sufficient circumstantial evidence to suggest that Blythburgh was a royal estate or *regio*; it was royal demesne in 1066; a place of pilgrimage in the eleventh century. The church of Blythburgh appears with two other dependent churches and extensive lands in the Domesday survey of 1086. The discovery in *c.* 1902 of a whale-bone writing tablet with eighth-century interlace ornamentation, together with three *styli*, on land once owned by Blythburgh Priory, might also indicate that there had once been a Saxon minster church there (Plate 12); more recently there have been finds of Ipswich ware also near the priory (Warner 1982, 75–8; Webster & Backhouse 1991, 81). Scarfe has also commented on the unusually large size of the ecclesiastical estate attached to Blythburgh and its two dependent churches in 1086 (Scarfe 1978, 155). The place-name of Hinton, which with Bulcamp and Walberswick all made up the very extensive parish of Blythburgh, means the *tun* of the *higna* or 'the monks or nuns' tun' (Ekwall 1960, 241). In the thirteenth century the men of Hinton still enjoyed a special relationship with the monastery at Blythburgh, feasting with the monks at Christmas time. The medieval Augustinian priory of Blythburgh was founded or re-founded some time after 1120, and may have incorporated one or other of the three Anglo-Saxon churches listed in the Domesday survey (Harper-Bill 1980, 2; Warner 1982, 80).

The fact that a place-name is not mentioned by Bede or one of the early sources does not exclude it from being an important royal vill or an early Christian site. At the time of the Domesday survey there were several large royal estates in Suffolk in excess of one carucate, which are not mentioned in early Anglo-Saxon sources. These include Thorney in Stowmarket, Bramford near Ipswich, Ringsfield, Stickingland in Yoxford and Bergholt, which had belonged to Harold before he became king fatefully in 1066. Stow, which means simply a 'holy place', and later gave its name to Stowmarket, was ancient royal demesne in 1086 and the capital vill of Stow hundred, in the same way that Blythburgh was the capital vill of Blything hundred (Hollingsworth 1844, 68). Here we may see another example of a lost minster centre, but without the chance mention of the name in Bede or other early sources.

Bramford near Ipswich is a particularly interesting example of a *regio* complex. It was 'ancient demesne', that is to say that like Blythburgh and Thorney it had belonged to Edward the Confessor before the Conquest, when there were two major estates, one of twelve carucates belonging to the king, another of ten carucates belonging to Bishop Stigand both in Bosmere hundred, and a smaller estate in Claydon hundred (DB ii, 247b, 281, 289). Scarfe has discovered that Sproughton in Samford hundred almost certainly represents the Bishop's estate, while Bramford in Bosmere hundred, with Burstall, which was always a chapelry of Bramford, formed the main royal estate (Figure 5.3) (Scarfe 1990, 173). Burstall, which appears as *Burgestala* in Domesday Book, means the place of the *burh* or fort (Ekwall 1960, 77). The discovery of an important rich Anglo-Saxon cemetery on the Boss Hall Industrial Estate, Ipswich, in 1990 prompted the excavator to conclude that this too might relate to the Bramford *regio* complex. Very near to the site of the excavation was situated the chapel of St Albright which lay in *Albrighteston*, a berewick or outlying part of Bramford

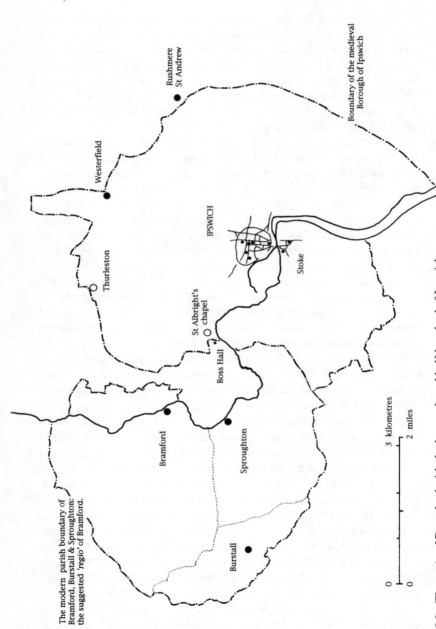

The modern parish boundary of Bramford, Burstall & Sproughton: the suggested 'regio' of Bramford.

Boundary of the medieval Borough of Ipswich

Rushmere St Andrew

Westerfield

Thurleston

IPSWICH

St Albright's chapel

Boss Hall

Stoke

Bramford

Sproughton

Burstall

0   3 kilometres
0   2 miles

5.3   The *regio* of Bramford with the borough and half-hundred of Ipswich parish (Newman 1991a). The dedication must be early for it recalls King Æthelberht of East Anglia whose head was struck off on the orders of King Offa of Mercia in *c*. AD 794 (Garmonsway 1972, 54). This dedication is one of six or seven known in Suffolk, including the church of the episcopal estate of Hoxne, and may represent a royal cult of kingly sainthood pre-dating the cult of St Edmund. The coincidence of ancient royal demesne with an early royal cult dedication argues for Bramford being an Early Saxon *regio*.

The relationship between the *regio* of Bramford and the early Borough of Ipswich is particularly interesting (Figure 5.3). The territory of the *regio* and the circuit of the medieval Borough boundary seem to complement each other either side of a double loop in the Gipping river. The chapel of St Albright, like the churches of Thurleston, Westerfield and Rushmere St Andrew, lay on the medieval Borough boundary. Nine of Ipswich's churches are listed in the Domesday survey, and there may have been more. The town has its origins in the seventh century as an estuarine trading place, and was probably under some sort of control from the 'Wuffings', the Anglo-Saxon dynasty of East Anglia (Biddle 1976; Wade 1988). Given the evidence from the Boss Hall site it now seems more likely that Ipswich was controlled from the adjoining royal estate of Bramford rather than from the more distant *regio* of Rendlesham. Ipswich had an important minster of its own, based on St Peter's church which had six carucates of glebe land in 1086, making it one of the largest landholding secular minsters in Suffolk (Blair 1985). But St Nicholas's church has the significant image of a boar on its Anglo-Saxon tympanum, which might link it to the 'Wuffings' (Galbraith 1973). Another early church and possible minster might well be the church of St Mary at Stoke, south of the river, which was held with the manor and mill on Stoke bridge, by the monks at Ely in 1086 (DB ii, 382b). Stoke is a place-name similar to Stow and means a holy place (Ekwall 1960, 445). It is often associated with rivers and river crossings and nearby markets, such as Stoke-by-Clare and Stoke-by-Nayland, on the Essex border; the latter was the burial place of the family of Ælfgar, ealdorman of Essex in the tenth century (Hart & Syme 1987).

The remarkable discovery of an important Middle Saxon site and early timber church at Staunch Meadow, Brandon, excavated in the 1980s by the Suffolk Archaeological Unit, clearly indicates that early ecclesiastical sites exist regardless of whether or not they are

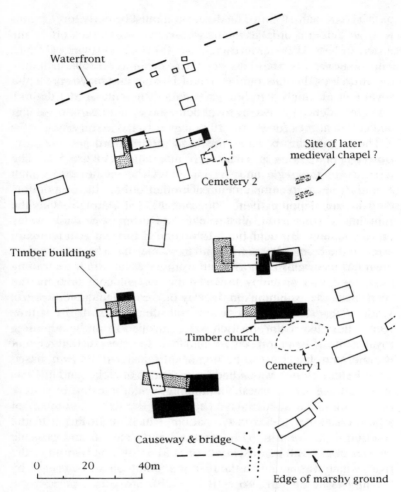

5.4 Brandon: the plan of a timber Middle Saxon church and other buildings from excavations at Staunch Meadow (drawn by R. Carr)

mentioned in Bede and early sources (Carr *et al.* 1988). Here, an early timber church and cemetery with skeletons of mixed age and sex were discovered together with ancillary buildings (Figure 5.4). The range of artefacts, including 234 bronze pins, some exquisitely decorated and dating from the seventh and eighth centuries, suggests a community of high status. The presence of three *styli* and a gold plaque of St John the Evangelist, either from a book-binding or from a crucifix, implies the practice of writing and reading, if not a scriptorium (Webster & Backhouse 1991, 81–8) (Plate 14). Such finds are rare and the only comparable material comes from the excavation of Hilda's famous monastery at Whitby, or the more recent excavations at Barking Abbey and Flixborough (Campbell 1982, 79; Webster & Backhouse 1991, 88–101; Whitwell 1991). The site at Brandon occupies a small low-lying island in the valley of the Little Ouse linked to the mainland by a timber causeway.

More than 52 buildings have been identified from post-holes and narrow trenches with the surviving ends of upright timber planks. Waterlogging had caused a high degree of preservation and excellent environmental evidence (Figure 5.4). The simple rectangular buildings average in size about 6.6 by 7.8 metres; some show several phases of building with the addition of gable-end extensions or 'annexes' adding substantially to their floor area. Near the river where there was likely to have been a timber quay there was evidence for a range of industrial activities including cloth dyeing, with seeds of flax, hemp, elder (*Sambucus nigra*) and dyer's rocket (*Reseda luteola*). There was also flax-stem waste, the result of retting flax for linen production. Marine fish and oysters were being brought to the site and rye, presumably grown on the lighter soils around Brandon, was probably the staple cereal. There was also evidence for barley, oats, wheat, peas and beans together with fruit stones of bullace, apple and walnut. Brandon is a typical Middle Saxon site in that Ipswich ware is the dominant pottery with a few continental imports. There was some glass ware including 130 fragments of window glass. Although extremely rare, window glass has been found on other early monastic sites such as Monkwearmouth and Jarrow (Campbell 1982).

The timber church and its associated graveyard was the most significant building (Plate 9). Developing from a two to a three-cell structure 24.5 metres long, it was a simple building with small chancel and nave, later gaining a western narthex matching the eastern chancel in size. At the east end of the chancel there was evidence of a substantial structure which was probably the altar. The nave was 6.5 metres wide and had opposing doors with massive timber thresholds set deep into the ground. Perhaps these supported heavily carved door frames, in the fashion of later Scandinavian churches. The chancel also had a smaller door facing south, clearly a priest's door which led across the graveyard towards a cluster of buildings, possibly the priest's house and glebe farmyard, if this small church had such a thing as glebeland at this period. This is the earliest timber church excavated in the county and one can only imagine that this represents a typical predecessor to many Anglo-Saxon churches. Brandon is all the more remarkable in that the plan is undamaged by later stone buildings which is the case in almost all other excavated churches in the country (Rodwell 1989).

The earliest evidence for activity on the site is associated with the clearance of scrub with a charcoal layer on top of the marsh peat. A radiocarbon date of AD 640 ± 70 and 660 ± 80 comes from this layer. Eight East Anglian *sceattas* (silver coins) from the site fall into the date range of *c*. AD 720–60 and a single Northumbrian *styca* (copper) coin of Æthelred II dates to *c*. AD 840. This and the small amount of Thetford ware suggests that the site was deserted in the last quarter of the ninth century. Perhaps this was linked to the presence of a Danish army at Thetford in AD 866 or 868, but there is evidence that the site moved 200 metres further south out of the flood plain and on to the slightly higher ground to the area of the present church of Brandon where later Saxon pottery has been found. There are also indications that the timber church had changed its function before the site was deserted; it had lost its chancel and the cemetery had moved 60 metres further north where, presumably, another church existed nearby. A small medieval chapel and graveyard associated with earthworks on the site were discovered in 1979; whether these are related to the Middle Saxon site remains obscure, but a continued religious presence is implied, even after the settlement had moved.

The main difficulty lies in placing Brandon in relation to other early Christian sites in Suffolk for it has no excavated precedent in lowland England. The mixed age and sex of the cemetery is no bar to the site being monastic, for Bede is very clear about early monasteries such as Ely having mixed communities of monks and nuns. The mixture of buildings might also be typical of a Celtic-style monastery. But how common were timber churches of this period? It is possible that Brandon simply represents the private church of a wealthy layman who could afford to support a priest or even a community of priests some of whom might well have had writing skills and a few books. The industrial nature of the site and the presence of a few coins is also consistent with an ecclesiastical community, but it could also be commercial which might account for the unusual wealth of the artefacts. Until more sites of this type are excavated these questions must remain unanswered, but how many more sites like Brandon are waiting to be discovered?

The dioceses of Dunwich and Elmham

Of all the early Christian centres in Suffolk, Dunwich is the most controversial, but since nearly all the archaeology has disappeared through coastal erosion, it is impossible to verify any statement about it. Here modern antiquarianism has run amuck. In truth all we know is what Bede tells us: that Felix established the first East Anglian see here in AD 630. Although there are records of nine or more medieval churches, all now under the sea, we have no reference to an early minster church at Dunwich, although there may well have been one. Theories about a cathedral church dedicated to St Felix at Dunwich are most unlikely, since Felix would hardly dedicate a church to himself. The presence of a monastic school at Dunwich could be implied by Bede, but it is not clearly stated. However, the *Liber Eliensis* does record a story about the miraculous cure of Ralph the school master from Dunwich through the influence of St Etheldreda. But this might well be a later tenth-century school and not the original foundation (Blake 1962, 271).

The best archaeological evidence from Dunwich comes from a section of the town defences undertaken in 1970. Eight small sherds of imported Pingsdorf-type ware and other early medieval wares suggest that Dunwich had a similar origin to Ipswich as a coastal Anglo-Saxon trading port (West 1970). Only three pieces of Roman pottery were found. The small number of Roman artefacts deposited in Dunwich museum and recorded elsewhere represent nothing more than the type of material that might be retrieved from any of the smaller Roman settlements in Suffolk; antiquarian references to Roman discoveries at Dunwich are incorrect (Gardner 1754, plate iv; Warner 1982, 68). The lack of any late Roman coin series for Dunwich compares most unfavourably with Walton shore fort, which, although lost to coastal erosion in the eighteenth century (Plate 7), has an excellent coin series (Moore 1948, 173; Warner 1982, 56).

Any suggestion, therefore, that Dunwich itself was a late Roman shore fort cannot be substantiated. The surviving road network leading into Dunwich is almost certainly Anglo-Saxon in origin and bears little relation to the Roman road system inland (Warner 1982, figure 17). Although a ninth-century copy of Bede refers to Dunwich as *Dommocceaster*, any attempt to equate the site with the lost settlement of *Sitomagus*, mentioned in the Antonine Itinerary, cannot be substantiated either archaeologically or on place-name evidence (Raven 1907, 28–9; VCH Suffolk 1911, 2; Johnson 1976, 19, 67; Warner 1982, 56, 68, 71). Another extraordinary controversy led to the suggestion that the site of Dunwich was in fact Felixstowe. Stuart Rigold, spoiling for a fight with Dorothy Whitelock, eventually conceded after a series of vitriolic articles, that the documentary evidence was insufficient to prove his point and there the matter must rest (Warner 1982, 68).

The sole relic of the East Anglian see from the pre-Viking period is the seal of Bishop Ethilwald, discovered at Eye in 1822. It is datable to *c.* AD 845–70, although the bishop's precise dates are unknown (Webster & Backhouse 1991, 238). In the eleventh century Eye Priory was granted 'all the churches which then existed or might subsequently be erected in the town of Donwich' (Gardner 1754, 52; Whitelock 1972, 4). In the sixteenth century the monks of Eye claimed that the 'Red Book of Eye' had belonged to St Felix and had come to them from their cell at Dunwich, washed away by the sea (Whitelock 1972, 4; Warner 1982, 73). Bishop Ethilwald's seal probably came to Eye in much the same way. Such circumstantial evidence supports the traditional view that Dunwich was indeed the site of the first East Anglian see.

The Domesday survey makes it clear that Saxon Dunwich was judicially dependent on the royal vill of Blythburgh. A thief caught in Dunwich had to suffer corporal punishment at Blythburgh, while his property remained to the lord of Dunwich. Dunwich had no mint, but there was a money-changer at Blythburgh (DB ii, 312, 312b). Such details emphasise the importance of Blythburgh as a royal administrative centre and as such it may well pre-date Dunwich. However, by the time of the Domesday survey Dunwich was the larger town and as a sea-port was rivalling Yarmouth and even Ipswich.

St Felix was buried at Dunwich and, during the time of Danish raiding, his remains were moved first to Soham near Ely and later to Ramsey (Whitelock 1972, 4). Bede fails to give us the names of Felix's successors until the division of the see after AD 673 at the time of Bishop Bisi's illness; his successors were Æcci and Baduwine (HE, IV, 5). The division of the see probably relates more to the pastoral needs of East Anglia and the desire to increase the number of bishops following the Synod of Hertford, than to any schism or desire to depose the infirm Bishop Bisi (Whitelock 1945). However, the formation of a new diocese of 'Elmham' poses the question as to which Elmham: North Elmham in Norfolk or South Elmham in Suffolk? The documentary sources are woefully inadequate and archaeological interpretation is fraught with difficulty; the result has been a controversy that has raged for over one hundred and thirty years (Seymour Stevenson 1927; Smedley & Owles 1970).

It must be said from the outset that the weight of argument over the years has always been in favour of the Norfolk site, yet recent work by Wade-Martins on his extensive excavations at North Elmham have failed to produce any convincing evidence for seventh-century occupation on the site consistent with a major diocesan centre (Wade-Martins 1975). Both the ruins of North Elmham Minster, and the so-called 'Old Minster' site at South Elmham are small and lacking in definitive architectural detail when compared with other known minster churches of the Early Saxon period. Although more work has been done on the fabric of North Elmham Minster, both structures have not been subjected to the sort of scrutiny now expected in modern church archaeology (Rodwell 1989). Both ground-plans are substantially different; North Elmham conforms to the long cruciform, apsidal plan favoured by later Saxon minsters, while South Elmham has a short apsidal plan with narthex favoured by the seventh-century churches of Kent.

The South Elmham minster needs to be considered not just as a romantic ruin in the landscape, but as a complex feature of earthworks and boundaries extending over a wide area of northeast Suffolk. Known as the 'Monasterium' or 'le Mynstre' from the early fourteenth century, it was granted with the manor of Elmham to the Priory of Norwich by Herbert de Losinga, the first Bishop of Norwich (Ridgard 1987). The property had been purchased from William de Noers, but Ridgard suggests that, because it was granted with the chapel of St Edmund at Hoxne, the Elmham manor and the minster were traditionally associated with the ancient diocese of East Anglia, and that the purchase was intended to secure such sites from the ambitions of Bury St Edmunds (Ridgard 1987, 198). However, the Old Minster at South Elmham is not mentioned in any sources earlier than the fourteenth century, and as Ridgard rightly concludes, our future understanding of the site rests firmly in the hands of the archaeologists.

It is the total morphology of the site that marks it out as one of the most interesting and formative ecclesiastical estates in the region, and, by implication supports the argument for South Elmham being the earlier of the two Elmham centres. The site now lies inside a massive square bank and ditch, with indications of a smaller outer bank and ditch to be seen on aerial photographs. The ruins of the Old Minster stand off-centre and at an odd angle to their surrounding earthworks, suggesting that they are of different dates (Plate 13). Tentative excavations in and around the ruins were undertaken by Norman Smedley and Elizabeth Owles in 1963. They concluded, on the basis of a fragment of re-used tomb-slab, that the present structure was no earlier than the eleventh century (Smedley & Owles 1970). This may well be true. However, at only one point did the excavation trenches extend for more than a metre out from the walls, and none of the interior was excavated except a small trench through the middle of the apse. None of the trenches went deeper than about a metre below the top-soil. Only two wheel-made potsherds of possible early medieval date were found outside the building.

On the basis of 'a few small sherds' of Roman pottery found in sections of the ditch and on the surface outside the enclosure, the enclosure itself was said to be Roman. Late Roman sherds and fragments of 'Romano-Saxon' wares were also found during trial trenching in 1984 (West & Barrett 1985). Recent field-walking in this area indicates the presence of many small Roman farmstead sites and a few sherds of Romano-British pottery may no longer be considered significant. The eighteenth-century topographer Gillingwater suggested that the enclosure contained a pagan cemetery of some kind with cremation urns. Suckling, writing in 1846 and probably copying Gillingwater, suggested that 'the frequent discovery by the plough of urns filled with burnt bones and ashes, seems to confirm the voice of tradition very current in the village, that the "Minster" occupies the site of a pagan temple' (Suckling

1846, 209; Ridgard 1987, 199). Further urns are said to have been found at a later date (Smedley & Owles 1970, 3).

In some respects, the earthwork enclosure is reminiscent of the Gallow Hill complex, Thetford, excavated by Tony Gregory in 1979, where a double-square ditched enclosure lay within a larger rectangle, and was thought to be a 'cult centre' of some kind dating to the middle Iron Age (Gregory 1981). The Thetford site proved to be remarkably free of domestic material although the central square contained three circular post-hole structures. Could the Elmham complex be a similar Iron Age cult centre, but this time with the main bank and ditch still upstanding? The Minster ruin, itself of much later date, could be an intrusion on a known pagan site. A comprehensive field survey and excavation programme is long overdue on this extraordinary monument.

Of even greater interest perhaps is the whole landscape setting of the Old Minster and its relationship to neighbouring boundaries and other Elmham place-names; the Old Minster is central to an unusual complex of villages all bearing the same name (Figure 5.5). The 'Ferding' of Elmham, originally one quarter of the hundred of Wangford, fits into the pattern of boundaries extending along the south side of the River Waveney, similar to the adjoining Mendham complex to the west and the Ilketshalls to the east. The Elmham and Ilketshall parishes seem to have developed in the same way in that each parish retained the name of its mother territory, each being distinguished only by its church dedication. The whole area is known locally as 'The Saints'; thus we have South Elmham All Saints, St Cross, St Margaret, St Peter, St Nicholas, St James, and Ilketshall St Lawrence, St Margaret, St Andrew and St John, to the consternation of visitors trying to navigate their winding lanes.

There are indications that Flixton and Homersfield were also part of this group and were included in the nine churches mentioned under Elmham in the Domesday survey. Both parishes, significantly perhaps, were held by the Bishop in 1086; Homersfield (*Humbresfelda*) bears the name of *Hunbeorht*; Scarfe suggests that this was probably Hunberht, bishop of East Anglia at the time of the martyrdom of St Edmund in the 870s (Ekwall 1960, 248; Scarfe 1986, 25). Place-name scholars warn about making such associations, but in this case it does reinforce the argument that the grouped parishes of Elmham together formed a Late Saxon

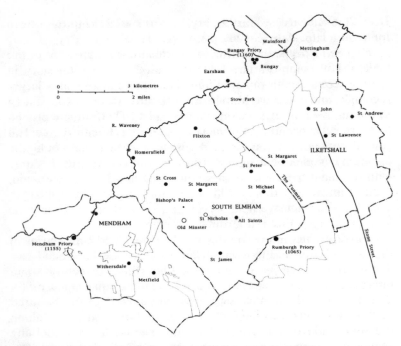

5.5 Minsterlands of Elmham and Mendham. Ilketshall represents the adjoining group of vills which are probably named after the great East Anglian hero of the Battle of Ringmere, ealdorman Ulfketill

episcopal estate. The boundary between Elmham and Ilketshall was formed by the great 'Tunmere' (Figures 5.5 and 3.4). To the east the Ilketshalls form a comparable group to the Elmhams, but here the historical associations are wholly secular. Ekwall put forward a strong case for associating *Ilcheteleshala* with *Ulfketill*, the ealdorman of East Anglia mentioned in the *Anglo-Saxon Chronicle* for 1004, who fought bravely against the Danes at Thetford, and again in 1010 at the Battle of Ringmere (Garmonsway 1972, 135, 140). Thus we have another example of a paired ecclesiastical and secular estate, the Elmhams belonging to the see of East Anglia and the Ilketshalls belonging to the ealdorman.

No archaeological centre has yet been identified for the Ilketshalls. However, Scarfe has hinted that the presence of Bungay, the later castle town of the Bigot earls, with its cluster of early churches and a later medieval monastic centre attached to

Holy Cross church (St Mary's), may have served as a minster centre for this group (Scarfe 1986, 280). To the west of Elmham lay another group of parishes around Mendham where there is a similar but less obvious pattern related to another early ecclesiastical centre. Mendham Priory was founded as a Cluniac house in the twelfth century, yet we know from the late Anglo-Saxon will of Theodred, bishop of London, that there was a minster with one hide of land at Mendham in the tenth century (Hart 1966, 53). The parish pattern of Withersdale, Metfield and Mendham is extraordinarily complex, suggesting that they once formed a single minster-land comparable to the Ferding of Elmham (Warner 1982).

Minsters and sokes

It is possible that in other areas the foundation of monasteries in the twelfth century simply disguises and regularises a pre-existing pattern of minster centres and their dependent churches. Some monastic churches have dual dedications and a persisting tradition that the local populace had the right to worship there. In some cases this resulted in the survival of part of the monastic church, usually the nave, as a place of worship after the Dissolution. For example, Rumburgh, near Halesworth, was dedicated to St Felix and St Michael, an unusual combination; the more important East Anglian cult dedication to St Felix probably relates to its monastic function. A Benedictine cell was established here as an outpost of St Benet's Abbey, Holme, in 1064; it appears under Wissett in the Domesday survey as a chapel with twelve monks (DB ii, 293). The secondary dedication of St Michael may relate to the secular use of this upland, clayland site – it is a rare example of a moated church – situated on the hundred boundary; it was originally a dependent chapelry of Wissett (Dougdale 1693, 615; Warner 1982, 90).

The dual dedication of Wangford church to St Peter and St Paul is not uncommon, but the present church is a rebuild of 1876 incorporating part of a medieval monastic church. The Cluniac priory of Wangford was founded in 1160 as a cell of Thetford. Early sources suggest that the parish church of Wangford was dedicated solely to St Peter in the late twelfth or early thirteenth century (Gardner 1754, 254). In 1206 there was an agreement between Abbot Samson of Bury St Edmunds and the cliff-top community of Southwold, an important supplier of herrings to the great Abbey in

1086, that they should pay the cellarer three marks a year for the services of a chaplain officiating in Southwold chapel. This was because the chapel at Southwold, with another at Reydon Smear, were dependencies of Reydon St Margaret, itself a possession of Wangford Priory, an alien house (Davis 1954, 150; Warner 1982, 89).

It seems that at the time of the Domesday survey, Wangford and Reydon were grouped as one vill; Wangford is not mentioned by name, but two churches are listed under the seven carucate estate of Toret, at Reydon, which was split up at about this time (DB ii, 414, 414b). The principal grange of Wangford Priory was an estate called 'Le Reye', which probably represents the core of this ancient estate. While the original estate boundary can be clearly recognised, as can the division between the two parishes running through Wangford Wood, it seems likely that Wangford represents a possible minster centre, the focus of a great pre-Conquest estate. Its dependent churches and chapels at Southwold and Reydon eventually grew to become the fully-fledged churches of neighbouring parishes.

Wangford and other similar twelfth-century monastic foundations usually incorporated pre-Conquest soke rights originally pertaining to the estates which formed their core benefactions. Thus the important Premonstratensian Abbey of Leiston incorporated the pre-Conquest soke of Edric of Laxfield, which extended into Fordley and other neighbouring parishes; it was still recognisable as *Leiston Sokene* in the late fourteenth century (Mortimer 1979, 25). This ancient soke is clearly indicated as part of the generous foundation gift of Ranulf de Glanville, although a charter of liberties granted by Henry II actually restricted the soke to lands held by the Abbey. However, the Abbot of Leiston was in difficulties when he sought to maintain his rights in later years. Mortimer, commenting on the charters of Leiston Abbey, says that: 'despite the centuries of history behind it, the Abbot was accused in 1399 of claiming a soke called "Leiston Soken" where he had none, and of preventing the king's sheriffs and bailiffs from executing writs, receiving plaints and delivering goods unjustly seized within it, insisting on holding such pleas in his court' (Mortimer 1979, 25).

In 1086, Leiston included three churches, two of which may have been Aldringham St Andrew and Knodishall St Lawrence. In the Norwich taxation of 1254, Leiston church was exceptionally wealthy, comparable to other minster churches such as Blythburgh. When the abbey moved from Sizewell in the fourteenth century, because of problems with flooding, it almost certainly moved to the site of Leiston church and a new church dedicated to St Margaret was provided for the local congregation, for the surviving ruins of Leiston Abbey incorporate within them remains of an earlier structure not all of which may have been taken from the earlier monastery (Mortimer 1979, 6–7). Although seemingly on a new site, Leiston had in fact gravitated to the centre of its principal possessions and the focus of an ancient pre-Conquest estate and jurisdiction which formed the core of its benefaction.

Although there is evidence to suggest that soke rights could be exchanged, rescinded, or even forfeited, as in the case of Edric of Laxfield, who forfeited his estates to Edward the Confessor after being declared an outlaw (DB ii, 311), most remained as legal rights attached to principal estates. Private sokes in East Suffolk were confined to small groups of adjacent vills with one or two more scattered socages relating to outlying landholdings. These private sokes are only known about through the Domesday survey, but in some cases they give the impression of great antiquity as for example, the case of 'Thorpe le Soken', which comprised the three vills of Walton, Kirby and Thorpe, grouped around the site of the late Roman shore fort of Walton. This *Liberty of the Soken* had a separate ecclesiastical court in which wills were proven and marriages granted. It included a special burial custom for strangers comprising 'his best upper garment and four shillings', the upper garment being given to the church 'according to the custom of the socken' (Warner 1982, 128–36).

Ancient soke-rights also survived at Rumburgh and probably derive from the Soke of Ralph the Staller of Wissett, a Breton minister in Edward the Confessor's court. At the dissolution of Rumburgh Priory, Dougdale mentions 'a courte called a Turne, which courte is ever kept after Michaelmas, and great appearance at the same. . . . The lordship is so free . . . that neither Sheriff exchequer nor coroner have none intermedeling with the same' (Dougdale 1693, 515). Such ancient soke-rights became incorporated into monastic property when they were granted along with large foundation estates and persist in some shape or form until the dissolution of the monastery or later. There is more than a hint that these soke-rights were becoming a liability as they were difficult to defend against the rising authority of the Norman sheriffs, hence they were off-loaded with generous gifts of land which the monasteries could not refuse. Like Rumburgh, at Bungay the survival of St Mary's church as the nave of a large monastic complex with other churches in close proximity is particularly interesting and suggests an early minster centre (Mann 1934). Bungay Soke, which belonged to Bishop Stigand, was extensive and widely scattered at the time of the Domesday survey. It came into the hands of Bungay Priory and was still important in 1453–4, when it was included in a survey of the manor of Bungay Burgh and Bungay Priory. In the eighteenth century it formed part of the appurtenances of Mettingham Castle estate, itself the residue of the religious foundation of Mettingham College (Warner 1982, 131).

Cult centres of the tenth century

The tomb of St Edmund was the most powerful cult centre in East Anglia in the late Anglo-Saxon period, and by the twelfth century it had raised over it the largest Norman church north of the Alps. The power of St Edmund was extraordinary. A relatively obscure young king in the 860s, but for his martyrdom and subsequent coin issues, he might well have remained almost unknown. His fame as a saint embodied all that was most attractive in popular religion. Countless cures and miracles were reported at his tomb; his martyrdom hinged on the fact that as a king he had accepted the greater lordship of God, and, demonstrating the ancient Anglo-Saxon bond of loyalty, he had died for his Lord defending Christendom from heathen hands. Above all he was an East Anglian saint; an embodiment of the virtues of the old East Anglian royal house surviving long after the unification of England, when East Anglia was under the rule of unpopular earls, mostly younger sons from the house of Wessex or foreigners elevated by Norman kings. But St Edmund was not just a local celebrity – his fame extended over the whole of medieval Christendom.

The power of the saint is hard for us to understand now, but as a king-martyr he inspired all the loyalty of national fervour combined with deeply-felt superstitious belief and genuine fear. The sheer terror that the wrath of the saint could inspire is amply illustrated by events. In 1014, Sweyn, the most powerful Danish war-lord in northern Europe was struck dead at St Edmund's t

136

for threatening to sack the town of Bury if he did not get a larger ransom. Leofstan, one of the eleventh-century abbots, had been paralysed when attempting to pull the head of the saint to see if it was indeed miraculously joined to its body. Thieves, who had attempted to break into the sanctuary at night and rob the shrine, had been found paralysed the next morning still frozen in fear perched up their ladders. Henry of Essex, Henry II's standard bearer, a well-known local figure with a castle at Haughley and an opponent of the Abbey, saw a vision of St Edmund admonishing him for his evil deeds while being defeated in a duel. This event took place in 1163 on an island in the Thames near Reading and, being a *cause célèbre* was witnessed by a great crowd of people. Henry was left for dead, but after a miraculous recovery lived out his days as a monk at Reading Abbey. These events and many others like them gave borrowed power to the monks who were the custodians of the shrine: 'The place is so deserving because of the worthy saint that it should be honoured and well provided with virtuous servants of God for the service of Christ' (Crossley Holland 1984, 233; Greenway & Sayers 1989, 61–3, 143).

The legend of St Edmund is more difficult to disentangle, but like all legends it has some basis in fact. That he was a minor king of East Anglia, killed by the Danes in AD 869/70 is not in doubt. This much is confirmed by the *Anglo-Saxon Chronicle* for 870, corrected by Dorothy Whitelock to the autumn of AD 869 (Whitelock 1969; Garmonsway 1972, 71). In almost every other respect the *Anglo-Saxon Chronicle* differs from that of other sources. His life and martyrdom is now so surrounded with Christian hagiography that it is difficult to substantiate more detail. The earliest surviving source dates from 1130 and is an illustrated life based on the *Passio Sancti Edmundi* of Abbo of Fleury, written sometime between AD 985 and 987. A later version by the great tenth-century scholar Ælfric, copied from Abbo shortly after AD 987, tells us that Abbo had the story from Archbishop Dunstan, who, as a young man, could remember Edmund's elderly armour-bearer telling it to King Æthelstan. Ælfric added a more flowing style of prose and the detail that Edmund was aged 21 at the time of his death.

In its earliest form therefore, the story must have been third or fourth-hand and already highly coloured with didactic Christian overtones. By the 1130s the story had been translated into English and copied out by hand many times. However, there are points in favour of its general reliability. First, we are told that Abbo presented his finished work to Dunstan for approval; second, the story was not written at the request of the monks of Bury, but instead was written while Abbo was based at Ramsey between AD 985 and 987, 116 years after the event, when the story may still have been current; third, Abbo's preface, addressed to Dunstan, says that he had heard Dunstan tell the story in front of the Bishop of Rochester, the Abbot of Malmesbury and other brothers, so stressing its reliability as an orthodox version.

There are details which suggest early attempts to authenticate the story as Dunstan said that he had heard it from a 'very old man' who told it on oath as the armour-bearer to King Edmund. Abbo first heard the story in about AD 985, three years before Dunstan's death. Dunstan may have first heard the story shortly after the coronation of Æthelstan in AD 925. If the armour-bearer had been aged 20 at the time of the martyrdom then he would have been about 75–6 years old when he made his statement to Æthelstan and Dunstan sometime after AD 925; the dates for the telling of the story would seem to fit. Coin evidence, although circumstantial, points towards the importance of the event at the time and its propaganda value to the English side. Just twenty years after 870, large numbers of coins were struck with the text *Sc Eadmund Rex*, 1,800 were found in the Cuerdale hoard alone, datable to about AD 903. These appear some time before the translation of the body of St Edmund to *Bedericsworth* (St Edmund's Bury) in AD 915.

Stripped of later embellishments, the story in essence is simple, but the manner of Edmund's death and certain miraculous hagiographical details may be incorrect: *Hinguar* and *Hubba* came with a Danish army to Northumbria and ravaged the land and killed the people. *Hinguar* then rowed south to East Anglia and came ashore secretly, attacked and destroyed a city, killing its inhabitants, and demanded the whereabouts of King Edmund while ravaging the district. Edmund was at *Haegelisdun*. *Hinguar* demanded his submission and a share of half his treasure. Advice was sought from a bishop, possibly Hunberht, who suggested surrender or flight. Edmund refused this easy option and sent word to the Danes that he would only submit if *Hinguar* first became a Christian. Edmund, who had thrown away his weapons, was then seized, brought before *Hinguar*, tortured and tied up to a tree. Enraged by his calls for Christ's help, they shot him with arrows until he bristled 'like a hedgehog or a thistle'. His head was then cut off and cast into a thicket in *Haegelisdun* wood. The miraculous recovery of the head (the 'country people' were led to it by a wolf calling 'here, here, here!'), and the re-joining of the head to the body, mark the first of many miracles associated with the saint (Whitelock 1969). To the medieval mind, preservation of the flesh was seen as incontrovertible proof of saintliness; Ælfric mentions a widow named Oswyn who dwelt at the tomb of St Edmund and, once a year, would cut his hair and pare his nails, keeping the relics in a casket.

Minor cult centres

By 1101 there was sufficient belief that Hoxne was the site of the martyrdom of St Edmund to incorporate a statement to that effect in the foundation charter of Norwich Priory, which was granted the church of Hoxne, with the chapel of St Edmund in the same vill 'where the same martyr was killed' (Whitelock 1969). Hoxne was a seat of the bishops of Norwich and central to the hundred of Hoxne, otherwise known as Bishop's hundred (Figure 5.6). However, the relationship between Norwich and Bury was a difficult one. During this period there were bitter arguments concerning the site of the new Norman bishopric which was moved, first to Thetford and then to Norwich. Attempts to move the diocese to Bury failed, but in the twelfth century Bury won exemption from visitations by both the Bishop of Norwich and the Archbishop of Canterbury, being subject only to papal legates (Gransden 1981). The fact that Norwich lost control over its most powerful abbey and with it nearly one-third of its ancient diocesan territory must have been extremely irritating. The statement in the foundation charter of Norwich Priory therefore has an air of churlishness about it and was not repeated in the confirmation charter of Henry II (Greenway & Sayers 1989; Whitelock 1969). Nevertheless, popular association of Hoxne with the cult of St Edmund has persisted to the present day and still has its ardent supporters (Carey Evans 1987).

Haegelisdun has also been identified with Hellesdon, Norfolk, by Whitelock and other writers on the basis of place-name evidence; Hellesdon appears as *Hailesduna* in 1086 (Ekwall 1960, 232). However, there is no supporting documentary evidence to link this

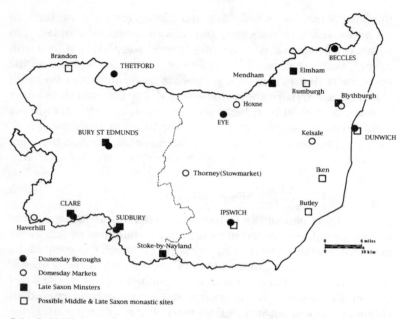

5.6 Suffolk: monastic centres of the tenth century and market towns of the Domesday survey

place with St Edmund and in recent years a much more convincing site for the martyrdom has come to light in Suffolk. In 1983, West, in a very brief note, proposed a site in Bradfield St Clare on the basis of a mid-nineteenth-century field-name *Hellesden*, no more than 8 kilometres (5 miles) south-east of the abbey. This in itself might not be convincing, were it not for two other place-names in close proximity, *Kingshall* in Rougham, suggestive of a nearby royal estate, and *Sutton Hall* between Bradfield Combust and Cockfield. Abbo suggests that the martyrdom took place at or near to a royal residence or royal estate, and in the 1090s Hermann of Bury locates the first burial of St Edmund at a place called *Sutton*, close to the site of the martyrdom (West 1983). Dymond noted that the two manors of Sutton Hall and Bradfield St Clare were not only still paying small rents to the Abbey until the time of the dissolution of the monastery, but also appeared juxtaposed in the list of rents (West 1983, 225).

There is no doubt that the new Bradfield St Clare site of *Hellesden* has a better claim than the *Hellesdon* of Norfolk, but defenders of the Hoxne site have not allowed the theory to go unchallenged (Evans 1987). While there can be no doubt that Hoxne was an important episcopal minster centre, also the capital vill of a large hundred, and that it had a long-standing association with the cult of St Edmund, there is no etymological link of any kind between the *Haegelisdun* of Abbo and the place-name of Hoxne. The later medieval belief that it had changed its name is not convincing. Hoxne has all the appearance of a very early hundredal name, first appearing as episcopal demesne in the will of Bishop Theodred of London before AD 951, when there was a church dedicated to St Æthelberht there (Hart 1966, 54). This suggests that it was in the hands of the bishops of London during the period of disruption caused by Danish conquest and therefore pre-dates the cult of St Edmund (Whitelock 1945).

It is the unbroken link between Hoxne and the diocese of East Anglia that must cause some concern and why, if Hoxne was ever a serious contender for the site of the martyrdom, Bury did not take steps to acquire it, or suppress it. The foundation of Hoxne Priory, a cell of Norwich, in 1110–19 is interesting but very late; the cell was not completed until 1267, and seems to have been a minor cult centre, constantly in debt, with very little evidence for popular support and pilgrimage. We must not forget that part of the St Edmund story involved, conveniently perhaps, the condemnation of a bishop of East Anglia for suggesting that Edmund should either surrender to the Danes, or flee. A later source, probably incorrectly, named him as Bishop Hunberht of Elmham, the man who was also supposed to have crowned King Edmund in AD 955 (Whitelock 1969). The Edmund saga was a thorn in the side of the Norwich medieval diocese, but it was powerless to act against the mighty St Edmund, or to intervene in the Liberty of the eight and a half hundreds of West Suffolk. Besides, the Abbey church of Bury was 50 feet longer than Norwich Cathedral – what a snub! Such petty rivalries and competitive church building formed the background to popular religion in the Middle Ages.

It is the association of Hoxne with the cult of St Æthelberht, the eighth-century East Anglian king-martyr, that is far more interesting. Clearly it was sufficiently important to be considered the seat for the bishop in Suffolk at the time of the Domesday survey.

Æthelberht was executed by his high-king, Offa of Mercia, in AD 794. Seeking marriage with Offa's daughter, Ælfthryth, he was seized while visiting his bride-to-be at Sutton Walls, Herefordshire. Offa then ordered his head to be struck off and took complete control of the East Anglian kingdom (Garmonsway 1972, 55). Other sources say that he was assassinated; his body was translated to Hereford Cathedral where the curative power of martyred kings generated many miracles. Hoxne was one of eleven churches in East Anglia to be dedicated to him, others in Suffolk include Herringswell, Falkenham, Hessett, Tannington and the chapel near Boss Hall discussed earlier in this chapter (Scarfe 1972, 104; Farmer 1985, 39–40).

Bures is yet another place associated with the cult of St Edmund, for it is here that he is said to have been crowned on Christmas Day in AD 855/6 by Bishop Hunberht of Elmham. The source, known as the *Annals of St Neots*, is relatively late, but may have been compiled at Bury in the early eleventh century (Whitelock 1969, 222). It is difficult to explain why Bures, so close to the southern boundary of the East Anglian kingdom with Essex, should be chosen, but the likely presence of a *regio* here at such an early date is interesting. Its proximity to Sudbury, where there had been a minster from the eighth century, associated with the cult of St Gregory, may be significant. The *Anglo-Saxon Chronicle* mentions the death of Bishop Ælfhun at Sudbury in AD 798 and his subsequent burial at Dunwich (Garmonsway 1972, 56). Other churches dedicated to St Gregory include Rendlesham, commonly associated with the *regio* of King Rædwald mentioned by Bede, and also Barnham and Hemingstone.

Suffolk has more than its fair share of cult saints, nearly all of them springing out of association with the Wuffings royal house and their known early royal estates. Flanking the tomb of St Edmund at Bury lay the bodies of St Botolph, transferred from *Icanhoh* in the tenth century and of St Iurmin, the son of King Anna of East Anglia, who is supposed to have been killed with him at the Battle of Bulcamp in AD 654. Bury clearly made some attempt to suppress this outlying cult of another martyred East Anglian king by transferring the body of St Iurminus to St Edmund's shrine, but Anna may well have survived at Blythburgh Priory. The tendency for cult centres to spawn obscure saints may quite rightly have been a cause of concern to the monks of Bury.

Ely had the same problem with cult centres associated with the three sisters of Etheldreda, daughters of King Anna: Sexburga, Withburga and Erminalda; and also her lesser known nieces, Eadnoth and Wendreda. In AD 974, Abbot Brithnoth of Ely seized the body of St Withburga where she lay at East Dereham in Norfolk and took the remains back by force to Ely. Abbot Elfsin likewise took the remains of Wendreda who was being venerated at March. By 1106 Ely had claimed the lot and one or two others, such as the body of Eadnoth, snatched on its way to Ramsey after the Battle of *Assandun* (Ashingdon) in 1016 (Farmer 1985).

6

The administrative frame

Introduction

In 1086, like other counties in eastern England, Suffolk was divided up into small administrative units called hundreds. Why 'hundreds'? The exact meaning of the term is lost in antiquity, but it is generally accepted by scholars that the term relates to one hundred hides, or a hundred variable units of land each sufficient to support an extended family unit, the *terra unius familia* of Bede (Loyn 1984, 36). Such terminology seems to lack precision, but in an age when there was no standard measurement this terminology meant something and allowed for a general reckoning of land values, taxation and population levels which are now lost to us. We know that Bede took great care to state the hidage of small islands and gifts of land in order to inform and impress his aristocratic audience; we, too, can only listen and try to understand the terminology.

In Suffolk the term *carucate* seems to correspond with the hide; it is understood to mean sufficient land for a plough, or a ploughland (Maitland 1897, 457–8). An early eleventh-century charter gives the bounds of a five-hide estate at Balsdon in Babergh hundred. The bounds have been traced by Norman Scarfe as occupying the northern half of the parish of Acton and correspond with the present parish boundary. By 1086 Balsdon was merged with the twelve carucates of Acton. Scarfe observed that the carucate seems to be equivalent to the hide in this area (Scarfe 1972, 131). This is very similar to an estate in Huntingdonshire where a tenth-century charter describes the bounds of Haddon, a five-hide unit, which corresponds closely to the modern parish boundary of Haddon (Hart 1966). The grouping of estates into five-hide units and in East Anglia into six-carucate units was commonplace (Loyn 1984, 165). An Anglo-Saxon law stipulates that five hides were the minimum landholding qualification for a *coerl* aspiring to the class of thegn, and we know from medieval sources that this corresponds very closely with the later feudal knight's fee (Stenton 1958).

For the vast majority of Suffolk towns, villages and hamlets, the name of the 'vill' in Domesday Book represents the first mention of a recognisable place-name. From the *Inquisitio Eliensis,* a parallel Domesday survey for the Abbey of Ely, we know that six men of the vill, the priest and the reeve represented the vill at hundredal level (Galbraith 1974, 34). But many of the smaller vills would have been hard pressed to find six men, let alone a priest, if they had no church, or a reeve if they had no sizeable manor. The vills were grouped into hundreds of varying size: the smallest hundreds had just two or three vills, while the largest had forty or more. The hundreds were in turn grouped into shires or, if they lay within the orbit of a great monastic foundation, into 'Liberties', such as those of Bury St Edmunds, or Ely.

These liberties were in effect the privately-owned shires of the great monastic houses, so that geld and other taxes were paid direct to them rather than to the Crown or the king's representative, the 'shire-reeve' or sheriff. The folk living within the liberties were notionally 'free' from direct royal control, but were certainly not free from taxation or the rigours of the law, for the abbots appointed their own sheriffs, reeves and bailiffs. Many hundreds lay outside the liberties, in 'geldable' areas, and were administered instead from their 'moot' courts, the profits from which were often shared between different lords. Thus Blything was shared between the king and the earl, while Ipswich was split with one-third going to the earl and two-thirds going to the king. In practice the king's reeves on the larger royal estates, and the earl and his reeves had more say in the day-to-day business within the 'geldable' hundreds; the Domesday survey for East Suffolk summarises disputes that had arisen between the reeves from different estates and the sheriff. The administration of some of the hundreds was shared between the king and the earl or, in the case of Hoxne, was annexed to the Bishop's manor, but this does not seem to have made administration any easier (Cam 1963, 82).

The pattern of vills, hundreds, and shires is a very ancient one. It was already fully developed by the time of the Domesday survey in 1086 and remained almost unchanged, as if set in concrete, until the boundary reorganisations of 1894. The system allowed for a process of limited representation among those free landholders who were qualified to attend the hundredal assemblies. It was a system that was deeply rooted in Anglo-Saxon society, but was not in any sense democratic, since none of its participants was elected. Many of the hundreds are synonymous with the place-names which were meeting-places. Every fortnight or three weeks the freemen of the hundred met and held their moot courts at these ancient landmarks. The Germanic tribal practice of moot courts is described by Tacitus in the first century AD and probably has its origins on the continent in the very remote past. Some hundredal names correspond with pagan Anglo-Saxon place-names or with sites of execution and one or two in other counties have produced evidence for pagan Anglo-Saxon cemeteries (Anderson 1934).

Following the Norman Conquest much of the power vested in hundredal moots was taken over by the function of manorial courts, which were in the hands of the great Norman lords. Matters of ecclesiastical law were separated into deanery courts after 1070, which also weakened the importance of the hundreds by reducing substantially their volume of business and judicial prestige. However, most of the hundred courts survived, some continuing as magistrate's courts into the seventeenth century. Just how old this system of hundredal administrative boundaries is remains a mystery. It has been argued that some parts may be much older than others. Many scholars believe that some of the later hundredal boundaries date from the re-conquest of the Danelaw; there is little archaeological evidence, however, to support the view that this was a particularly formative period of history. There is undoubtedly a Danish element, but it is almost impossible to quantify as the Scandinavian system of rural administration, typified by the Wapentakes of Lincolnshire, was essentially the same; the supposedly Danish Wapentake of Loveden, Lincolnshire, for example, met on Loveden Hill, which was the site of a pagan Anglo-Saxon judicial cemetery. It has also been argued that some hundredal boundaries in Suffolk, particularly those to the east of the county, date back at least to pagan Anglo-Saxon times and others may even incorporate elements of Roman, or even pre-Roman, tribal land divisions (Warner 1988). Some of these arguments will be rehearsed in this chapter.

The county boundary

Suffolk, itself a relatively late county, incorporates at least two ancient shires or 'Liberties'; the eight and a half hundreds of Thinghoe, which comprise the separate county of West Suffolk, a possession of the Abbey of Bury St Edmunds, and the five and a half hundreds of Wicklaw, which comprise the parishes grouped around Woodbridge which belonged to the Abbey of Ely. Both groups of hundreds served as counties in their own right, while the remaining area, known as the 'Geldable' had for its county town, Ipswich, which was itself a half hundred (Figure 6.1). Within the geldable area there was the very large hundred of Blything, which has all the appearance of an ancient shire. Thus, the oldest boundaries are not necessarily those of the county, although it must be understood that most physical boundaries are multi-purpose, frequently serving as parish, hundred, liberty and county boundaries at one and the same time; a clear example is the boundary between East and West Suffolk (Figure 6.1). Significant deviations between some parish boundaries and the county boundary appear as early as the Domesday survey and suggest that the county boundary was imposed on a pre-existing pattern of local estate and parish boundaries, which was itself much older.

The county boundary probably dates from about the time of the Norman Conquest. A charter, purporting to date from the time of King Alfred, was once quoted as evidence for an early division between Norfolk and Suffolk, but this has since been exposed as a forgery (Hart 1966, 40). The earldom of East Anglia was not divided until some time after the Norman Conquest, while the office of sheriff was shared by both counties until the sixteenth century (Scarfe 1972, 42; Warner 1988). A division of the diocese followed the Synod of Hertford in AD 673, but was undefined before the reign of Edgar, and it was reunited afterwards, so that it is not possible to determine whether the division in the seventh century corresponded with the line of the Waveney valley (Whitelock 1945). The diocese in the Middle Ages bears a striking resemblance

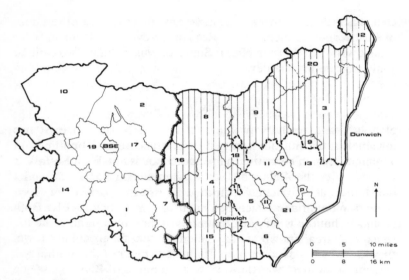

6.1 Suffolk hundreds

1 Babergh; 2 Blackbourn; 3 Blything; 4 Bosmere & Claydon; 5 Carlford; 6 Colneis; 7 Cosford; 8 Hartismere; 9 Hoxne (Bishop's); 10 Lackford; 11 Loes; 12 Mutford & Lothingland; 13 Plomesgate; 14 Risbridge; 15 Samford; 16 Stow; 17 Thedwastre; 18 Thredling; 19 Thinghoe; 20 Wangford; 21 Wilford; P Parham half-hundred; BSE Bury St Edmunds.
The boundary between the eight and a half hundreds of Thinghoe (West Suffolk), or the Liberty of St Edmund, and the Geldable Hundreds (East Suffolk) is marked by a dotted line.
    The five and a half hundreds of Wicklaw, or the Liberty of St Etheldreda, belong to Ely.
    The shaded area represents the Geldable Hundreds of East Suffolk with the half-hundred of Ipswich.

to what must have been the old kingdom of East Anglia, extending up the River Stour to Haverhill then along the Devil's Dyke to the River Cam, north through the fens to Wisbech and the Wash, coming out close to the mouth of the River Nene, thereby taking in extensive areas of fenland west of Norfolk (Jessopp 1884) (Plate 1). This probably corresponds with the ancient tribal territorial unit of the Iceni, and also formed the administrative district, or *territorium*, of the Roman period centred on Venta Icenorum. It is this to which the smaller shires of West Suffolk and Wicklaw relate; indeed, they could be as old as the tribal territory itself. Some clearly represent sub-divisions or shires within the ancient kingdom of East Anglia.

The division of Norfolk and Suffolk along the line of the Waveney and Thet valleys was convenient, but arbitrary. Similarly the southern boundary with Essex may have been imposed over pre-existing estate and parish boundaries. In both areas there are examples where parishes extended across both sides of the county boundary and seem to pre-date it. Diss, a Norfolk parish, was included in the Suffolk hundred of Hartismere in 1086. The old parish of Diss ran more than a mile northwards to take in Heywood Green and parts of Burstall, within the extensive area of coaxial prehistoric field systems identified in south Norfolk by Tom Williamson. Perhaps this extension of Diss into Norfolk represents Suffolk's share in what must have been a very large area of wood-green pasture, similar to that identified north of Halesworth (Warner 1987). Thetford also lay in Suffolk in 1086 and, until the Divided Parishes Act of 1876, a large part of the parish of Mendham lay over the River Waveney in the county of Norfolk, extending as far as Harleston. The territory of the minster-land of Mendham once included its two dependent vills of Metfield and Withersdale (Figure 5.5), and may also have included this northern extension into Norfolk before the county boundary was formed (Hart 1966, 53; Warner 1986). On the southern boundary, Bures lay partly in Suffolk and partly in Essex, while Nayland lay in Essex, but was geldable in Suffolk in 1086 (Davis 1954, xliv).

The liberties

The eight and a half hundreds of West Suffolk, which comprise the Liberty of St Edmund, are first mentioned under the name of *Thinghog* in a charter of 1044, from which time they belonged to the Abbey of St Edmundsbury. The control which the abbey exercised over its estates and the extensive rights granted to it by successive kings rendered this territory a separate shire. A county within its own right, West Suffolk enjoyed autonomy until the local government reforms of 1974. Even now it still retains its own shire courts and Bury St Edmunds has all the flavour of a county town. Of the eight and a half hundreds, Blackbourn (Bradmere), Cosford, Lackford, Risbridge, Thedwastre and Thinghoe counted as single hundreds, while Babergh was a double hundred, but counted as one, and the town of Bury St Edmunds was a hundred and a half. The names of these hundreds date back to the eleventh century, but Thinghoe, which lends its name to the whole group and served as the central meeting-place for all of them, may be the oldest.

Historians are agreed that the pattern of hundreds in West Suffolk was essentially a post-Danish imposition, but that it overlay a much earlier system of administrative boundaries, elements of which it incorporated. The original meeting-place of the whole district of West Suffolk was at one of a group of four mounds, called the *Thinghogo* (Thinghoe), which lay at the junction of Thedwastre, Thinghoe and Bury St Edmunds hundreds (Figures 6.2 and 6.5). The *thing* place-name element means an assembly and suggests a Scandinavian origin for this group of hundreds (Anderson 1934, 95–6). That the point of assembly lay outside the town of St Edmund's Bury is not surprising, indeed the meeting-places of other early towns, such as Ipswich and Dunwich, also lay just outside the town defences. Lobel suggested that the town of Sudbury was substituted for Bury St Edmunds when Bury was granted to the Abbey for the feeding of the monks (*ad victum monachorum*) (Lobel 1935, 3). Although the town of Bury counted as a hundred and a half, in the early Middle Ages the area of the town itself was very small, but the *banleuca*, the area outside its walls, was more extensive and included several small suburbs, hamlets and separate communities. It seems that while the size of early medieval towns, such as Bury, was small their influence over the surrounding district and market catchment area was great.

The liberty of the town, or its *banleuca*, was marked by four crosses, and was probably established by 945 (Lobel 1935; Hart 1966) (Figure 6.2). The body of St Edmund was said to have been found incorrupt in AD 915 and was translated to Bury in or before 925 (Farmer 1985). Early charters indicate that Bury was acquiring substantial landholdings from 951, when the community was probably re-established by Bishop Theodred of London, following the period of disruption caused by Danish raiding. These estates included Whepstead, Nowton, Ickworth and part of Horningsheath. Further lands were granted by Eadwig in the later 950s, including Elmswell and the distant herring fishery of Beccles. Chelsworth and Cockfield reverted to the Abbey on the death of Æthelflæd of Damerham in 1002 and with them other lands intended for the

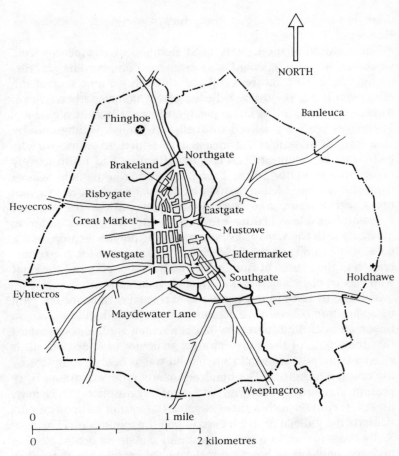

6.2 Bury St Edmunds: the bounds of the *banleuca* marked by four crosses as described in a charter of AD 945 (from Lobel 1935)

foundation of a monastery at Stoke-by-Nayland. It has been suggested that the tenth-century collegiate minster of Bury St Edmunds, intended to house the relics of the saint killed in *c.* AD 870, was an outpost of Ramsey Abbey in the fens of Cambridgeshire (Hart & Syme 1987). Certainly, Ramsey had estates close to Bury and the first life of St Edmund was probably written at the request of the Ramsey monks between 985 and 987, but by this time Bury had been established for at least thirty-four years and there is nothing to suggest that Bury was a satellite house of Ramsey.

The creation of the Liberty of St Edmund owes much to King Cnut, but the politics behind this move were complex. His generosity may have been motivated partly through genuine fear of the saint, who it was popularly believed had struck his father, Sweyn, dead at the tomb in 1014, and partly through political expediency. There was probably a need to quell anti-Danish feeling and, by endorsing East Anglia's principal cult figure, to atone for the bloodshed of conquest. The fact that Ramsey had been actively involved in supporting King Edmund Ironside in the fight against Cnut at *Assandun* (Ashingdon) in 1016, may have resulted in a final break with Ramsey if any such dependency existed. The death of Edmund Ironside at Oxford a few weeks after the battle, following his treaty with Cnut, may have prompted the poignant choice of the date of the anniversary of the Battle of *Assandun* for the consecration of the church at Bury, which contained, of course, the saint who was Ironside's namesake (Hart & Syme 1987).

The rise of Bury in the tenth and early eleventh centuries, with its acquisition of extensive estates in West Suffolk culminating in the creation of the Liberty in 1020, is a strong argument to suggest that the whole of the administrative structure of West Suffolk is substantially post-Danish in origin and was probably complete by the mid-tenth century. The hundreds neatly grouped around Bury present a relatively uniform pattern of organisation. They may, however, contain within them elements of earlier structures, particularly the judicial centre focused upon the mounds of Thinghoe. Sadly these mounds no longer exist and remain an archaeological mystery; could they have been the burial mounds of the pagan Anglo-Saxon rulers of West Suffolk? We shall probably never know.

The five and a half hundreds of Wicklaw, which formed an outlying part of the Liberty of St Etheldreda, present a very different picture. Their comparatively small size and disjointed appearance make them distinctively different from the hundreds of West Suffolk; Loes had one and later two detached portions, while Parham half-hundred lay in two small parts corresponding to the parishes of Parham and Wantisden (Figure 6.3). The hundreds are first mentioned in 970, when Ely was re-founded as a Benedictine house by Bishop Ethelwold, but there are good reasons to believe

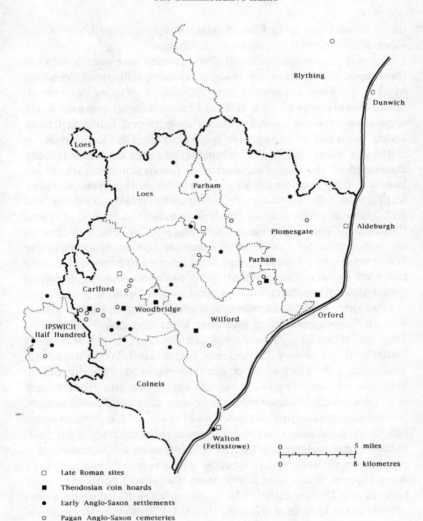

6.3 The Wicklaw hundreds: the distribution of late Roman and early Anglo-Saxon sites

that they are much older. The territory of Wicklaw may in fact have been part of the original endowment of Ely, established by Etheldreda, the daughter of King Anna of East Anglia, in 654 (Warner 1988). There is a body of circumstantial evidence to link the area with the early East Anglian kings and possibly to a late Roman administrative unit in the landscape.

The original meeting-place of Wicklaw may have been a site near the manor of Wicklows, known as Gallow Hill, near Wickham Market. Gelling has argued that *wick*, appearing as the first element in a place-name such as Wickham, may be a Latin loan-word, suggestive of some degree of overlap between Romano-British Latin word-users and early Anglo-Saxon Germanic-speaking settlers (Gelling 1977). An extensive late Roman site has been excavated in the adjoining parish of Hacheston (Selkirk 1976). Isolated finds of Anglo-Saxon material within the Wicklaw territory at places such as Waldringfield, Butley, Parham and Rendlesham, either side of the Deben valley, suggest that it was the focus of early settlement (Newman 1992b). The presence of the royal cemetery of the Wuffings at Sutton Hoo, opposite Woodbridge, and another princely cemetery at Snape overlooking the Alde estuary, suggests that this area developed into the main power-base of the early East Anglian kings (Figure 6.3).

A wealthy late Roman presence is also evident. A cluster of late-Roman hoards containing gold and silver coins of the Emperor Theodosius (AD 379–95) and some of Honorius (AD 393–423) from Little Bealings, Butley, Orfordness, Sutton Hall, Woodbridge and Tuddenham St Martin, have been found in the middle of the Wicklaw territory (Figure 6.3). An impressive late Roman coin series, including 240 fourth-century coins, has been recorded from private collections for Felixstowe and the site of the Roman shore fort at Walton, now eroded by the sea (Moore 1948, 173). Such material, particularly the hoards, is suggestive of discontinuity – where people have failed to return and recover their carefully buried fortunes. But they also witness a wealthy late Roman presence in the Deben valley, where perhaps the Roman shore fort offered some kind of protection. By AD 410, following the removal of Roman troops to the continent, that protection was lost. In consequence, wealthy colonial families, some in a supporting role to the troops, also left the area intending to return when their safety could be assured, but alas, it never could. Eventually, by the mid-sixth century, political control had fallen into the hands of the Wuffings, an aristocratic family with a Scandinavian and continental background. Thus the Deben valley was both the cradle and the resting-place of the early East Anglian kingdom.

We must now ask ourselves how this territory, comprising the five and a half hundreds of Wicklaw with its distinctive pattern of boundaries, found its way to Ely. Scholars will always argue about the problems of continuity at such an early period, but people and institutions are territorial by nature and where land ownership and boundaries are concerned, collective territorial memory becomes part of the evidence of title. The rigidity of the territorial framework of boundaries in Suffolk from the time of the Domesday survey to the late nineteenth century is testimony to that fact. Although first mentioned as the five and a half hundreds of *Wicklawan* in a charter of 970, at a time when Ely was being refounded after the period of Danish conquest, it is unlikely that the hundreds were then new, or that they owed their appearance to Danish influence. The pattern of hundreds is quite different from those of West Suffolk and is more akin to a system of boundaries associated with *letes*, a system of territorial organisation which was concerned with the collection of geld (Warner 1988).

The Ely chronicles refer to the island of Ely as the 'dower' of St Etheldreda given with her marriage to the short-lived prince of the South *Gyrwe* in or before AD 654/5 (Miller 1951). Although Bede says that this was part of a *regio* of about six hundred hides in the province of the East Angles, it is clear that the territory of the South *Gyrwe* lay on the very edge of East Anglian territory (HE, IV, 19). The island of Ely must have been of some strategic importance as it lay on the border with Mercia. The acquisition of this land through marriage was undoubtedly an astute political move on the part of Etheldreda's father King Anna of East Anglia, but it may also have inflamed the dispute with Mercia which resulted in his death at the hands of Penda, the powerful pagan king of Mercia, in AD 654 (Warner 1988). Ely was probably not the dowry of Etheldreda but her 'morning gift', the traditional contribution made by the husband the morning after the marriage.

Bede was at great pains to stress that Etheldreda preserved her virginity through two marriages. So the marriage with Tonbert was never consummated; there was a marked difference between the partners' ages and Tonbert died soon afterwards. If the gift was conditional on consummation of the marriage, and the land was not returned to the South *Gyrwe* after Tonbert's death, then Penda would have had a valid dispute with the East Anglian kingdom. How poignant, then, that the island of Ely should be chosen for the site of a monastery by St Etheldreda in AD 673, knowing that it had, in effect, been the cause of her father's martyrdom. But why does Bede not tell us this? Bede was writing an exemplary history about the works of early Christian kings, for other kings who needed reminding about their moral duties. So for the purposes of such a story, an early Christian king like Anna could do no wrong in the eyes of Bede. He tells us only what he wants us to hear.

If this island of Ely had been the 'morning gift', then possibly the Wicklaw territory was the dowry, given with his daughter by King Anna to the prince of the South *Gyrwe*. The Wicklaw territory was very extensive, but it included the old lands of the pagan Wuffings and the site of their ancestral burial ground at Sutton Hoo. The early Christian kings of East Anglia were buried elsewhere; Sigeberht was probably buried at *Bedericsworth* (Bury St Edmunds), and Anna was buried at Blythburgh; both sites are well away from the Wicklaw area. By choosing to be buried at consecrated Christian sites these kings may have set a trend which eventually resulted in the abandonment of all the old pagan Anglo-Saxon folk cemeteries throughout the kingdom and the establishment of new Christian cemeteries. The decision to grant away the old lands may have been linked to the idea of the new religion and a desire to distance the royal family from its pagan past and particularly the old *regio* of Rendlesham tainted by association with the apostate King Rædwald.

It seems likely, therefore, that the territory of Wicklaw represents an early shire, possibly the homelands of the Wuffings dynasty, who in AD 654, when the time seemed right, granted it in dower in order to gain control over an important border outpost, the island of Ely. But the plan went badly wrong; the husband died before the marriage was consummated and the resulting dispute with Mercia cost King Anna his life. Yet twenty years later the island of Ely was used for the foundation of a great monastery and the lands which had caused such a bitter dispute became its principal endowment.

The framework of hundreds

In 1086 there were twenty-five hundreds, half-hundreds and double hundreds in Suffolk. Some, such as Mutford and its neighbouring half-hundred of Lothingland, should really be regarded as one, whereas others, such as Blackbourn and Bradmere, are really double hundreds, like the double hundred of Babergh (Lees 1911; Anderson 1934). In spite of minor changes – the tiny half-hundred of Parham was to disappear by the thirteenth century and the hundred and a half of Samford became a single hundred, and there were one or two changes of name – the hundreds of 1086 are very much the same as those listed in the Hundred Rolls of 1274. The pattern of Domesday hundreds is further complicated by fractions of hundreds. The Ferding of Elmham, a quarter of Wangford hundred, has its closest parallel in Wisbech, which was a quarter part of the hundred of the Isle of Ely; other ferdings are found at Ludham in Norfolk, and in Huntingdonshire. Thredling hundred or the 'Trelling of Claydon', also a possession of Ely, was a third of Claydon hundred. Thredling does not appear until 1188, but by 1275 it had been upgraded into a half-hundred (Stenton 1922; Miller 1951; Davis 1954; Warner 1988). The financial advantages to Ely of upgrading fractions of hundreds in this way is significant when we come to look at the pattern of small hundreds in Wicklaw.

A glance at Figure 6.1 reveals that among the hundreds of Suffolk there is a wide variety of size. A small hundred such as Stow, with approximately 22,000 acres, is but a fraction of one of the larger hundreds such as Blything with approximately 87,000 acres. Indeed, the single hundred of Blything is substantially larger than the 71,000 acres of the double hundred of Babergh. While the poor sandy soils may account for the large size of the Breckland hundreds such as Lackford and Blackbourn compared with their neighbours in the five and a half hundreds of Thinghoe, it cannot account for the very small size of hundreds on the similarly poor soils of East Suffolk, particularly Wilford with 31,500 acres and Colneis with just 17,000 acres. Other reasons must be found to explain the small size of the Wicklaw hundreds.

By contrast Blything hundred dwarfs its southern neighbours in the Wicklaw territory. The name Blything means simply the people of the River Blyth; presumably this included all those living within the catchment area of the river, for the boundary of the hundred follows remarkably close to the watershed (Figure 6.4). To north and south the hundred is bordered by two minor rivers both called 'Hundred River', again emphasising the arterial nature of the River Blyth. At the lowest crossing place on the River Blyth stood Blythburgh, a royal vill and meeting-place of the hundred, the

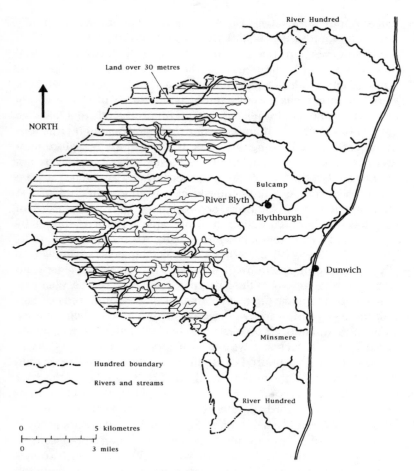

6.4 Blything hundred: the watershed territory

importance of which has already been discussed. It appears an ideal topographical model, yet few hundreds have territories as clearly defined as this. Similar hundredal territories with names linked to river dwellers have been noted by David Dymond at Loddon and Happing hundreds in Norfolk (Dymond 1985). There seems little doubt that in Blything we see an ancient *regio*, or small shire, a sub-division of the East Anglian kingdom. We can imagine that the people of the River Blyth would once have had the same sense of their own identity as cricketers or football players would associate with their modern English county or shire.

Blything hundred is a particularly striking example of the water-shed model, but it is not unusual for ancient shires of this type to have boundaries which coincide with watersheds; similar territorial units have been recognised as far apart as the Laths of Kent, parts of Mercia, Northumberland and southern Scotland, where they are recognised as the primitive pattern of landdivision underlying later administrative structures (Maitland 1897, 266–7, 410; Taylor 1957, 58–9; Barrow 1973, 8, 11). Minor anomalies to the watershed boundary of Blything can be detected, but they can be accounted for in later documentation, such as the appearance of Rumburgh Priory on the northern border with Elmham in 1065, which caused the parish of Rumburgh to be formed partly out of Blything hundred and partly out of Wainford hundred. To the south the parish of Kelsale-cum-Carlton forms a detached portion of Hoxne or Bishop's hundred and was probably taken partly out of Blything and partly out of Wicklaw when Kelsale became the administrative centre for the pre-Conquest sheriffs in East Suffolk. Taken as a whole, Blything hundred is about the same size as Wicklaw and is directly comparable in that Wicklaw takes in the territory of the River Deben, the only difference being that Wicklaw is sub-divided into smaller hundreds. The reason for this anomaly must now be examined.

Letes and vills

The grouping of vills into letes, or what were later known as *ville integre*, in East Anglia is one of the more obscure aspects of early medieval administration. The term 'lete' is distinct from 'leet', as in leet court, which could also be applied to a meeting-place of a leet court, such as Leet Hill at Dunwich. The principal function of letes was to assist in the levying of geld within each hundred. There could be urban as well as rural letes. The borough of Ipswich, being itself a half-hundred, was divided into letes or wards (Martin 1954, 11). The payment of Danegeld to Viking war-bands is well documented in the *Anglo-Saxon Chronicle*, but the payment of geld may have become a regular form of taxation in later Anglo-Saxon England; certainly by the time of William the Conqueror it was being raised every year.

Geld entries are sporadic in the Domesday survey for Suffolk, and letes, generally speaking, are not given at all, although they do appear in the Norfolk hundreds of Clacklose and Greenhow (Dodwell 1969). However, there are several medieval sources which enable the reconstruction of letes in Suffolk. The *Kalendar of Abbot Samson*, a twelfth-century document, lists the letes of the eight and a half hundreds of Thinghoe; hence it is possible to reconstruct the pattern of letes for the whole of West Suffolk by using the hundred of Thinghoe as a model (Figure 6.5) (VCH Suffolk 1911, 412–16). Under Cosford half-hundred it states that when geld was raised, 'every lete gives thirteen shillings and six-pence and divides it within itself' (Davis 1954, 60–1).

When geld was levied it was imposed as a fixed sum, usually 20*s*, on the hundred. But how could this burden of taxation be equitably raised among the hamlets, villages and farms each with a different ability to pay? The solution was to group the vills into more or less equal clusters, called letes, and ask each cluster to raise an agreed proportion of the whole by dividing the burden among its constituent vills. In order to achieve these clusters, vills might be combined from different parts of the hundred, so that a lete did not necessarily contain adjacent vills, but might consist of several vills scattered about the district. The pattern in East Suffolk is highly distinctive, but in West Suffolk, where reorganisation of hundreds had taken place after the re-conquest of the Danelaw territories, the letes are neater and more compact, suggesting that the new hundredal pattern had taken into account the need for letes and the raising of geld. However, even in the eight and a half hundreds of Thinghoe where some of the hundreds were divided into as many as twelve letes, the portions of geld raised by each lete was not exactly equal, and there must have been room for much argument among the constituent vills. In reality it has to be said that a large number of vills in the Domesday survey of Norfolk and Suffolk are given no geld assessment, and where they are there is little evidence for equality, even where the letes can be reconstructed (Warner 1988, 26–32).

By using later medieval sources it is possible to arrive at a reconstruction of letes in Blything hundred where, like other hundreds in the geldable area, figures for geld assessment are substantially incomplete in the Domesday survey. There survives a fourteenth-century list of *ville integre* among the documents of the Sibton

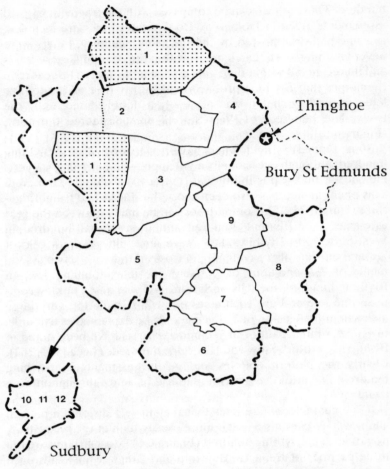

6.5 Thinghoe hundred: divided into letes (after Round 1911, 412)

1. Barrow, Flempton, Lackford; 2. Risby with Higham; 3. Westley, Saxham (Great & Little); 4. Hengrave, Fornham; 5. Ickworth, Chevington; 6. Brockley, Rede, Menston; 7. Whepstead; 8. Hawstead, Nowton; 9. Horningsheath (Horringer); 10, 11, 12. Sudbury (three letes).

Abbey estates in the British Museum (Denney 1960). This and the ordering and grouping of vills listed in taxation documents, such as the Lay Subsidies of 1327 and 1334 and the *Nomina Villarum* of 1316, enable a tentative reconstruction of letes over the whole hundred. These in turn can be compared with the fragmentary geld assessments given in Domesday Book. Not all vills are included, as some had disappeared by the fourteenth century, others were never anything more than hamlets within the orbit of larger estates and therefore fell within their geld assessments. Out of this exercise it emerges that Blything probably had twenty-four or twenty-five letes, suggesting that it was originally a double hundred, if the twelve-lete hundreds of West Suffolk are considered the norm (Figure 6.6).

Some Domesday landowners have two lists of vills for Blything hundred, although occasionally a vill appears in both lists, suggesting once again the possibility that Blything was a double hundred. This phenomenon has also been spotted in Essex and Cambridgeshire (Hart 1974, 15). Comparisons can be made between the geld assessments of Blything hundred and Cosford half-hundred in West Suffolk. In Blything there were nine vills paying a geld of $7\frac{1}{2}d$ and one lete also paying $7\frac{1}{2}d$; in Cosford there were two assessments of $7\frac{1}{2}d$ and four or possibly five letes totalling 15d. In Blything hundred, the vills of Sibton, Walpole and Cookley comprise one lete and are each assessed at $7\frac{1}{2}d$, while the very large assessment for Leiston of 3s $1\frac{1}{2}d$ can only be explained as five units of $7\frac{1}{2}d$. A similar pattern of $7\frac{1}{2}d$ and 15d units have been noted in Bishop's, Carlford, Stow and Risbridge hundreds (Lees 1911, 362). Clearly the pattern of letes and geld assessments in Blything hundred fits into the general pattern of letes throughout the county.

It is a characteristic of letes that they have a disjointed pattern and nowhere can this be seen more clearly than in the reconstruction of letes in Blything hundred (Figure 6.6). Most striking are the three parishes of Benacre, Bulcamp and Brege, whose vills once made up one lete, also Halesworth with Cratfield, and Chediston with Blyford. Their size, appearance and general pattern is very similar to the hundreds of Wicklaw to the south; they compare well with Loes and Parham half-hundred, both consisting of vills some distance apart (Figure 6.3). Surely we are looking at the same pattern in the landscape, but in Blything they are called letes and in Wicklaw they are called hundreds. It is known that Ely upgraded some letes into hundreds in this area in order to enhance its revenue. Certainly the 'Trelling' of Claydon, once a third part of Claydon hundred and often grouped with the Wicklaw hundreds,

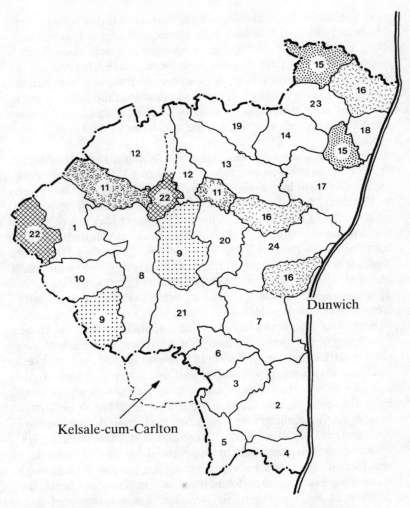

6.6 Blything hundred: the pattern of letes (after Warner 1982)

1. Huntingfield (with Linstead); 2. Leiston (with Sizewell); 3. Theberton; 4. Thorpe, Aldringham; 5. Knodishall (with Buxlow); 6. Middleton, Fordley; 7. Westleton; 8. Sibton, Walpole, Cookley; 9. Bramfield, Peasenhall, Mells; 10. Ubbeston, Heveningham; 11. Chediston, Blyford; 12. Wissett (with Spexhall), Holton, Rumburgh; 13. Sotherton (with Westhall), Henham; 14. Uggeshall, Frostenden; 15. Henstead, Cove; 16. Benacre, Bulcamp, Brege (Dingle); 17. Reydon (with Wangford), Southwold, Easton Bavents; 18. Northales (Covehithe); 19. Brampton, Stoven; 20. Thorington, Wenhaston; 21. Darsham, Yoxford (with Stickingland); 22. Halesworth, Cratfield; 23. Wrentham; 24. Blythburgh (with Walberswick and Hinton).

was upgraded as Thredling hundred sometime before 1188 (Warner 1988, 22). The only possible explanation is that the hundreds in Wicklaw are in fact letes upgraded into hundreds. If this is the case then the pattern must have been in existence before the five and a half hundreds of *Wicklawan* are first mentioned in the charter of Edgar in AD 970. It also suggests that the administrative system of letes must be substantially older than this date, possibly pre-Viking. So just how old are the hundreds, or one-time letes of Wicklaw?

There is reason to believe that the hundredal pattern within Wicklaw is very much older than the time of Edgar. The meeting-place of Wilford hundred was at the river-crossing now marked by Wilford bridge and probably lay within the boundary of the suggested *regio* of Rendlesham (Chapter 5). Above the ford at Wilford was a place of execution; the hill-top gallows are clearly marked on John Norden's map of Bromeswell in 1601 (Figure 5.2). Wilford looks as if it may have its origins in the early Anglo-Saxon period, but was this the meeting-place of the lete, before Wilford was upgraded into a hundred, or is it possible that the organisation of letes in Wicklaw is older still?

How is it that one can have two valleys, the Blyth and the Deben, occupying a very similar stretch of Suffolk coastline, with very similar settlement patterns and yet they end up with such markedly different territorial organisation and boundary patterns? Let us consider briefly their similarities and differences. Both territories have at their core an ancient royal estate, Blythburgh in Blything hundred and Rendlesham in Wicklaw; both have their royal burial places, Blythburgh and Sutton Hoo; and both correspond to river valley territories described by the watersheds of the rivers Blyth and Deben. They also have good evidence for pre-existing settlement from prehistoric to Roman times. On the other hand, their differences are quite marked. Wicklaw has a number of pagan Anglo-Saxon cemeteries; none have yet been found in Blything. Wicklaw has at least six important late Roman hoards containing coins until the reign of Honorius in the early fifth century; none have yet been found in Blything. Wicklaw has up to four Latin loan-words among its place-names, including the name of Wicklaw itself, while Blything has just one, the place-name of Bulcamp. Wicklaw once had a late Roman shore fort at Walton, but, allowing for coastal erosion, as far as we know Blything had no comparable defensive site in the late Roman period. Of course there remains the other major difference, that Wicklaw has five and a half hundreds, whereas Blything is a single large hundred or possibly a double hundred.

These differences between the two areas, particularly the differences in their administrative boundaries, reflect two fundamentally different social and economic histories. Blything was relatively unaffected by early Anglo-Saxon settlement, but Wicklaw was an area profoundly affected and eventually dominated by Anglo-Saxon migrants, who were to produce the family which came to rule the whole kingdom of East Anglia. These royal associations eventually brought Wicklaw to the foundation of St Etheldreda's monastery at Ely, where careful management resulted in the division of the territory into small hundreds along the line of letes. In contrast, Blything continued unchanged and survived as a very large hundred until the nineteenth century. Such contrasting history from two adjacent areas of the county highlights the great complexity of the origins of the shire. The history of the county of Suffolk is very much the history of its constituent parts, for territories such as Wicklaw and Blything were shires within their own right long before the county of Suffolk came into existence. They are the salt and the seasoning which gives the county its distinctive flavour.

The rebirth of towns

The rebirth of towns in the post-Roman period is one of the most significant developments in the history of northern European society. In Ipswich, Suffolk can claim to have the earliest Anglo-Saxon town; if Suffolk was the cradle of early English kingship, as represented by Sutton Hoo, then it was also the cradle of English towns. In 1086, Ipswich was a medium-sized county town comparable to Maldon; by comparison, the town of Bury St Edmunds was a hundred and a half, while Norwich and Thetford counted as single hundreds. Dunwich, on the other hand, sent just two or three representatives to Blything hundred court, and does not seem to have a separate hundredal assessment (DB ii, 312; Ballard 1904, 63).

Although Ipswich now lacks both castle and cathedral, simply because its castle was dismantled in 1176 and Norwich was chosen as the diocesan centre, it nevertheless has all the qualities of a county town. Ipswich was badly damaged by German bombing during the Second World War; many of its timber-framed buildings which had not been removed before the 1940s burnt furiously in the Blitz. In the 1950s and 1960s it suffered from greedy and inept development, but in recent years there has been a marked improvement in the quality of its modern architecture and, at last, some care is being taken over the preservation of its few surviving timber buildings (Colman 1976). The result is a town which is beginning to be proud of its past, with good reason.

Although the significance of Middle Saxon Ipswich ware was understood before 1957, and there were a number of small rescue excavations by Stanley West in the 1960s, it was not until 1973 that the Scole Committee pointed out the archaeological riches that lay underneath the devastated town (West 1963; 1973). Systematic rescue excavation began the following year with the setting up of Suffolk County Council's Archaeological Unit. If residents now appreciate the archaeology and early history of Ipswich they should thank Keith Wade who worked tirelessly under the most difficult of circumstances to salvage what he could from the wreck of the town's development. Up to 1988 there were 24 excavations. The resulting archaeological sample is very small when compared to other historic centres such as Canterbury, Norwich, or Hamwic, the predecessor of Southampton and Ipswich's closest English parallel; it is fractional when compared to Dorestad, Ipswich's closest early medieval continental trading partner (Wade 1988).

Wade has established that Ipswich was a *de novo* Anglo-Saxon settlement, without any significant Roman urban precursor. This marks Ipswich out as being of special importance, for most early Anglo-Saxon towns grew up among the ruins of old Roman provincial walled cities, while the old Roman port of London continued as the 'emporium for many nations who come to it by land and sea' into the eighth century (HE, II, 3). It has been suggested that there was a direct relationship between the development of Ipswich, the production of Ipswich ware, and the East Anglian Wuffinga dynasty (Scarfe 1972, 101–3; Dunmore *et al.* 1974). Ekwall has even suggested an early Swedish link in the place-name of *Gipeswic,* an argument which in retrospect may seem to have been overworked (Ekwall 1960, 266). Early Anglo-Saxon towns such as Ipswich, *Hamwic* (Southampton), Sandwich, *Eborwic* (York) and even

Lundenwic (London), were estuarine trading settlements each corresponding with the separate kingdoms of East Anglia, Wessex, Kent, Northumbria and Essex respectively (Biddle 1976).

As more evidence comes to light for the size and economic strength of Ipswich, this question of royal patronage does not go away, but seems less significant. We have to ask, was it the power of the early Anglo-Saxon kings which stimulated trade and urban growth, or did the development of trade and urban growth generate a more sophisticated and cosmopolitan style of kingship? Before the Norman Conquest two-thirds of Ipswich was held by Queen Edith and there were another sixteen holdings in different ownership; Ipswich was in reality a composite free borough under the king, a fact which was more clearly stated in its charter of 1200. It is this freedom, guaranteed through the authority of kingship, which was more likely the key to its success, and not any direct royal intervention or stimulus from above.

Some degree of self determination existed in Ipswich before that glorious day, on 29 June 1200, when the townsfolk assembled in the churchyard of St Mary-le-Tower to consider the formation of a sworn council composed of twelve 'Capital Portmen . . . as there are in other free boroughs of England' (Martin 1954, 8). Martin has suggested that the royal charter of 1200, which granted Ipswich its borough status and liberty from the sheriff's courts, was a 'legal abstraction' and that the first *Portmanmote* held at St Mary-le-Tower was also the last appearance of a much older folk court (Martin 1954, 23). This may well be true, but there is no supporting evidence. After 1200 the Portmanmote met every alternate Thursday and was the equivalent of the hundredal court of rural areas. Petty pleas were also heard twice a week. The initial panel of electors was formed out of four freemen chosen from each of Ipswich's twelve parishes. Thus the twelve portmen may each have come from a separate parish, with the bailiffs and coroners elected from among their number. Over them all presided the Alderman of the Guild, chosen by the guild and independent of the borough structure.

In 1290–91 a further panel of 24 of the 'better-advised men of the town' was elected to recollect and re-draft the written customs of the borough which had been stolen by the town clerk eighteen years earlier. Thus the classic borough oligarchy composed of the 'twelves' and the 'twenty-fours', to be found in many other English towns, was constituted. The relationship between the 'Great' and 'Petty' courts, held within the walls of the borough, and the moots held on St Margaret's Green, known as the *Thingstead*, just outside the town, is not entirely clear. This may have been the site of the pre-Conquest *Burg-mote*, which according to the laws of Edgar (AD 962) was to be held three times a year. In the time of Henry I the *burg-motes* were held just twice a year to bring them into line with shire-motes (Ballard 1904, 121). The *Thingstead* on St Margaret's Green was an important shire court, relating not just to Ipswich, but also to the Geldable Hundreds of East Suffolk. As such it was very similar to the mound which served as the meeting-place of the eight and a half hundreds of Thinghoe, just north of Bury St Edmunds. It was similar also to Colchester's 'Leet' court which met three times a year (Martin 1954, 17), and to Dunwich's borough court which met on a hill, called 'Leet Hill', which still survives just outside the defences. Later moots at Ipswich were summoned by a moot horn and met within the defences near St Mildred's chapel close to the site of the medieval Moot Hall, Guild Hall and Town Hall, near Corn Hill, the supposed site of the Norman Castle (Redstone 1948, 68–72).

The free borough of Ipswich grew in direct response to an increase in overseas trade and the demand for high-status objects which are evidenced in the later pagan Anglo-Saxon princely graves, such as Sutton Hoo and Boss Hall. Ipswich ware, the first post-Roman wheel-made pottery to appear in England, was mass produced in the town; waste from the kilns extended 160 metres along the south side of Carr Street. It was exported inland throughout the area of the East Anglian kingdom. A few sherds of Ipswich ware have been found as far afield as Lincolnshire, the Midlands, Essex, London and the north Kent coast (Wade 1988, 97). No other production centre has been confirmed, thus the distribution of Ipswich ware clearly indicates the importance of the early town and its far-reaching trade contacts. The presence of imported seventh-century continental pottery types, such as Black-ware pitchers and early Badorf wares, link Ipswich with the Merovingian ports of Quentovic, near Boulogne, and Dorestad, the early trading settlement near Utrecht, at the junction of the rivers Lec and Rhine (Wade 1988).

It is now known from the concentration of Ipswich ware that the Middle Saxon town extended over 50 hectares. In its earliest phases the town had small ditched enclosures, probably arable and pasture fields, on its periphery. The settlement was undefended, and the irregular street pattern led down to a waterfront revetted with timber. Most of the evidence for Middle Saxon Ipswich comes from pits and wells within the built-up area. It is not until the ninth century that there is evidence for substantial buildings, some of several phases, with cellars facing on to, in one case, a metalled road, the precursor of the modern street pattern. Evidence for crafts such as iron-working, horn- and bone-working, and leather-working, particularly shoe-making, have been found together with spindle-whorls and loomweights suggesting woollen cloth production. Quantities of goat horn may have been supplied with goat hides from the dry heathland soils of the Sandling region north of Ipswich.

The waterfront was clearly a hive of activity with evidence for successive phases of timber and wattle revetting encroaching on to the river frontage. The church of St Peter, and possibly later St Mary-Quay along College Street were built very close to the waterfront; St Peter's is mentioned in the Domesday survey. As a result of this riverside encroachment these churches now stand some distance from the quayside, but clearly they were intended to serve a population residing near the old port. It was here no doubt that the *windraghers*, or porters who worked on the Common Quay, lived (Martin 1954, 11). Both bridges at Handford and Stoke were in place with a settlement on the south side of the river before the Conquest, grouped around St Mary at Stoke and the now lost church of St Augustine. The settlement at Stoke, which belonged to the Abbot of Ely in 1086, was active in the Middle Saxon period as attested by the presence of Ipswich ware and may be as early as the pagan Anglo-Saxon cemetery found in 1906 at Hadleigh Road to which it may relate (DB ii, 290b, 382b; Ozanne 1962; Scarfe 1972, 22; Dunmore *et al.* 1974, 61).

Defences in the form of a bank and ditch were added in the tenth century, possibly in response to Danish raiding. The defences cut off the outer fringes of the street pattern leaving 'lost' lengths of Anglo-Saxon streets and reduced the number of entrances, causing roads such as St Clement's and St Helen's Street to veer north towards the nearest town gate (Figure 6.7). As far as one can tell, the line of the Anglo-Saxon ditch corresponds closely with the line of the medieval town wall and is still evident in the gentle curve of

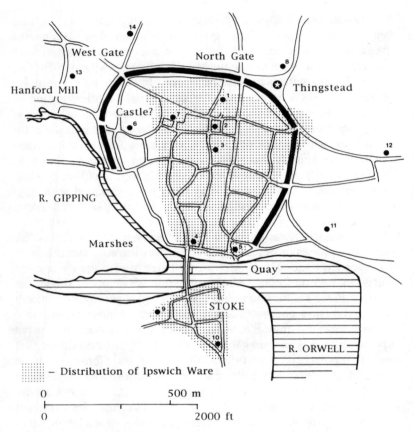

6.7 Ipswich: the Late Saxon and Norman town. The shaded area indicates the distribution of Middle Saxon Ipswich ware

The churches are those believed to be in existence by Norman times. 1. St Mary-le-Tower; 2. St Lawrence; 3. St Stephen; 4. St Peter; 5. St Mary-Quay; 6. St Mary Elms; 7. St Mildred; 8. St Margaret; 9. St Mary Stoke; 10. St Augustine; 11. St Clement; 12. St Helen; 13. St Matthew; 14. St George

Crown Street and Tower Ramparts, and the line of Old Foundary Road, known in the eighteenth century as Margaret's Ditches. On the north and east the defences were probably more substantial, while on the west and south the marshes and river frontage provided some sort of protection against all but sea-borne raiders.

Ipswich suffered miserably from pirate raiding from the tenth to the twelfth centuries. In AD 991, prior to the Battle of Maldon, Olaf Tryggvason stood off Folkestone with 93 ships and after harrying outside the town and attacking Sandwich they closed on Ipswich, 'overrunning all the countryside' (Garmonsway 1972, 126–7). It is hard to see how Ipswich could have escaped the attentions of Sweyn in 1003 when Norwich and Thetford were sacked, although the town is not mentioned in the *Anglo-Saxon Chronicle* for that year. 1005 was the year of the great famine and in 1010, the Danish host of Thorkell the Tall, that had over-wintered in Kent, landed at Ipswich after Easter and attacked ealdorman Ulfketill's levies and scattered them. The Danes took possession of East Anglia that year and destroyed Thetford and Cambridge; 'for three months they harried and burnt that land, even penetrating into the unin-habited fens, slaying men and cattle, and burning throughout the fens' (Garmonsway 1972, 138–40). In 1016 the host of Cnut left London and sailed into the Orwell, and from there went into Mercia, 'destroying and burning everything in their path as was their custom' (Garmonsway 1972, 150).

The Domesday survey describes a town in a desperate state. Ipswich may not have escaped undamaged either during the period of the East Anglian rebellions or the post-Conquest disturbance between 1069 and 1075. In 1085, King William ordered the laying waste of coastal districts to counter the threat of invasion from Denmark and Flanders (Garmonsway 1972, 216). The survey lists 538 burgesses held by Queen Edith in 1066, but by 1086, 100 were too poor to pay anything more than one penny a head in geld, and 328 burgages lay waste (DB ii, 290). Of the 41 burgesses held by Suane of Essex, 15 were dead (DB ii, 402). There were also six vacant burgesses on the land of Richard son of Earl Gislebert (DB ii, 392b), and three others are mentioned under the lands of Walter the Deacon, which may be included with those of Queen Edith (DB ii, 427).

Stoke seems to have escaped damage, but perhaps as much as two-thirds of the town north of the river was desolate. In spite of its crushed state Ipswich, like all the other county boroughs in Eng-land, did not escape the humiliation of a Norman castle being built within its ancient defences. A few of the waste burgages may have been caused by the building of the castle. The earth mound of the motte with its timber tower was probably near to St Mary-le-Tower, while the outer circuit of the bailey was probably formed by Tower Ramparts and the north-west corner of the Saxon town defences (Figure 6.7). Here Hugh Bigod was besieged by King Stephen in 1153; the castle was eventually dismantled on the orders of Henry II in 1176, together with other Bigod castles in the region (Redstone 1948).

If Ipswich was laid waste as a result of the Norman Conquest and the effects of castle building, there are indications that it was flourishing again in the later twelfth century when it began to expand beyond its tenth-century ramparts and the quay area was extended eastwards with the appearance of St Clement's parish. Ipswich had a mint in the tenth century when it was minting coins during the reign of Edgar; coin production is a good indication of borough status and importance. Coins were also being produced in the thirteenth century, at least until 1272. By 1200, Ipswich had acquired its first charter of liberties and became an incorporated royal borough (Martin 1954, 7).

Of the other pre-Conquest towns in Suffolk we know remarkably little (Figure 7.1). Hardly any urban archaeology has been done outside of Ipswich; most of our delightful Suffolk market towns have not been subjected to the same sort of ruthless post-war commercial development and therefore remain unavailable for archaeological sampling. The only detailed documentary source for towns is the Domesday survey and one or two early charters. The mention of burgesses in 1086, however few, the presence of a money-changer or a mint, and above all, a market, are the definitive features of urban status, but rarely do they all coincide with perfect clarity. As well as Ipswich, there were burgesses in Sudbury, Dunwich, Clare, Eye and Beccles.

There is no mention of a market at Ipswich or Dunwich; their sea-ports were clearly the focus of trade and markets are not always recorded in Domesday Book. For example, in Essex, no markets are recorded in 1086 where clearly a number must have existed at towns such as Maldon and Colchester which had burgesses (Darby 1952, 251). We must be thankful that any markets are recorded in the Domesday survey for Suffolk at all and accept that there may well have been others unrecorded. Domesday markets in Suffolk are mentioned at Thorney and Blythburgh, both important ancient royal manors, at Hoxne, which was the bishop's seat in Suffolk, and at Kelsale, which was the sheriff's manor in East Suffolk, and at Haverhill, where a third part of a market was worth 13s 4d (Darby 1952, 202–3). Of these, Blythburgh and Sudbury had money-changers and Ipswich had a mint (DB ii, 282, 286b, 290). There is no doubt that Bury St Edmunds also had a mint, from the evidence of its coins, but no mint is listed, presumably because it belonged to the Abbey.

St Edmund's Bury was a burgeoning urban community in 1086; 342 houses had been built on demesne land of the Abbey since the time of Edward the Confessor, yet Bury had no burgesses for it was not a free borough. It existed solely for the sustenance of the 118 monks and to house the 75 bakers, ale-brewers, tailors, washer-women, shoemakers, robe-makers, cooks, porters and agents of the Abbey (DB ii, 372). Lobel did her best to demonstrate that Bury was a borough before 1086, while accepting that any proof of the importance of the town was lacking. It is indeed very likely that Bury was an important town before the Norman street-plan was laid out – it was valued at a hundred and a half – but it was originally a royal vill granted to the convent for the feeding of the monks and as such it was not a free borough. This was a bone of bitter contention between the townsfolk and the Abbey through-out the Middle Ages (Lobel 1935). The town, in 1086, is described as contained within a great circuit, indeed the gridded streets are clearly visible today as the very model of a planned Norman town (Figure 6.2). The design was probably the work of Abbot Baldwin, while the unit of measurement was the chain of four poles or perches of $16\frac{1}{2}$ feet (Crummy 1979). There may in fact have been several phases of planned development with a later extension of the town to include the northern suburb of Brakeland.

So what can still be seen of the old centre of *Bedericsworth*, the predecessor of St Edmund's Bury? A square for God and a square for man, which constituted the rectangular form of the Abbey Precinct and the planned Norman town, are clearly at odds with some elements of the street pattern which appear to pre-date this Norman angularity. In particular the circularity of Maynewater Lane and the configuration of streets around St Mary's Square, the *Elder* or older market, once the site of the old Horse Market, may indicate part of a pre-Norman defensive circuit, but this has not been confirmed by excavation (Carr 1975). The path of South Gate Street and Northgate Street once joined up underneath the Abbey

Precinct; the cross-roads thereby formed with East Gate Street in the area of the Mustow must be significant. The latter place-name may derive from 'mot-stow' meaning a meeting-place (Smith 1956, II, 44), or possibly it may indicate the minster-stow, which preceded the later Abbey.

Near here, in the early twelfth century, stood the large manor house of Adam of Cockfield with its wooden belfry 140 feet high (Hart 1966; Greenway & Sayers 1989, 123). Such secular towers may have been a feature of the pre-Conquest urban skyline; certainly the 'famous' Earl Ælfric son of Wihtgar, Lord of Clare, owned a tower in which his son was living, for it is mentioned in the foundation charter of the secular canons of Clare c. 1044–65 (Hart 1966, 71). The charter is referred to in the Domesday survey and it is clear also that the market at Clare once belonged to the Anglo-Saxon earl (DB ii, 389b). Ælfric's estate at Clare extended to twenty-four carucates, and this, with his adjoining estate of twenty-five carucates at Hundon, made up the largest single block of land in secular ownership in Suffolk before the Conquest. It is tempting therefore to suggest that these high belfrys, which had a secular function, were for the regulation and control of major market centres and were not just status symbols of the thegnly class (Stenton 1958). By 1086, Clare was a substantial urban community, the focus of the earl's estates, with 43 burgesses, 30 villeins, 30 bordars and 20 serfs, in all upwards of 123 households. The manor of Clare and all the other extensive estates of Earl Ælfric were seized by King William and granted to Richard, son of Count Gilbert.

Sudbury was an important borough in 1086. It had been held by Alveva, the mother of Earl Morchar, before the Conquest and then became royal demesne kept by two members of King William's household, William the Chamberlain and Otho the Goldsmith. Sudbury was an outlying portion of Thinghoe hundred and the place-name of *Sudberie* suggests that it was the 'southern burh' or fort controlled from the centre at Bury St Edmunds (Ekwall 1960, 452). Extending this theory, the royal manors of Exning and Thorney (Stowmarket), and the town of Thetford might possibly be considered the western, eastern and northern defences of the Liberty of St Edmund. Recent excavations suggest that Sudbury was once a late Iron Age defensive site, but was abandoned for 700–800 years before becoming an important Late Saxon settlement. The *Anglo-Saxon Chronicle* mentions in a laconic entry for the year 798 that Bishop Alfhun passed away at Sudbury, but was buried at Dunwich (Garmonsway 1972, 56). Clearly Sudbury was a place of some significance to have been mentioned at all. A Middle Saxon pit, 125 metres south of St Gregory's church, was excavated in 1991 and a few sherds of Ipswich ware were found, but this does not make a Middle Saxon town (Newman 1991b). However, further work may well unearth more Ipswich ware so that this view will have to be revised.

The Late Saxon defensive circuit of Sudbury seems to follow the line of a late Iron Age triple-ditch system and is clearly reflected in the horseshoe shaped street pattern formed by Friars' Street, Burkitts's Lane and Croft Road (Newman 1990). Anyone who has not had the pleasure of walking around this circuit among Sudbury's well-conserved buildings and delightful streets should do so; they will soon appreciate the small size of the enclosed Saxon town (Freeman 1986). St Gregory's church is mentioned by name in 1086 and this was clearly the most significant feature of the town, dominating the Stour valley from an elevated position in the northern corner of the defences (DB ii, 286b). Sudbury had a total of 118 burgesses and others are recorded in Essex at Hedingham and Hinckford hundred; there may have been as many as 142 households (Darby 1952, 197, 252). Links with Essex are not surprising given Sudbury's location at an important crossing of the River Stour; it was usual for composite boroughs to have links with larger manors in the surrounding district. Ipswich, for example, had links with Clare, Bergholt, Nacton and Bramford. These links seem to have arisen through the need for large estates to have a town property, but it is just possible that some may have originated through the process of burh-work and military service. Perhaps Sudbury was one of the *burhs* constructed by Edward the Elder in the early tenth century; unfortunately there is insufficient evidence as yet to substantiate this attractive theory.

Beccles may have had as many as 48 burgesses; 22 of them are listed under Norwich as having moved to Beccles, possibly because they had been displaced by the building of Norwich castle and other traumas which had beset the city (Darby 1952, 140, 196). But it is not clear whether the 26 burgesses listed in Suffolk included the 22 burgesses from Norwich. However, the larger figure of 121 households based on all listings of burgesses and unfree tenants seems likely. The king had the fourth part of Beccles market (DB ii, 283b), while the Abbot of Bury held the other three parts (DB ii, 369b). Bury had been granted the manor of Beccles with Elmswell by King Eadwig in the 950s, thus indicating that the settlement at Beccles had once been a royal estate (Hart 1966, 248). The manor rendered 30,000 herrings before the Conquest, but this had been doubled to 60,000 by 1086 (DB ii, 369b–370).

The commanding hill-top position of St Michael's church, Beccles, with its view north over the River Waveney, is reminiscent of Sudbury's view south over the Stour. Perhaps this was the single church mentioned in the Domesday survey, but there was another close by, St Peter's, which served the old fish market east of the present market site. Remains of its fabric can still be seen inside St Peter's House. Today, Northgate Street leads eastwards out of the town towards Beccles bridge. *Gata* means a street, so this was once the northern street of the old town. The open market area south-west of St Michael's church and the configuration of streets around it may be of Norman date, initiated perhaps by the influx of bur-gesses from Norwich, while the large and important fish market represents both the nucleus and the specialised function of the Late Saxon borough. The fish market itself could well be a rare example of a planned Late Saxon market centre, below which there must lie a riverside quay rich in waterlogged archaeological deposits. There have been some missed opportunities in the archaeology of Beccles and it has suffered from over-development with housing estates; sadly, there is little awareness of the town's importance so that Beccles now lacks the civic pride of Sudbury and this shows up painfully in its conservation area.

The creation of Eye as a castle town and market centre by William Malet may disguise an earlier focus of the estates owned by Edric of Laxfield before the Conquest (DB ii, 319b–320). Edric was one of the largest Late Saxon landholders in East Suffolk. But the market appears to be a new creation for there are complaints under the entry for the Bishop's manor of Hoxne that since William Malet had set up a market on Saturdays under his castle at Eye, the market at Hoxne, traditionally also a Saturday market, 'has been so far spoilt that it is of little worth' (DB ii, 379). The Hoxne market changed to Fridays and continued as a small but successful market town into the late Middle Ages. At Eye, the castle, its park and the 25 burgesses dwelling in the market were all new after the Conquest. There may have been as many as 144 households in 1086, which could make Eye comparable with Beccles in size of population.

Of all the towns discussed in this section, the one that is most elusive, as ever, is Dunwich. Already by 1086 Dunwich had lost a carucate of land to the sea and this irreversible process of coastal erosion was to continue throughout the Middle Ages and eventually brought about its destruction (Warner 1982, 8–11). Dunwich had 120 burgesses before the Conquest, rising to 236 in 1086. There were also 24 Frenchmen and another 80 burgesses living in the suburb of Alneton, Westleton. Even though 178 poor men are also listed, the impression given is of an expanding and successful community which seems to have escaped the devastation evident at Ipswich and Norwich (Darby 1952, 194; Warner 1982, 16, 80). Perhaps some of the 116 new burgesses at Dunwich had been displaced from other less fortunate coastal towns.

Two churches had been added to the one listed pre-Conquest church at Dunwich, presumably to serve a rising population. The total number of households in and around the town in 1086 may have been as high as 600. Darby argues for a population in the region of 3,000, which means that Dunwich was comparable with Ipswich and considerably larger than Yarmouth, its other sea-port trading rival. As the principal pre-Conquest landowner had been Edric of Laxfield, the main manor had come to William Malet, the new Norman lord and castilian of Eye. Malet may well have been responsible for developing the town and sea-port. In 1086 it was worth the huge sum of £50 and, like Beccles, paid 60,000 herrings, but before the Conquest it had only been worth £10 (DB ii, 311b–312).

With Dunwich we can only reflect on how much history and archaeology has been lost – it is as if one threw a city the size of Ipswich or Norwich into the sea and forgot all about it. There is no doubt that in Dunwich the county of Suffolk has lost one of its principal Saxon and medieval towns and we can only speculate in the vaguest terms about its Saxon street pattern, its churches and markets, its harbour and about the thousands of lives that were lived out within its defences.

7

Domesday Suffolk

Making the survey

Domesday Book is the central source for our understanding of the early shire; not just for the history of its boundaries and sub-divisions, but for the history of the folk who articulated this ancient administrative system. The circuit of the great survey which comprised East Anglia, including the counties of Norfolk, Suffolk and Essex, was contained in a separate volume known curiously as 'Little' Domesday, or volume two (DB ii). It is in fact substantially larger than volume one, known paradoxically as 'Great' Domesday (DB i), which contains the main survey for most of the other counties of England. The detail contained in DB ii is formidable especially when compared to other counties in DB i. So, for example, in the main volume (DB i) the county of Kent occupies 28 pages while in DB ii, Suffolk occupies 200 pages. The reason for this anachronism has been explained in the way the survey was brought together in the months before King William's death, and if we accept the cogent arguments of Galbraith, the 'Little' Domesday survey of the eastern counties would eventually have been compressed down to the more manageable size of the counties in the main volume. It is, he says, 'no more than a very hasty fair copy of an earlier draft and is, as we should expect, full of errors' (Galbraith 1974, 59).

The entries of Little Domesday Book have also been described by H. C. Darby as 'cumbrous and untidy' when compared with

DB i (Darby 1952, 97). It is cumbersome in that it contains much detailed information about stock held on the larger manors and untidy because of the many small entries which relate to freemen and sokemen holding small acreages. There are also frequent 'exotic' entries referring to legal disputes in the hundredal courts, arguments over land ownership, the commendation of freemen and other petty squabbles between reeves on the royal estates and the sheriff. In Suffolk there are over eighty such entries about half of which refer to business in the hundredal courts. Clearly these entries do not agree with Darby's concept of the 'tidy' Midland manor. That as a primary source it seems to be full of perplexing detail does not necessarily mean that DB ii is also 'full of errors'; indeed, perhaps we should try harder to understand what this 'cumbrous' detail is all about, and whether the 'errors' are really errors or merely misconceptions and misunderstandings based on an empirical knowledge gained from volume one. Let us therefore, without prejudice, rummage in the most untidy and potentially erroneous parts of DB ii for the county of Suffolk.

Tidiness and lack of error are not qualities that one normally expects to find in primary source material; indeed it is a luxury which most local historians learn to live without. The past, like the present, is not a tidy place and we cannot assume that the eleventh-century pattern of landholding was necessarily any more tidy than our own. Furthermore, untidiness, clutter and the unconsidered trifles of the past, are not just the charm of history, they are its evidential dynamics; they are the clues which reveal that basic human truth of 'deeply ordered chaos', which rules all our lives. Furthermore, when historical sources are found tidy and error-free it is usually because somebody has made them so; the suspicions of the historian must be aroused, for, like a detective fresh on the scene of a crime, we must consider what is missing and why. It could be argued, therefore, that the very qualities in DB ii condemned by some historians are the ones which reveal its unadulterated honesty as an historical document.

Domesday Book would indeed have been unremarkable had it been a survey of a few large and tidy estates – the fact that it covers a great many small landholdings, some of just a few acres, means that it is a survey of unparalleled size and complexity. It is in DB ii, and also in one or two of the satellite surveys such as the Exeter Domesday and the *Inquisitione Eliensis*, that we can appreciate the full complexity of the first draft. Little Domesday Book, as far as we know, was never successfully compressed into the concise format of volume one. That this was intended seems highly likely, but either William's death, or the sheer enormity of the task prevented it from happening. The mass of detail does, however, indicate one of the central problems which lies behind the making of Domesday Book – the difficulty of knowing 'what or how much each man who was a landholder here in England had in land or in live-stock, and how much money it was worth' (Garmonsway 1972, 216).

In Little Domesday Book there is also a fourth dimension, that of time. DB ii has a better memory than DB i, including sometimes three valuations: one *Tempore Rex Edwardi* (TRE), in fact the valuation taken on the day when King Edward was both 'alive and dead'; another *tunc*, probably taken when the property was entered upon by its present incumbent; and *modo* – the valuation in 1086. Sally Harvey pointed out the way that Domesday Book must be dependent upon earlier surveys and information recorded at a local level (Harvey 1971). The eclectic character of DB ii raises serious questions about the function of the survey; we know that it was not just concerned with the collection of gelt or with the valuation of manors. It seems however to be concerned with all landholders great and small and the changes which had taken place in the pattern of landholding as a result of the Norman Conquest and local disturbances that followed in its wake.

The survey records many 'invasions' or encroachments and disputes which exercised the hundredal courts. Wormald has identified 25 lawsuits mentioned in the survey for Suffolk, Norfolk has 20 and Essex 27, making the eastern counties, with Lincolnshire, the most litigious counties (Wormald 1990). However, at least forty incidents can be noted in Suffolk where the hundred 'testifies' or 'bears witness' in disputes of all kinds. These involve the folk-memory of the court and test its reliability as a legal entity. At Stow, Nigel, a sergeant of Count Robert, *invasit* 11 acres belonging to Stow church and added them to the manor of Combs – 'but he is dead, and there is none to make answer thereupon, And the Hundred testifies that they were Alms lands belonging to the church' (DB ii, 291b). Following the Conquest and the rebellions under Earl Morchar and Earl Ralph, the mortality and attrition rate among freemen in the hundredal courts must have been high. The whole of the upper end of the old Anglo-Saxon seignorial class including many wealthy freemen had been swept away. Five entries clearly indicate the hundred's inability to come up with answers. At Thorney, in Stowmarket, the hundred did not know if a second church, built on the edge of Stowmarket's churchyard by a group of freemen, had been consecrated (DB ii, 281b). Neither did the hundred know who had ownership of a certain freeman's 9 acres at Onehouse, possibly because 'it rendered no customary dues in the hundred' (DB ii, 291b). In a protracted dispute involving the land claims of Roger Ramis the hundred denied knowledge of two of them but supported a third (DB ii, 338–338b, 449b, 352). 'Nor was there anyone on his behalf who could say by what title' he made his claim.

In certain important respects the survey supplanted the function of the hundredal courts in that it provided a sound corpus of knowledge that was not dependent on folk-memory and the witness of the hundred. There are a few cases where the hundredal testimony clashed with the sheriff and the reeves. In a lengthy land dispute between the sheriff Roger Bigot and the burgesses of Ipswich, 'the half-hundred of Ipswich bears witness that this [land] belonged to the church in the time of King Edward, and Wisgar held it, and they offer to prove it' (DB ii, 393). At Buxhall, the sheriff, who also had overall responsibility for the royal demesne, used the land of one of his freemen to make up an estate at Baylam in an adjoining hundred, 'but the hundred has seen neither writ nor feoffor' (DB ii, 336). But more often the hundred appears to support the sheriff and royal reeves, as at Belstead where 'two manors were taken by judgement from Ralph Taillebosc and Phin into the King's hand, and afterwards Aubrey received them without livery of seisin, as the reeve and the hundred say' (DB ii, 418b).

The most heated debates are those which relate to ownership and commendation where associations with those that were in some way disgraced might affect title to land. At Fordley, there was Edric, a freeman, with a number of others who had been commended to the Saxon landholder Edric of Laxfield. During the reign of Edward the Confessor, Edric of Laxfield had been outlawed, probably for his sympathies with the house of Wessex. All his land was seized by the king, including the free-holdings. There followed a reconciliation and the king granted him back his lands. 'He gave him too a sealed charter [*breve et sigillum*] that whosoever of his freemen under commendation might choose to return to him, by his grant they might return'. But the hundred saw no sign that the freeman, also called Edric, had returned to his lord: 'he himself says, and offers proof by ordeal that he did return' (DB ii, 310b). Land lost in some way as a result of this type of forfeiture could be redeemed, but it was an essential part of the title that redemption should be in open court and witnessed by the hundred. In Loes hundred three freemen forfeited their lands to the Abbot of Ely for reasons that are not explained; 'and the hundred has not since seen that they have redeemed it' (DB ii, 443b). It is clear from this entry that while these freemen were not commended to any lord, other than perhaps the abbot, their five fellows were and held their lands securely.

Loyalty and commendation

The Domesday survey effectively upholds one of the basic principles of Anglo-Saxon society: that no man should be 'lordless'; the chosen lord of a freeman was usually of the highest rank, the King or Queen, the Earl, the Bishop or a thegn (Maitland 1897, 99). Although commendation may in certain respects have bound the land, it was of little financial value; to hold land 'merely by commendation' was probably the smallest landholding obligation (Maitland 1897, 103) (DB ii, 201). Yet there are few freemen or sokemen in the eastern counties whose commendation was not recorded with meticulous care. Why was this necessary? The same cannot be said for the recording of gelt, and other aspects of the survey seem to be haphazard, such as the recording of land attached to churches, or meadowland and common pasture, where substantial differences occur between counties.

The recording of commendation was important because it had a direct bearing on the process of the hundredal court meetings. When we look at the freefolk of the eastern counties in the eleventh century, we must remember that we are looking at a markedly hierarchical society. Although the freemen met regularly at their hundredal courts where all aspects of local government and land transactions were enacted, this was not a democratic society in the modern sense (Loyn 1974). The freemen who attended the three- or four-weekly meetings were not elected representatives; they attended by virtue of their landholdings and their inherited status. Neither were they there to represent their own personal opinions or to play at politics for its own sake. The law required that they be somebody's 'man' and that unquestionably required them to support their lord in the assemblies, even when all the odds were against them.

For example, a group of freemen maintained that Burchard of Mendlesham was their lord, 'and they have not any testimony except themselves; and yet they are willing to prove it by any means' (DB ii, 285b). As Burchard was a man of Earl Ralph and his lands were in the king's hands under Godric the Steward, this insistence that they were Burchard's men cannot have helped their position. Thus the acquisition of land and the commendation of freemen brought with it the support of votes in the hundredal courts; this point has not, in the view of this writer, been given due consideration by Domesday scholars. Little Domesday Book, by recording the pattern of kinship and commendation in the old Anglo-Danish order, was providing information about the different political factions, at local and county level, and the bonds of loyalty which had the potential to re-emerge as opposition to the new Norman regime. Alternatively a change of commendation might cause trouble through political in-fighting at the hundredal assemblies, or cause a shift in the local political power-base with possible wider repercussions. Having detailed knowledge of 'what or how much each man who was a landholder here in England had', was not just a fiscal exercise to maximise taxation, it was a political exercise by a conquering power that had, first and foremost, every intention of maintaining control at national and local level (Garmonsway 1972, 216).

In recording commendation the survey constantly refers to 'predecessors', or the pre-Conquest pattern of commendation and how this had changed as a result of an incoming lord. For example, at Northales (Covehithe), one of the freemen of Roger Bigot, 'by name Harding, held 20 acres under commendation to Ulketle, predecessor of William de Warrenne' (DB ii, 333b). Sometimes there was more than one level of commendation and commendation itself could be divided between lords. This process of sub-commendation and divided commendation can be seen at Chediston where there was 'a freeman, Ulsi with 13 acres over whom one who was himself under commendation to Robert Malet's predecessor had half commendation, and the Queen the other half in the time of King Edward' (DB ii, 332/332b). A significant number of 'predecessors' were for various reasons *persona non grata,* the mere association with whom might threaten title to land.

In East Anglia the list of persons who had forfeited their estates was unusually large due to the disturbances and rebellions following the Conquest. There were the freemen and king's thegns who had been directly commended to Harold Godwinson, or his brother Gurth, both of whom had been earls of East Anglia at different times, and those who had fought against William in the Battle of Hastings. Harold held soke over his principal manor in Suffolk at Bergholt, and the hundred and a half of Samford (DB ii, 287b). Earl Gurth's freemen, men such as Ulsi of Mutford, find a prominent place in the royal demesne which Roger Bigot the Sheriff kept for King William (DB ii, 283). Gurth had also held one-third of the borough of Ipswich (DB ii, 290). All these estates had large numbers of freemen under commendation.

There were also those who had supported Earl Morchar in 1071 and the resistance movement in the fens led by Hereward the Wake. The town of Sudbury, with Cornard and Groton, once held by Alveva, the mother of Earl Morchar, lay safely in the king's hands being kept by William the Chamberlain and Otho the Goldsmith, both members of the royal household (DB ii, 286b, 373b). In this respect even the Abbot of Ely was not above suspicion; how useful to know therefore, that Guthmund the Thegn, who had married the daughter of Earl Alfgar and who had held extensive lands in Livermere, Stanstead and Occold, was the brother of Uluric, abbot of Ely, and that although Guthmund had lost his lands there were more than 55 freemen and sokemen still living in surrounding vills who had been commended to him (DB ii, 406, 408, 410b; Hart 1966, 71–2).

The rebellion of Earl Ralph had also singled out, through his personal family connections, an alliance with the Bretons, which further highlighted the factional nature of East Anglian society. Not only does the survey go out of its way to establish loyalty to 'predecessors', but there are constant reminders of kinships which must have had a bearing on the potential loyalty of likely rebels and members of the old order. For example, it is made clear that two important freemen, Ulsi of Mutford, who was commended to Earl Gurth, and Uluric (Aluric), who was probably a king's thegn, and shared lands at Bungay, were in fact brothers (DB ii, 283, 288, 296,

300). Similarly, a seemingly harmless reference to 'Godwin, Alsi's Sone, Queen Edith's Thegn' (DB ii, 306), takes on added significance when we are told that Alsi was Earl Ralph's nephew (DB ii, 322).

The problem with DB ii is that it covered a circuit which contained the three most populous and wealthy counties in England. Furthermore the social structure of its freefolk was such that complex relationships of kin and commendation created a vertical heterogeneity within what was a markedly horizontal and hierarchical society. Here the Domesday survey was hoist on its own petard – the need for all this detailed information caused the sheer mass of collected material to overwhelm the system designed to handle it. Compression may have proved impossible because of the number of small landholdings in East Anglia, particularly the holdings of countless freemen scattered through the three counties, which, because they each represented a political pawn in the game, did not lend themselves to simplification. These freefolk were the very core of the East Anglian social structure. Therefore the survey describes their landholdings and the complex web of loyalties established through the process of commendation whereby every free person was somebody's 'man'.

It has been suggested recently that the question of loyalty may be one of the prime functions of Domesday Book, that it was in many respects a survey of loyalty to the Crown; evidence from Little Domesday would seem to substantially support this view (Wormald 1990, 61). However, in East Anglia, through the process of commendation the chain of loyalty was exceptionally complex and detailed. It was further complicated by a succession of minor rebellions following the Conquest and by a tangled web of family relationships. In order to appreciate this almost paranoiac obsession with detail in DB ii, it is necessary to understand something of the historical background of East Anglia and the disturbances following the Conquest.

Treachery and rebellion

East Anglia was certainly the most populous part of England regardless of any bias there may have been in the Domesday survey for the eastern counties. Massive castles were built in the centres of population at Thetford, Ipswich and Norwich, destroying many

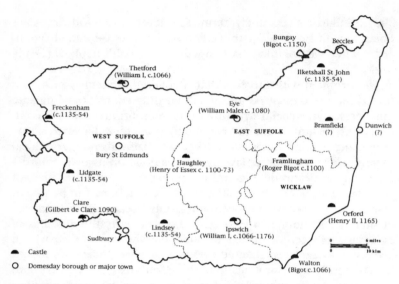

7.1 Suffolk: Norman castles, boroughs and major towns

burgage plots (Figure 7.1). Ipswich, according to the Domesday survey, was a town in ruins. Sufficient numbers of freemen from Suffolk had been involved in the fight at Hastings to warrant an early writ from King William granting all their lands in West Suffolk to Bury St Edmunds. In 1071, Bishop Æthelwine and Earl Morchar escaped by ship to Ely and there joined up with Hereward, who, with the men of Peterborough, had been leading a resistance movement in the fens since 1070. William moved quickly to surround them by land and sea. Only Hereward escaped. The king captured Æthelwine and Morchar and all their followers 'and delt with them as he pleased' (Garmonsway 1972, 208).

Then there was the fiasco of Earl Ralph de Gael's wedding in 1075, when he, Earl Roger of Hereford, Earl Waltheof of Huntingdon and several senior clerics conspired against the king. Potentially this was a serious matter. Ralph's father, known as Ralph the Staller, was a Breton serving in the court of Edward the Confessor, with lands in Norfolk and Suffolk (Douglas 1964, 231; Garmonsway 1972, 210). His family connections in East Anglia may have been extensive and well connected (DB ii, 306). However, this 'foolish plot' involved the loyalty of other Bretons in

William's army and a 'pirate host' was also drawn in from Denmark. In fact the two principals in the conspiracy grossly overestimated the support they hoped to gain from their respective earldoms, in particular from a folk who were already well acquainted with the power of their new king; 'the garrisons of the castles ... together with the inhabitants of the country, opposed them and did everything to hinder them' (Garmonsway 1972, 212).

Ralph fled, abandoning his wretched bride in Norwich Castle, the Danes turned north, and as for the Bretons 'some were blinded, some were banished, some were brought to shame. So all traitors to the king were laid low' (Garmonsway 1972, 212). In 1076 William followed up with further campaigns against the Bretons in their homeland, unsuccessfully besieging Earl Ralph and others in the castle at Dol (Douglas 1964, 234). It must have been at this time that Norman, the sheriff of East Anglia, was ordered to deliver the lands forfeited by Walter de Dol in Mendlesham and Ashfield in Suffolk to Ralph de Savigny, 'as the hundred witness' (DB ii, 371, 377). Also, the lands of Walter de Douai, a Fleming, at Rushmere may have been forfeited at this time (DB ii, 407b). Among the freemen of Roger Bigot there were many who had been commended to Earl Ralph, his father, and others implicated in the plot. In 1086 they were all effectively in the custody of the sheriff.

From the time of Earl Ælfgar, East Anglia had been ruled by earls whose stance was at times openly hostile to the Crown. In the years immediately before 1066 both Harold Godwinson and his brother Gurth had held the earldom. The Domesday survey for Norfolk and Suffolk lists many freemen who had once held lands under commendation to both Harold and Gurth. Many of them must have been either killed at Hastings or were subsequently exiled. Of the 210 sokemen that had been on Earl Gurth's holdings in Samford hundred, only 119 remained (DB ii, 287). But as well as those that survived there existed beneath them a complex pattern of sub-commendation, of lesser freemen who still occupied their farms and whose loyalty to William must have been suspect. The wedding plot of Earl Ralph only served to further confuse the issue, for there must have been enmity between those members of Ralph's family and their local supporters who had survived and other locals who had either failed to support them or who had obstructed the conspiracy. It is no wonder then that the Domesday survey of Norfolk and Suffolk seems paranoid over just who was commended to whom and where the complex web of intrigue and the patterns of loyalty extended.

Sheriffs and reeves

The Domesday survey mentions some twenty sheriffs throughout England, most of whom were tenants-in-chief to the Crown. Four of these left heirs who within two generations became earls and established regional dynasties (Morris 1927, 49; Green 1983). One of these was Roger Bigot, a central figure in the Domesday survey of Suffolk and Norfolk and sheriff of both counties. It was he who held the principal royal and ancient demesnes in hand for the king. These are listed in the first four folios of the county (DB ii, 281b–284b). There is no doubt that Roger Bigot was a man of extraordinary administrative ability, with a very strong right arm. Sheriffs are usually portrayed as the perennial 'bad guys' of medieval local government; they were, of course, appointed by the king to enact unpopular policies and to ensure that taxes raised in the shires came into the Royal Exchequer. It goes without saying that only certain men had the qualities to succeed in such a post; a desire for popularity was not one of them (Morris 1927, 36).

Bigot became the founder of a local dynasty. It has been suggested that his name was derived from 'le Vigot' or Visigoth, but we know very little about his origins other than that he was the son of a knight closely attached to the fortunes of the Conqueror (Planche 1865, 93; Morris 1927, 47). After the Conquest he was rewarded with 117 lordships in Suffolk, but most of these were freemen with small manors, and just six lordships in other counties (Planche 1865, 94). More importantly, he married Adelica, the daughter of Hugh de Grandmenisle, and thus must have been accepted into the higher echelons of Norman society. By her he is said to have had seven children and there are other indications of an extensive family from witness lists on early charters (Planche 1865, 94–5). He was sheriff of Norfolk by 1069 and sheriff of Suffolk twice before 1086. Later he became *Dapifer*, or steward to William Rufus. The sheriffs were not usually of aristocratic background, but they soon aspired to baronial status; thus his second son, Hugh, became the first Bigot earl of Norfolk in 1140, and for the next 167 years the Bigot family dominated the region (Morris 1927, 49).

Roger Bigot appears as the seventh listed tenant-in-chief in Domesday Suffolk; most of his holdings appear to have been transferred from the previous sheriff, Norman, who may have been sheriff from 1065 to about 1069 (DB ii, 330b–334). There follows an extraordinary list of 'Freemen under Roger Bigot' which extends for eleven folios and represents a comprehensive record of the 537 freemen held by the sheriff (DB ii, 334-345b). A similar but smaller entry for Roger Bigot's freemen appears in Norfolk (DB ii, 178). He also held one or two persons in the custody of the sheriff with their lands which appear at the end of the county (DB ii, 446b). The distribution of these freemen is central to an understanding of why there is so much detail included with them, in particular their commendation to 'predecessors'. First, they are concentrated in East Suffolk, particularly along the coast (Figure 7.2). Second, they cluster in relation to important estates, some of which had either been ancient royal demesne or the estates of Harold Godwinson and his brother Gurth. Two clusters relate to the estates of Edric of Laxfield at Eye in Hartismere hundred, and the estates of Norman, the previous sheriff, at Kelsale and Walton.

There are indications that the post of sheriff had changed hands a number of times. Concerning the freemen in the soke of Bergholt: 'when Roger Bigot first had the shrievality his ministers ordered that they should render £15 annually. . . . And when Robert Malet had the shrievality his ministers increased them to £20. And when Roger Bigot had them again in like manner they gave £20' (DB ii, 287b). Bigot may have temporarily forfeited his estates after the rebellion of Earl Ralph in 1075 (Morris 1927, 47). We hear also of Toli the Sheriff who had held the office before 1065 (DB ii, 140, 334). Toli is mentioned in a writ along with Grimketel who was bishop of East Anglia from 1038–1047 (Morris 1927, 23–4). Norman the Sheriff was one of eight pre-Conquest sheriffs to survive in England, indeed, he continued to hold three of his manors, at Saxmundham, Yoxford and Peasenhall, which were specifically granted back to him by the king and he also continued in the service of his successor, Roger Bigot, as one of his *ministri* (DB ii, 333, 338b; Warner 1982, 146, 157).

The sheriff held certain lands for his term of office, some of which were acquired through the process of his official duty as, for example, the two burgesses of Ipswich held by Norman, one in pledge and another for debt (DB ii, 438), or the two freemen with

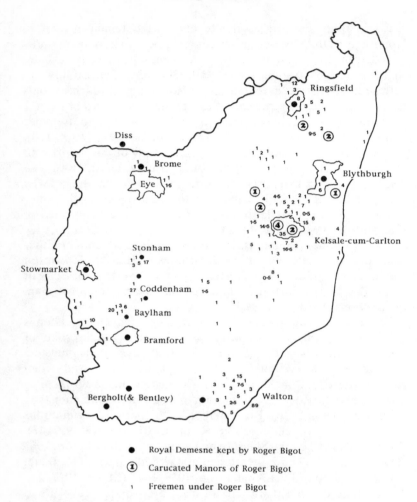

●   Royal Demesne kept by Roger Bigot

①   Carucated Manors of Roger Bigot

¹   Freemen under Roger Bigot

7.2   East Suffolk: the freemen of Roger Bigot

18 acres over which Berenger had encroached. Berenger was at the king's mercy, but he was sick and could not attend the pleas. 'Now [the lands] are in the sheriff's custody' (DB ii, 449). These lands in temporary custody contrast with estates such as Kelsale, which had been held by Norman the Sheriff before Roger Bigot took up his post. Kelsale-cum-Carlton was a detached part of Hoxne, Bishop's

hundred (Figure 6.1). Ekwall searched for a personal name to fit the first element of the place-name *Keleshala*, but admitted that no such name could be found (Ekwall 1960, 270). In fact the earliest spellings of Kelsale are *Cheressala, Cheresala, Chylesheala* and *'Kireshala'* (DB ii, 334b, 338b, 339). This suggests that the first element originally began with a soft consonant 'C' and as *Chere* may be equated with Old English *scire* (shire). Thus Kelsale was the 'Shire's-place', a name which perfectly fits its function as the estate held for the use of the sheriff during his term of office.

Kelsale also had a market in 1086 and there were 35 freemen who could sell and give their lands, suggesting a degree of freedom approaching burgage status. If Kelsale was the sheriff's official manor there may well have been sufficient traffic to make it proto-urban in character. Two similar estates are known from the county of Dorset (DB i, 83, 133; Morris 1927). In Cambridgeshire, Ordgar, King Edward's sheriff, held the manor of Isleham, where two men of King Edward found cartage for the sheriff (DB i, 194a, 199b). And at Orwell, in the same county, a freeman found escort for the sheriff while others were lent by the sheriff to the Earl for holding his pleas, but failed to return (DB i, 193c). Campbell has recently pointed out that, 'the number of men, below the level of sheriff who were in some sense agents of government, was very large' (Campbell 1987, 205).

Such estates and the men who lived on them were in effect Crown property reserved for the use of the sheriff during his term of office. As both Kelsale and Carlton were part of the same outlying portion of Hoxne hundred, Carlton must be considered in the same light as Kelsale. The importance of Carlton place-names has long been recognised, meaning the *tun* of the *ceorls* or free peasants, usually linked to royal manors and estates (Finberg 1964). It was the house-carls who were in effect the 'standing forces' used by later Anglo-Saxon kings to enforce tax collection (Hooper 1984; Campbell 1987, 203). Thus we see in Kelsale-cum-Carlton the remarkable fossilisation of an ancient pre-Conquest administrative system; the freemen under commendation to the sheriff clustering in adjoining vills were clearly an extension of that same system (Figure 7.2).

The freemen under Roger Bigot were held by a group of about eighteen individuals who were probably the *ministri* or agents of the sheriff. Some, such as Bernard, Turold, Hugh de Corbun,

Ralph de Turlaville, Robert de Curcun, Robert de Vals and William de Nemore seem to have Norman names, but others, including Ausketil the Priest, who we are told was Roger Bigot's chaplain, bear Anglo-Saxon or Anglo-Scandinavian names (DB ii, 334b). These include Thurstan son of Wido, Wihtmar, Cus and Akile Surfreint. Others have a history within the Domesday survey which suggests that they had turned their loyalty away from the old Anglo-Saxon order to serve their new Norman lords. Such was Godwin son of Tuka who had been Earl Gurth's man in the time of King Edward (DB ii, 335b). Ulmar, the king's reeve of Bramford, enjoyed Roger Bigot's support (DB i, 446, 448b). Norman, the previous sheriff who has already been discussed, must have been a particularly useful agent and that no doubt was why he was allowed to keep three of his manors (DB ii, 338b).

There were probably as many reeves in Anglo-Norman England as there were farms and manors that needed their skills in estate management. At Bury St Edmunds there were also 'thirteen reeves over the land who have their houses in the said town' (DB ii, 372). Because the town formed part of the convent's property these town reeves served the monastic community by raising £40 per annum for lighting the great church. Before Abbot Hugh's death the reeves were appointed by the convent, but after that date, following a dispute, they were appointed by the abbot (Greenway & Sayers 1989, 64–5). The abbot himself had reeves, such as Orgar and his predecessor Aluric who appropriated two freemen in Wickham (DB ii, 371). The importance of these men varied with the size and importance of the estates for which they were responsible. They are the middle-managers of the Anglo-Norman world and as such their attendance was expected at the hundredal courts where the king's reeves acted as Crown prosecutors; much has been written about them (Loyn 1984).

There were also lesser reeves, who, with the priest and men of the vill, might represent the interests of the local community at assemblies. These were probably not elected reeves, but the equivalent of a farm manager on the largest manor in the vill. From the *Rectitudines Singularum Personarum* the impression gained is of a man sensitive to his duties who must 'learn the laws of the district lovingly if he is to win good opinion on the estate' (Crossley Holland 1984, 260). But many reeves must have found themselves in a difficult position with the transition to Norman masters who were clearly more demanding than their predecessors. Many large estates were in the hands of the Crown as a result of recent forfeitures, but were being 'kept' for the king by the sheriff, Roger Bigot. There are a number of entries which illustrate the difficult relationship between reeve and sheriff.

The king's reeves who managed the various royal estates were key men in the county community. As both reeves and sheriff were royal appointments, close cooperation between the sheriff and the royal reeves was important, although there was no love lost between them. Ulmar, the reeve of Edward the Confessor's manor of Bramford, got on particularly well with Roger Bigot and between them they added a number of freemen to the estate. At Hemmingstone, two freemen were joined to the manor; one of them, called Alwin, was previously under commendation to Earl Gurth, the brother of Harold Godwinson. 'Ulmar the reeve conjoined this freeman to the King's farm of Bramford and Roger the Sheriff is warrant to him for so doing and he renders every year 5s' (DB ii, 446). At Olden there were four freemen 'added to the farm in King William's time, and Roger is warrant thereof to Ulmar the Reeve, and Roger did not know that they were so added, and they used not to belong to any farm' (DB ii, 446). The 12 acres of the freeman Uluric at Somersham had been held by Earl Ralph at the time when he made forfeiture following the abortive rebellion: 'On this Ulmar the king's reeve encroached, and he gave security. Roger Bigot is his surety. And it is now in the king's hands' (DB ii, 448b). Between them, Roger Bigot and Ulmar must have added substantially to the royal revenues, and, one suspects, to their own.

Life was not so easy for those reeves who were in charge of estates that were not under the direct supervision of the sheriff. Aluric Wantz had charge of the manors once held by Harold Godwinson in Bergholt and of Harold's brother Earl Gurth at Bentley and Shotley. Although Aluric Wantz was reeve of these confiscated estates just as if they were royal demesne, he accounted and paid the estate dues to the sheriff who could therefore apply such pressure that there were arguments about the render from these estates which clearly threatened Aluric's position.

And when Robert Malet had it the whole together rendered £60 by weight, and £8 by tale as a fine, and the same amount the manor rendered to Roger Bigot as the reeve himself says. But Roger says that it rendered 40s more by tale and one mark of gold. But Aluric the reeve contradicts and Roger is willing to prove [what he says] by those men who were present at his agreements. The said Aluric now renders £60 by weight, and he so holds of the king by such an agreement that he is bound to make the king [payment of] £60 out of the profit, and of this he vouches the king to warrant. So he says himself and he says too that this does not hold good in that he does not make that [much] profit. (DB ii, 287b)

In complete contrast to the cooperation Roger Bigot received from the reeves on the ancient demesne, where freemen were 'conjoined' to the estates and rents exacted, on the confiscated estate of Harold at Bergholt, Aluric Wantz released the freemen of the heavy burdens which had been imposed on them by the sheriff.

Those freemen who in the time of king Edward belonged to the soke of Bergholt each gave freely to the reeve annually a gratuity of 4d only, and rendered soke as the law required, and when Roger Bigot first had the shrievality his ministers ordered that they should render £15 annually, which they did not do in the time of King Edward. And when Robert Malet had the shrievality his ministers increased them to £20. And when Roger Bigot had them again in like manner they gave £20, and now Aluric Wantz holds them in the like custom as in the time of King Edward. (DB ii, 287b)

The two arguments must be related and they illustrate well how powerful the king's reeves were in being able to challenge the authority of the sheriff in this audacious way.

In other respects Aluric Wantz followed the Norman line. He also had responsibilities for the freemen confiscated from Ulsi of Mutford, the man of Earl Gurth, in the hundred of Lothing (Mutford). Over the 87 freemen, scattered through nine vills, he imposed an annual render of £30, which in the time of King Edward had been a mere 13s 6d. This was done 'in King William's time under Roger Bigot' (DB ii, 283). In the adjoining half-hundred of Lothingland there were more freemen previously under Earl Gurth's commendation; 'All these men rendered in the time of king Edward 20s to the farm [of the manor] and afterwards in Roger Bigot's time Aluric the reeve increased [it] to 100s and in the time of H[ugh] de Hosdena to £50, as the men say' (DB ii, 284b). The relationship between the Mutford estate and Carlton Colville is an interesting one and we may see here the more shadowy remains of a similar administrative set-up to that already described above at Kelsale-cum-Carlton.

Freemen and freewomen

Darby estimated that freemen and sokemen comprised more than 41% of the total number of persons included in the Domesday survey for Suffolk and a similar figure for Norfolk. Of this figure freewomen form perhaps less than 2% (sokewomen are extremely rare). Over England as a whole freemen represent 14% of the Domesday population, but this figure disguises the fact that the majority are to be found in East Anglia and the north. In Norfolk, sokemen outnumbered freemen, but in Suffolk they amounted to only a ninth of the freemen. This discrepancy between the two counties, which is highlighted in the distribution of ancient royal demesne, may be caused by the retention of important freemen in Norfolk by King William while most of the freefolk in East Suffolk were allocated to Roger Bigot and were given a separate entry. All the freemen with lands in West Suffolk who had fought at Hastings were granted by royal writ to the Abbey at Bury St Edmunds, consequently we get fewer names and less detail about freemen in West Suffolk than we do in the complex entries for the freemen of Roger Bigot.

There have been a variety of theories about the origins of freemen. Loyn went so far as to suggest that 'such free peasants constitute the tribesmen warriors of the first consolidated settlements' (Loyn 1962, 195). This is unlikely as the distribution of Domesday freemen, spread throughout both counties, does not relate to concentrations of pagan Anglo-Saxon cemeteries found around the fenland basin and in other areas of East Anglia. Domesday freemen are mostly found in the clayland vills of central Norfolk and Suffolk where early Anglo-Saxon cemeteries are largely absent. Scholars have suggested variously a Frisian, Danish or Scandinavian ancestry for these freemen (Douglas 1927; Dodwell 1939; Stenton 1943; Homans 1957). A few bear Danish or Scandinavian personal names. Only 8.5% of the freemen belonging to the Abbot of Bury St Edmunds had Scandinavian personal names, but many names have indeterminate origins and the work of von Feilitzen upon which this calculation was based was too selective (Feilitzen 1937). In Norfolk and Suffolk there is no correlation between the distribution of freemen and supposed Scandinavian place-names, in particular the concentration of *by* endings in the Broadland area of Norfolk (Davis 1955). We must be cautious not to equate the few Scandinavian personal names of Domesday freemen with the initial phase of Danish settlement in East Anglia, some 200 years earlier, the density and character of which remains a matter for debate (Sawyer 1958; Loyn 1977; Brooks 1979).

That freemen were well established as a complex social class, forming more than 40% of the population throughout the region before 1086, is beyond doubt. Anglo-Saxon society was not one to change overnight and we can be reasonably certain that some of them had been established in the area well before that date. While we cannot place freemen in any ethnic group, it may be reasonable to assume that they were of mixed backgrounds with a few perhaps of Danish ancestry. The liberty of pre-Conquest freemen probably varied considerably with their position in the social hierarchy, and the Domesday survey makes it clear that freemen were commonly found at nearly all levels of society, consequently they represent a very wide spectrum of material wealth. In pre-Conquest times theirs was essentially a liberty from manorial control; they were not, like the Domesday villeins, bordars and serfs, listed among the ploughs and chattels of the manor.

A three-tier structure of commendation can be recognised in the Suffolk Domesday entries, which in turn relates to three broad classes of freemen. Most important were freemen of the seignorial class, many of whom were probably of old Anglo-Saxon or Anglo-Danish stock. One such was Edwin, described as *vir gloriosus lauerd Edwinus* by the monks of Bury St Edmunds to whom he was a benefactor. His will would have left them extensive but very scattered estates in Norfolk and Suffolk, had not the events of 1066 overtaken him (Whitelock 1930, 86–9, 199–201; Hart 1966, 67). Edwin was of the thegnly class, but in Blyford, as elsewhere, he held his lands as a freeman and there is nothing to distinguish him from other freemen. It is clear therefore that thegns held their lands as freemen and in consequence are not always referred to as thegns in the Domesday survey. There were many classes of thegn, from a king's thegn such as Scula, King Edward's thegn who held Barnham in Bradmere hundred, and Orth, Harold's thegn at Freckenham (DB ii, 296, 381), to queen's and bishop's thegns and others who appear to have no distinguishing rank. The holdings of these great men were swallowed up by Norman tenants-in-chief who supplanted them and retained their largest manors as demesne.

A second, or what might be called a middle-class, of named free-persons held, or shared, substantial, even carucated, lands and manors. Thus we find seven named freemen, all with separate commendations, holding one carucate at Darsham (DB ii, 334). *Swarting, Agar Herewold* and *Osfert* held 27 acres in Fordley, all being under commendation to Edric of Laxfield, except for *Osfert*, who was only half-free and was under commendation to *Toli the Sheriff* (DB ii, 314). At Stoven, *Gooday* and *Langaein* held just 14 acres, both being under commendation to *Godwin son of Tuck* (DB ii, 333b). The Domesday survey for Suffolk is packed with information about this class of named and commended freemen; they are given more attention than any other social group. A few entries indicate ties of kinship; thus at Stickingland (Yoxford), where there were five freemen who were *Ulf's* men, *Gode, Alfwin* his brother, *Bunde the Smith [Bunda faber]*, *Aluric* the son of *Bunde* and *Osketel*, who together held 60 acres – four out of these five freemen were related to other members of the same group (DB ii, 334b). At Maiston there were six freemen, one *Alfoh* being the son of *Wibald* (DB ii, 339b; Darby 1952, 170). The name *Blackman*, which appears in five different places in Colneis hundred and twice in Blything hundred, may not necessarily be the same person and there are obvious difficulties with variations in spelling (Dodgson 1985).

There are other indications of kinship groups. At Stowmarket there were four brothers, freemen under Hugh, who built a chapel on land of their own hard-by the churchyard of the mother-church (DB ii, 281b). That groups of freemen were active in collective church-building at or before the time of the Domesday survey is well attested. The example at Stowmarket serves as a model for more than forty others in East Anglia, mostly in Norfolk, where two or more churches appear to have been built in the same churchyard (Warner 1986). There are examples noted by Barlow at Wantisden, where half a church belonged to twenty-two freemen and the other two-quarters were held by two freemen and one freeman respectively; at Stonham there was a church with 20 acres, which nine freemen had given for the salvation of their souls

(BD ii, 306b, 307, 344, 428; Barlow 1963, 193). There are many examples of freemen holding several parts of churches in Suffolk, including Helmingham, Braiseworth and Willingham (Redstone 1908, 27; Redstone 1930, 41). It is likely that in some cases groups of freemen combined with lords of the manor to build churches which would be large enough to serve the whole community. Their varying degrees of participation in church-building can be taken as an indication of their varied wealth and standing in the local community.

Members of the third and largest class of freemen are unnamed; they are usually found in small groups sometimes holding pitifully small acreages. There can be little doubt that they represent a relatively humble but numerically important section of society. Stenton saw them as living on 'resources which can have been little more than adequate for bare subsistence' (Stenton 1943, 517). These groups of lower-class freemen are mainly concentrated in remote clayland vills in upland wood-pasture situations, places where green-side settlement is evident in the later medieval landscape (Warner 1987). Stoven is a good example, with most of its settlement on the edges of greens. The place-name *stofn*, meaning stem or tree-stump, suggests woodland clearance (Smith 1956, 157; Ekwall, 1960, 448).

Before the Conquest, there were four freemen at Stoven with 50 acres between them, another two freemen held just 14 acres and under them were two bordars (DB ii, 333b, 406). Part of the rent was paid in herrings, so fishing must have supplemented their meagre acres. Likewise pasture from the greens and commons, not mentioned in 1086, may have provided additional income. After the Conquest, Hugh de Montfort took the largest 50-acre freeholding in hand as demesne and the freemen who had shared it were reduced from four to three. The other two freemen were listed under the lands of Roger Bigot.

At Chippenhall in Fressingfield, a vill with extensive commons and green-side settlement and which once 'abounded in woods', there were nine freemen with two and a half carucates, another freeman with 60 acres and two villeins; Walter held four sokemen with one carucate and there were another three sokemen with 80 acres, all under different lordships (DB ii, 329, 441; Hart 1966, 249). This pattern of groups of freemen with small acreages under divided lordship is highly characteristic and it has been argued that it relates to a protracted process of piecemeal enclosure around greens and commons on the claylands of Norfolk and Suffolk. As one holding became consolidated so it established other, smaller, dependent freeholdings in colonising situations about it. The process is reflected not only in the three-tier social structure of commendation so laboriously described by the Domesday survey, but also in the surviving pattern of green-side settlement itself, where dispersed tenements lie on the periphery of older estates (Warner 1987, 29–38).

If freemen have been little studied, some modern scholars might be forgiven for not knowing that freewomen even existed. It is startling that freewomen find no place even in the index of major works on Domesday studies which have lengthy entries for freemen. Male and female scholars seem to be equally guilty and the one book on Anglo-Saxon women by Christine Fell does little to redress the balance (Fell 1984). Historians can draw their own conclusions from this omission; however, gender-bias may not be entirely to blame as there are some serious problems with the identification of women in the survey. Domesday Book itself has difficulties in recognising freewomen as a minority submerged within the great mass of freemen.

The process of commendation required all freefolk over the age of twelve to be commended publicly in the hundredal courts to either superior free-persons or aristocrats, but only women who were landholders, or who stood to inherit land, may have been subject to commendation (Loyn 1984, 147). Consequently it was not uncommon to have husbands and wives with different commendations; at Sibton we find Blackman; 'but the wife of this man was Bishop Stigand's man [sic]: and he had commendation over the woman' (DB ii, 313). It is also clear from this and other entries that women are sometimes referred to as men. In the case of the freewoman *Goda*, a name which in itself could be either gender, she is almost certainly referred to on one occasion as a man (DB ii, 376b, 396). Gender can sometimes be established from the spelling of names; thus *Lefquena* and *Leofleda* are probably female, but *Mansura* is probably not, since variations of the name appear as *Mansuna* and *Manesuna* (Manson), which must surely be male (DB ii, 419, 342, 340).

It will also be appreciated that there are wide variations in spelling caused by dialect differences and Norman-French pronunci-

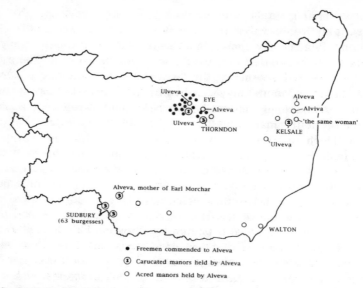

7.3 Suffolk: the lands of Alveva, the mother of Earl Morchar

ation of Anglo-Saxon and Anglo-Scandinavian names. Thus *Alveva*, the mother of Earl Morchar, may appear as *Alviva, Ulveva* and *Uveru*, but from a parallel entry in the *Inquisitione Eliensis* and from earlier sources it would seem that the correct Anglo-Saxon form of this relatively common name was *Alfgeve* (DB ii, 354b, 385b; *Inquisitione Eliensis*, 158). When the lands of Alveva in Suffolk are seen together on Figure 7.3, it becomes clear that they cluster in relation to her main holdings at Sudbury, Eye and Kelsale in such a way as to link together variations in her name. Similarly, the juxtaposition of a *Godgeva* and a *Modgeva*, both described as freewomen and both holding land at Wortham in Hartismere hundred, suggests a simple scribal error, a confusion of the letters G and M.

There are nine entries in the Domesday survey for Suffolk which mention the wives of freemen, including the wife of a priest, who held land either jointly or separately with their husbands. In some cases the wives were commended to different lords from their husbands and therefore merit special mention. None of these wives are named, but there are indications that a few named free-women lie undetected as wives within the survey. For example at Wyverstone in Hartismere hundred we are told that there were four freemen, but then six are listed by name. There was 'Ulmar, Alfleda and Ulwin, and Alwin and Alflet, and Alwin' (DB ii, 321b). The punctuation would seem to indicate two married couples, the wives being Alfleda and Alflet. Both couples presumably held land jointly and were regarded as a single freeholding. Other freeholdings may well have been held jointly, but in the name of the freeman only.

In fact there are relatively few ambiguities in the survey, more often than not the entries are explicit: 'a certain freewoman' or 'the same freewoman'; such is clear enough. We are told that *Esmonda* was 'wholly the woman of Toli the Sheriff' and that 'Brihtmar her son was the man of Brihtmar, Robert Malet's Reeve, and [he was so] in respect of the sixth part of the land'. Such precision is much more characteristic of Little Domesday Book, but this in itself leads to other more complex problems of interpretation.

Freewomen parallel freemen in some respects but not in others. They follow the same pattern of commendation; they represent a wide range of society from the very rich to the relatively poor, from landowners with just half an acre worth one penny, like *Aldith* at Creeting in Bosmere hundred (DB ii, 446), to *Edith the Fair* with over thirty carucates and six churches. There is little difference in their legal status as landholders, only that there were apparently far fewer women than men. We find women giving their land to monasteries and entering into life-leases jointly with their husbands. Of the two carucates *Leveva* held in Topesfield (Cosford hundred) she 'gave half a carucate to Holy Trinity [Canterbury] after her death in return for another half carucate which she held of the Archbishop in her lifetime. This agreement was made TRE, and Leveva was living in King William's time, and was seised thereof' (DB ii, 372b; Hart 1966, 68). At Norton (Blackbourn hundred) 'Edith, a certain freewoman', probably Edith the Fair, had also made arrangements of her own: 'This manor belonged to the demesne of the Abbot of St Edmund; and Edith held it by arrangement with the Abbot the agreement being such that after her death the Abbot was to have it back, and so [she] held the manor on the day on which King Edward died' (DB ii, 286; Hart 1966, 68). At Gislingham (Hartismere hundred) a freeman *Alsi* (Aelfsige) and his wife took a life-lease from Abbot Leofstan of two carucates as a manor in the time of King Edward, 'by such an agreement that after their deaths the Abbot should have back his manor and another manor of Alsi's, Eustuna [Euston] by name' (DB ii, 44b; Hart 1966, 71).

In other respects there is a sharp distinction between freewomen and freemen. It has long been appreciated that some freemen suffered substantially as a result of the Norman Conquest (Loyn 1962, 256). In Suffolk there were certain highly privileged groups of freemen attached to royal estates. Thus in Wangford hundred under the royal demesne which Roger Bigot kept, 83 freemen of the hundred were added to Hugh de Montfort's estate after 1066, twelve of which in Ringsfield paid 'no custom at all' in the time of King Edward, 'but now they render £15' (DB ii, 282b). Other examples have already been given from Bergholt (DB ii, 287b).

As a consequence of King William's writ, almost all freefolk in the eight and a half hundreds of Thinghoe owed commendation and soke to St Edmund, so there are fewer references to named predecessors than in East Suffolk. Apart from the most important freewomen and aristocrats, some of whom held their own sokes, such as Queen Edith, Edith the Fair, Edith the Rich and Alveva, mother of Earl Morchar, who owned Sudbury, only three or four other women landholders are mentioned by name in West Suffolk. Two held substantial carucated manors; at Hargrave, *Alviet* held a manor of four carucates and a church, while at Topesfield, *Leveva* held the two carucates, one half of which was leased from Canterbury (DB ii, 435, 373b–374, 372b). *Alflet* or *Elflet* of Stonham (Bosmere) and Stanningfield (Thedwastre) may be the freewoman who gave her name to Alpheton (Scarfe 1986, 73–5). *Alflet* was commended to Harold and she may well have lost her husband at the Battle of Hastings.

Most of the widows of freemen in West Suffolk who lost their lands after the Conquest were exiled or fled abroad. The *Anglo-Saxon Chronicle* tells us that in 1067, while some men and women found sanctuary with King Malcolm in Scotland, *Gytha*, the mother of Harold, went to the Island of Flatholm 'and the wives of many good men accompanied her.' From there they fled to Saint-Omer (Garmonsway 1972, 202). The choice of Saint-Omer may relate to the fact that Judith of Flanders, the wife of Tostig, was established there where her husband had been exiled; however, it may also be linked to a long-standing affinity between this area of northern Gaul and the English aristocracy. As early as the seventh century princesses of the East Anglian royal house had sought refuge and instruction in the monasteries of Brie, Chelles and Andelys-sur-Seine (HE, III, 8).

Naming the landscape

In the absence of all but a few pre-Conquest charters, the Domesday survey provides us with the first recognisable spelling for the majority of our Suffolk place-names. However, there is as yet no detailed study of Suffolk place-names. Margaret Gelling has recently produced a brief summary of a supposed chronology of Suffolk place-names based on the work of Ekwall, but she herself would admit that this is a poor substitute for the sort of survey which the English Place-Name Society has carried out in other counties (Gelling 1992). The etymology of place-names is now a highly specialised subject. It has come in for criticism in recent years as it has updated and revised its interpretations of early place-names, but this should not detract from its credibility as a subject. Because they have lacked the necessary detailed research, historians of Norfolk and Suffolk have been forced to speculate at length about the history of place-names, sometimes with disastrous results. Indeed, it is almost impossible to write a history of the county of Suffolk without indulging in some speculation about early place-names and the reader must accept that this final section will have to be rewritten when eventually the English Place-Name Society survey is completed.

The reader will also be aware that earlier chapters have touched upon the significance of Latin loan-words in Suffolk place-names such as Wickham, Wicklaw, Bulcamp and Campsey; these are recognised by Gelling as indicators of contact between an indigenous population with the use of some Latin words and incoming Germanic-speaking settlers; true to form these names cluster in the area of the Wicklaw hundreds (Gelling 1992). Of the earliest Anglo-Saxon place-names, it has been accepted since the work of Dodgson that place-names ending in *ingas* are not indicative of early settlement since they do not correlate with the distribution of pagan Anglo-Saxon settlements and cemeteries (Dodgson 1966). The exception to this may well be names which apply to settlement groups associated with river watersheds such as Gipping, Thredling and Blything. Since Dodgson's work, *ham* and *ingaham* place-name endings have been thought to be significantly early. The mention of Rendlesham by Bede would seem to confirm this view. The use of the genitive 's' indicates a personal name – somebody's *ham* or farmstead. Bucklesham, Chattisham, Hintlesham, Martlesham, Mendlesham, Redisham, Shottisham, Walsham, Wattisham and Witnesham may belong to this relatively rare group.

There are many other *ham* place-name endings in Suffolk, such as Elmham, which lack the genitive 's'. Elmham is not in fact mentioned by Bede although the name Elmham appears in early sources without the distinction being made between North Elmham in Norfolk and South Elmham in Suffolk. Place-names which combine *ingaham* such as Icklingham and Helmingham may be equally early. There is nothing to say that these are not as early as the Rendlesham group, it is just that they do not happen to be among the very few place-names mentioned by Bede. The difficulty with *ham* place-names is that some may belong to the later generic *hamme* meaning low-lying meadowland. Until more detailed study has been done names such as Syleham and Mendham, with churches in low-lying positions in the Waveney valley, must remain suspect even though there may be other reasons to indicate that they are early places. Since Dunwich is also mentioned by Bede and because Ipswich produces a mass of seventh–eighth-century archaeological material, both place-names must be accepted as early.

Religious sites and holy places are indicated by *stow* and *stoke* of which Suffolk has several examples; some, such as West Stow, Stow Park near Bungay, Stoke-by-Nayland and Stoke near Ipswich have already been touched upon in relation to early *regios* and estates in earlier chapters. Others at Felixstowe, the original spelling of which was *Filchestou* (1254) and therefore clearly not associated with St Felix, and at Stowmarket and Stowlangtoft, may be equally important (Gelling 1992). Place-names which contain the early English generic *worða* are generally recognised as being among those place-names which appear later than *c.* AD 750 (Gelling 1992, 57). Significant among these are *Bedericsworth*, the old name for Bury St Edmunds which could well be earlier than 750, Braiseworth, Chellesworth, Dagworth, Dunningworth, Halesworth, Hepworth, Ickworth, Ixworth and Worlingworth. Without exception these are interesting places, some have substantial Domesday entries and a few have monasteries or early Christian associations. The work of Ridgard over many years at Worlingworth and the detailed study of Brixworth in Northamptonshire suggests that these 'worths' should be studied as a group (Ridgard 1989).

Just as there are place-names which must be significantly early, so there are place-names which are demonstrably late. Many of our *tun* place-name endings are associated with individuals who are known to have lived in the later Anglo-Saxon period or who are mentioned in the Domesday survey. For example, Euston is associated with the moneyer called *Efe* who minted coins for King Beorna in the mid-eighth century (Archibald 1985; Gelling 1992). Alpheton has been noted by Scarfe as associated with *Elflet* or *Alflet*, a freewoman mentioned in the Domesday survey for Stanningfield and Stonham (Scarfe 1986). Gelling also suggests that some *tun* place-names may be renamed places. Ekwall and Scarfe have noted that Homersfield appears to bear the name of *Hunbeorht*, equated with Hunberht, bishop of East Anglia in the 870s (Ekwall 1960, 248; Scarfe 1986, 25). Both writers make a similar association between Ilketshall and Ulfketill, the great ealdorman of East Anglia who fought bravely against the Danes in the early eleventh century (Ekwall 1960; Scarfe 1986). Although nationally there are ten *feld* place-name endings recorded before 730, it would be rash to conclude that any of our Suffolk *felds* are earlier than the second half of the eighth century. Indeed many of our *feld*, *tun* and *hala* place-names may be of much the same date as the few identifiable, but demonstrably late, Scandinavian place-names. The dangers of trying to formulate a chronology of Suffolk place-names where early charter evidence is lacking and all our sources are either very Late Saxon or early Norman must be apparent.

Gelling recognises 29 Suffolk parish names in *feld*, a generic which like the old Dutch *velt* means 'open country', particularly grassland (Gelling 1984, 235–9). Six of these are combined with *inga* as in Stanningfield, Fressingfield, Waldringfield, Bedingfield, etc., and as such may be of similar date to some *ingaham* endings. There may be dangers in this argument in that *inga* can also combine with *tun* as in Thorington and with *hala* as in Rickinghall; not all such place-names can be early. Gelling argues for places with *feld* endings being indicative of land that was pasture in the early Anglo-Saxon period, but was then broken into by the plough as

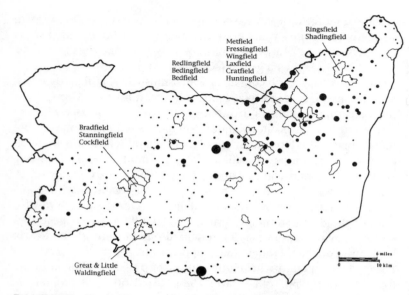

7.4 Suffolk: Domesday woodland (after Darby 1952) and nineteenth-century parish boundaries with '-feld' place-name endings. Only clusters of '-feld' parishes are listed

part of an early expansion of settlement (Gelling 1992). Scarfe has written eloquently about *felds* and the way that they cluster and coincide with concentrations of woodland recorded in the Domesday survey (Scarfe 1986, 13–26). Most noticeable are the two separate clusters around Fressingfield and Bedingfield (Figure 7.4), but not all clusters of *feld* endings coincide with Domesday woodland, as for example, the clusters around Bradfield and Waldingfield, and there are other isolated *feld* place-names many of which have no Domesday woodland (Figure 7.4). There is no obvious explanation for this discrepancy, neither can we be sure that *felds* relate to the late Roman landscape as Scarfe has suggested, since we would expect two or three Roman sites to be found now in all Suffolk parishes. *Hala* place-name endings are more scarce, but there is one important cluster formed by the Ilketshall parishes with Spexhall and Westhall, which can be linked to a concentration of woodland listed in the area of Halesworth and Wissett in 1086 (Warner 1982).

This association between *feld, hala* and Domesday woodland is particularly significant for the history of the Suffolk landscape, yet not all *feld* place-names had woodland recorded in 1086 (Figure 7.4). In particular the two clusters of *felds* around Bradfield and Waldingfield in West Suffolk have few entries, perhaps because woodland had been lost here due to the building of the new town at Bury St Edmunds. The Domesday survey records the state of woodland, both pannage woods and coppice woods, as in marked decline (Figure 7.4). Darby records 38 places where the yield of pigs from pannage wood-pasture had declined by 1086, but this should be seen against a backdrop of a decline in plough-teams in many areas and the laying waste of resources following the Conquest (Darby 1952, 180–4). In other words a decline in yield may not necessarily indicate a decline in woodland. When considering *feld* place-name endings we must bear in mind one of the principles of naming, which is that names do not always accord with that which is most common-place; they record the significant, the unusual, the landmark, which singles out a place and makes it different from others around about.

Thus in a landscape where woodland predominated, open space and grassland was sufficiently unusual to give rise to place-names with *feld* endings. That *felds* cluster as they do suggests that there were certain areas of clayland Suffolk where open space and woodland alternated in a patchwork of trees and grass. At Bradfield, where fine coppice woods can still be seen, there are few woods recorded in 1086. In other areas such as Fressingfield and Cratfield, the woods have gone, but we know that the monks at Bury chose Chippenhall in Fressingfield in the eleventh century, 'because it abounded in woods' (Hart 1966, 249). There is just enough evidence to link some *felds* with greens and commons. In Fressingfield the open common of Chippenhall Green still survives unenclosed whereas the larger Norwood Green in neighbouring Cratfield was enclosed in the nineteenth century. The North Wood in Cratfield once adjoined the green; the name survives in a group of field-names. In essence this pattern is duplicated in many clayland parishes; in some cases open commonable moorland lay on the clay plateau of the interfluves with trees growing on the better drained slopes above the valleys (Warner 1982, 33–6).

Gelling has identified only twenty examples of Scandinavian place-names in the Suffolk landscape (Gelling 1992, 62–3). They all lie along the coastal belt none further inland than Kettleburgh and Ubbeston. Barnby, Ashby, Lound and Lowestoft must be seen as part of a concentration of Scandinavian place-names in the Broadland area of Norfolk, most of which have *by* endings. Sibton and Ubbeston are hybridised Anglo-Scandinavian place-names and may not be significant, although it has been suggested that the *Ubba* of Ubbeston could be identified with the Danish leader who was involved in the martyrdom of St Edmund. Kettleburgh and possibly Grundisburgh may also record the names of Danish leaders who built *burhs* to defend their newly acquired lands, but here again we are in the realms of speculation. There is evidence for a late shift in dialect from the soft 'c' to the hard 'k' in place-names such as Kirton and Kirkley, derived from Old English *cyrice* meaning church (Gelling 1992). This shift is generally thought to indicate Scandinavian influence, however, we have already seen how the spelling of Kelsale appears three times in the Domesday survey with the first element beginning 'Ch' and only one spelling beginning with 'K', which may indicate that this shift in dialect comes considerably later than the period of Danish settlement.

More Scandinavian place-names will come to light as early field-names are recorded and mapped; this is already proving to be the case where Gwen Dyke and others have been working on the Deben valley place-names (Dyke *et al.* 1977). Large numbers of Scandinavian field-names have also been found in Lincolnshire and Fellows-Jensen has used this as evidence for Scandinavian settlement (Fellows-Jensen 1974). But the evidence for these names comes from very late sources and it is not possible to be certain that they all relate to the formative period of Danish conquest. We must not forget that there is a continuum of Scandinavian influence from the migration period in the sixth century through to the coming of the Normans in the eleventh. A Danish–Viking presence represents just one phase in that continuum. The small number of Scandinavian place-names suggests that Danish settlement was not significant in Suffolk except along the coast. This is borne out by the almost complete lack of archaeological material outside the major urban centres. Sadly, the Danes in Suffolk, although well documented in the *Anglo-Saxon Chronicle*, must remain a figment in the imagination of nineteenth-century antiquarians.

Scarfe, in his work on the Suffolk landscape, mentions the small farms grouped in the Shotley peninsula on the Suffolk coast with names such as Morston Hall, Grimston Hall, Kembrooke Hall, Candlet, Gulpher, Alston Hall. He suggested that these might be linked with Domesday Book in that they, 'largely comprised the successors of the small groups of freemen farming fifty small estates scattered through the seven or eight parishes of Coleness Hundred' (Scarfe 1972, 164). He also noted that personal names such as Woolnough, Thurston, Surman, Levitt, Gooding, which appear in the Domesday survey, still persisted as surnames in the same area to the present day. He went on to point out other examples where manorial names seem to suggest a degree of continuity from 1086.

Apart from some manorial names such as Burnaville, a distinctly Norman-French place-name, there is no exact correlation between the body of personal names represented by Domesday freemen in the Shotley peninsula and the modern recorded landscape. Scarfe's theory of continuity is a very attractive one; he took care not to overstate his case and suggested the subject would be 'worth following in microscopic detail'. There are indeed many hundreds of named freemen listed in both counties in the Domesday survey, but as they appear in many cases attached to small landholdings, they are difficult to relate to the modern landscape or even to later medieval documents. However, large numbers of named tenements comprising relatively small landholdings are described in later medieval land surveys or extents for some manors in East Suffolk. Thus it is possible to test Scarfe's theory where concentrations of named Domesday freemen can be compared with names from medieval surveys and later map evidence. Just such a concentration of names was found in the area of Yoxford, Darsham, Middleton and Westleton where over 400 tenement names survive in medieval surveys of the Cockfield Hall estate, which could then be compared with the names of 27 Domesday freemen from the same area (Warner 1987, 35).

The result suggested that there was in fact widespread dislocation of personal names in relation to landholdings although the survival of Domesday personal names as surnames in the region cannot be denied; one only needs to look at a modern telephone directory to establish that fact. Just one name, that of Leuric Cobb, one of four named Domesday freemen in Darsham, could be found to correlate with a later deserted medieval tenement in Darsham called Cobbe's (Figure 7.5). An extent for Westleton manor dated 1463 describes what may be the original holding or that of Leuric

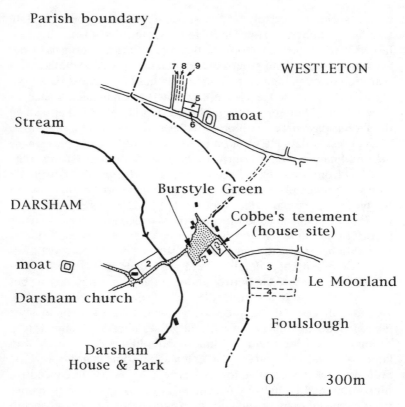

7.5   Cobbe's tenement, 19 acres in nine pieces, around Burstyle Green, Darsham, based on evidence from a survey of 1463 and the nineteenth-century Tithe Award map (Warner 1987)

Cobb's descendants. Under the lands of Thomas Clampe, there were '19 acres of copyhold land called Cobbestenement . . . lying in Darsham [and Westleton] where the first piece is an enclosure once built on . . . butting onto Burstyle green' (Warner 1987, 36).

The house site and its eight other appended lands can be identified around Burstyle Green by reference to the nineteenth-century tithe map and 'Brussel's Green Farm' which now stands on the site of Thomas Clampe's engrossed farm. Cobbe's tenement is very typical of the smaller deserted green-side sites found in great numbers on the claylands of Suffolk. Its nine pieces were scattered over

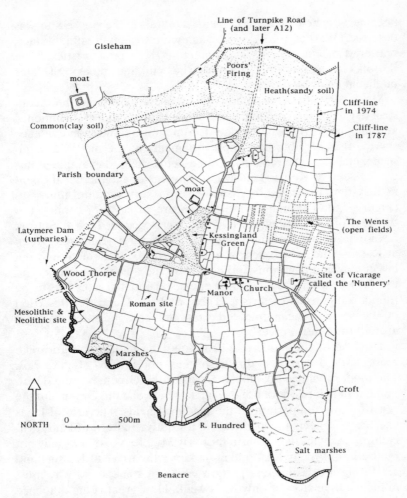

7.6 Kessingland parish: greens, commons enclosures and common fields in 1787 (Warner 1982)

the parish boundary in areas of secondary colonisation bearing names such as *le Moorland* and *Foulslough*, once clearly areas of waste. In Cobbe's tenement at Darsham we see the survival of a small peasant land unit of a type that was common in the Suffolk landscape. As the burden of labour services was effectively transferred from the individual to the land, so the name of Cobbe became attached to the tenement, even after the house site was deserted (Warner 1987, 35–8). Such were the small landholdings, scattered around greens and commons, so characteristic of the Suffolk landscape, that became the building blocks of later medieval engrossed farms.

Many other peasant tenements, of various sizes, can be reconstructed from map evidence and from later medieval documents, and in some cases, where good documentation and map evidence survive it is possible to glimpse fragments of the medieval landscape, including the remains of open-fields. A good example of this can be seen at Kessingland where remains of the medieval open-field system, truncated by coastal erosion, survived until the 1930s (Figure 7.6). The manor and church are in close proximity, but the rest of the settlement is widely scattered in typical Suffolk fashion. The relationship between the central triangular green at Kessingland, which acts as a loose focus of settlement and the larger clayland commons and heaths on the northern periphery of the parish, where several large medieval moated sites are to be found, is highly characteristic. There is also evidence for desertion in the several vacant moated sites and gaps between cottages around the central green.

The line of the modern A12 follows the path of the turnpike road, marked here as a double broken line in 1787 (Figure 7.6). The modern village now fills the area of the Green, but the development of a network of holiday chalets between the Green and the coast follows the pattern of the medieval fields. The grid of lanes and tracks reflects the ancient and formative pattern of land ownership, which has its origins in the early Middle Ages. They may not realise it, but today the holiday-makers who arrive at Kessingland are fitting into a timeless pattern which in some small way must influence their lives, if only for a week. How great is the influence of this landscape on those of us who have the pleasure of living in it for a lifetime?

Conclusion

So what is the significance of this type of history? What is the relevance of a subject which focuses upon so remote a period that only archaeology and ancient texts can elucidate it? If the reader has been surprised at all by the contents of preceding chapters, it may be the extraordinarily formative character of the shire, established so firmly, so long ago.

The county reflects our origins as a community; out of it came our local administrative boundaries, our judicial system, our system of taxation and to a certain extent our system of social order. But do ancient rural communities like this matter any more? The shire was formed at a time when perhaps only 10–15% of the population lived in towns and although Suffolk is still a rural county, as far as the rest of Britain is concerned, more than 80% of us live in towns. Our rural origins in the shire may therefore seem remote and irrelevant. And yet it seems that we can never really divorce ourselves from our rural past, or if we do, we do so at our peril.

The past is a very big place. We can easily get lost in it and forget any bearing that it may have on the present, or indeed the future. To some it can serve as a pleasurable distraction from the realities of life, while to others it may seem claustrophobic and restrictive in a modern society; alternatively it can also serve as an inspiration for change, as a renaissance for new thinkers. The past is whatever you make of it. If you identify yourself with a particular county, then by definition you identify to some extent with the past of that county, with its boundaries, its rivers, its towns and villages, its cricket team, its courts and its churches. Indeed, the more you know about your county the more you have reason to identify with it. So, if when you began reading this book you regarded yourself as 'from' Suffolk, and you have persevered this far to the end of the book, you should have become more than ever an adherent of the county.

Knowing our roots is not just an idle phrase, it is a reality which, for good or bad, influences all our lives to some degree or other. So if the shire becomes more and more a living reality in our lives, if in other words we gain from an added knowledge when we go about our daily business, when we drive along a certain road, or walk along a certain street, or visit a certain town or village, are we in some sense a better person for the experience our additional knowledge has given us? Unfortunately, knowledge in itself is not a virtue, but caring about things and people is. It is not the past itself that matters, but the things and places which survive from the past to enrich and stimulate our lives, and which we know can enrich and stimulate the lives of other people, particularly the young. So without knowledge our sense of caring is limited, or at best, misguided. One of the more distasteful aspects of modern life to an historian is the way so many of our streets and buildings have become a superficial pastiche of the past. This goes for many of our urban conservation areas and indeed, for some our country houses, even those in the hands of the National Trust. Here we have a re-enactment of our ignorance about the past set to popular themes and folklore, or what we might call theme-park history. It is the stuff of advertising and superficial tourism. There is no reason to care at all about such a vision of the past, unless you own a commercial interest in it.

If this book reveals anything, it is that there is so much surviving from the past, in some cases from very remote periods of time, that it must be difficult to know what is worth preserving from it. But first we must know what is old and what is interesting before any judgements can be made. Clearly it is not in everybody's interest that everything that is old and interesting should be preserved. We have to live in a practical and economically viable environment as well as one which is visually and intellectually stimulating. The point is that our judgements in relation to conservation should be based on sound knowledge.

In the 1960s and 1970s many hundreds of miles of hedgerows in Suffolk were destroyed to make way for farm machinery. At that time it was not appreciated how many of our hedges marked ancient boundaries which could be pre-Roman in origin. If that knowledge had been available, it might not have stopped the hedgerows from being grubbed up, but it would have allowed an informed decision to be made and might well have led to the preservation of some of them. The same might well be said of the shops and timber buildings of a town such as Ipswich. Few people would now doubt that we are the poorer for some of the ill-informed decisions of a generation ago which resulted in the loss of countless historic buildings and landscape features.

Today we still face the same sort of problems as our predecessors faced a generation ago. Many hundreds of listed and unlisted archaeological sites in the county are currently being plundered by treasure-hunters using metal-detectors. The majority of these machines are being used by very responsible people who work legally and record and report their finds for posterity, but sadly a minority of them are not. It seems that we have utterly failed to give this minority the knowledge and the wherewithal to care significantly about their own past. Knowledge can make us care, even where the cash value of objects enters into the balance. This was clearly demonstrated by the exemplary action taken recently by the finders of the Hoxne hoard, one of the richest hoards ever excavated by archaeologists in this country. If we are to share in a common heritage, the knowledge of what is worth preserving or recording must be shared by all sections of society so that we all have reason to care about our past. If only one half of society has access to a knowledge of their heritage and attempts to preserve it, the other half can hardly be blamed if they destroy it in ignorance.

It is, of course, the purpose of any book to disseminate knowledge, and for you, the reader, to use that knowledge as you see fit. But it stands to reason that only a very small section of society will read a book of this type, the responsibility therefore weighs heavily on the reader to disseminate what knowledge they may have gained and to be a voice that cares about our shared past. For what it is worth, I have shared this knowledge with you, now you must share it with others, particularly with the young. One of the more enlightened aspects of the National Curriculum now being taught in our schools is the provision for different aspects of local history at primary school level. It is comforting to know that our younger children may have the chance to discover for themselves different aspects of the ancient local communities in which they live. Surely, such knowledge must lead to a more caring society and one that can be visually stimulating and exciting for us all to live in.

Appendix: Gazetteer of sites

Aldeburgh

Museum in the Moot Hall. A delightful place to visit. Objects from the excavation of the Snape cemetery, including clench-nails from the boat-burial excavated by Septimus Davison in the nineteenth century.

Blythburgh

Church of Holy Trinity. Mostly fifteenth century, but look for small fragments of Norman corbel-table re-used among stones on the north wall and buttresses. The church and its setting are magnificent. Excellent walks in all directions. The Priory ruins can be visited by arrangement with Mrs Hubbard, owner of the site.

Bradfield Woods

Good example of ancient coppice woodland still being managed in the traditional manner. Wonderful flora and fauna. Open to the public in season.

Bungay

Remains of Earl Hugh Bigot's castle including the tunnel under the corner of the keep, part of the intended slighting of the castle ordered by Henry II. Delightful walks around the town. The two churches of Holy Trinity and St Mary's in close proximity with ruins of the medieval nunnery. Late Saxon round tower. Bungay Museum is definitely worth a visit.

Burgh Castle (Norfolk)

Burgh lies outside the county boundary, but within the Parliamentary constituency of Lowestoft. Roman shore fort and church with round tower. Magnificent views over Breydon Water into Norfolk. Good walks.

Burgh-by-Woodbridge

Medieval church. The remains of the banks and ditches of the Iron Age and Roman fort can be seen with difficulty if the crops are not too high.

Bury St Edmunds

Moyses Hall Museum (including display of Anglo-Saxon objects from West Stow and Westgarth Gardens cemeteries). Abbey Ruins Visitors' Centre in the ruins of the western south transept. Norman Tower, fourteenth-century Abbey Gate and planned Norman town.

Clare

Clare Castle and Clare Camp are two separate sites. Clare Camp is thought to be an Iron Age lowland fort. The Castle is Norman. Clare Priory, which is now a Roman Catholic retreat, can also be visited. Delightful architecture in the town and a wonderful medieval church.

Devil's Dyke (Cambridgeshire)

You can walk along the top of the ditch for approximately 7 miles. Park at Reach, Fair Green, and walk south-east towards Newmarket racecourse. Alternatively park near the roundabout at junction of A1303 and A1304 2 miles south-west of Newmarket and walk north-west. There is also a parking space beside the B1102 where it passes through the Dyke, and the best views can be had from Hangman's Hill 300 yards south-west of this point on top of the Dyke.

Dunwich

Excellent museum. Children will love this, but join one of the guided talks. Buy a footpath map. Cliff-top walk and ruins of Grey Friars monastery now open to the pubic. Ruins of Norman leper chapel close to modern church. Excellent walks, in particular King John's Road, one of the old roads out of Dunwich. Also the lane once leading to Middle Gate which now disappears over the cliff. However tempted you may be, keep clear of the top and bottom of the cliffs, which are unstable and very dangerous, or else you will become part of the archaeology of this extraordinary place.

Eye

Norman castle town with concentric plan. Recent conservation work has made Eye a delightful corner of Suffolk. The magnificent fifteenth-century church tower is one of the sights of the county.

Framlingham

Castle of Earl Hugh Bigot. Delightful architecture in the town and walks around the outer ditches of the castle. The medieval church contains the magnificent renaissance tombs of the later Dukes of Norfolk removed from Thetford Priory.

Saxstead Green and English Heritage Windmill. The Green is a good example of a surviving open clayland common with settlement dispersed around its edges. The mill, like many other windmills, was built in the middle of the green and encroached upon it with its house and buildings in the nineteenth century. A Late Saxon/Viking sword was found here some years ago.

Fressingfield

Chippenhall Green is one of the best preserved Suffolk unenclosed commons. Find the low circular medieval mill-mound in the centre of the green marked by a clump of bushes next to the road junction. Marsh and meadow orchids to be seen on the common in late April and May. On the north side, the road follows the line of a Roman road heading south-east towards Peasenhall. Fressingfield village with its fifteenth-century church and the 'Old Stables', a fourteenth-century raised-aisle hall, are well worth visiting.

Hoxne

Church and supposed site of the martyrdom of St Edmund.

Iken

Church and Anglo-Saxon cross-shaft. Good views of the River Alde and excellent walks.

Ipswich

Ipswich Museum, Museum Street: in desperate need of refurbishment, but this does not detract from the quality of the material on display. Probably one of the best collections of fossils outside the Natural History Museum in London. St Nicholas's church, Anglo-Saxon tympanum.

Lidgate

Delightful village. Remains of the motte and bailey castle can be seen in undergrowth. Take a good map.

Lindsey Castle

Norman earthworks and medieval chapel.

Orford

Castle of Henry II built to counter the growing power of Earl Hugh Bigot in East Suffolk. Excellent for children. Ruins of Norman chancel at east end of Orford church.

Polstead Church

Norman church with apparent early use of tile-bricks. Long-and-Short work also evident indicating overlap of Saxon and Norman building techniques.

South Elmham

Old Minster. Take a good large-scale map and follow the footpath from South Elmham St Cross. Footpath maps are available from the Halesworth and Bungay Book Shops.

Stowmarket

Abbot's Hall Museum of Rural Life.

Sudbury

St Gregory's church and walk around the circuit of the Iron Age and late Saxon defences. Friars' Street, Burkitts' Lane and Croft Road. Good views of the River Stour and delightful old buildings.

Sutton Hoo

Visitors' Centre, mounds only are visible. For the objects from excavations of 1939 and the 1980s you must go to the British Museum.

Take the Melton road out of Woodbridge across Wilford Bridge on the A1152. At the roundabout immediately after Wilford Bridge take the Alderton/Bawdsey road (B1083). After half a mile follow signs for parking and walk to the site. Good views of the River Deben and walks.

Thetford Castle (Norfolk)

Norman motte and bailey castle built inside earlier Iron Age oval fortification. Stiff climb to the top with good views. Earthworks of Anglo-Saxon town south-west of Three Bridges.

Wattisfield

Watson's potteries welcome visitors at Wattisfield. Follow signs south off the A143. Pottery showrooms and remains of Roman kilns. Evidence of post-medieval industrial archaeological interest.

West Stow

Country Park and Visitors' Centre. Book early if you want to bring a group. Anglo-Saxon Village reconstructed buildings and craft exhibition. Costume and craft days. Excellent for children.

Wissett

Church with Late Saxon round tower and early Norman work in south door.

Woodbridge

Woodbridge Museum with excellent small display illustrating the Sutton Hoo excavations. You will have to go to the British Museum to see the real thing, but this is almost as good. Shire Hall, built by the Seckford family, in the market place. 'The most attractive Suffolk Market town'. It lives up to its reputation. The Bull Hotel, where the excavators in 1939 refreshed themselves before departure to London with the gold and garnet jewellery from Sutton Hoo in their pockets for safe keeping.

Bibliography

ABBREVIATIONS
PSIA Proceedings of the Suffolk Institute of Archaeology.
TRHS Transactions of the Royal Historical Society

Allen, D. F. (1970) 'The coinage of the Iceni', *Britannia* **1**, 1–33.
Anderson, O. S. (1934) 'The English hundred names', *Acta Universitas Lundensis*, **30**(i), 1–174.
Archibald, M. (1985) 'The coinage of Beonna in the light of the Middle Harling hoard', *The British Museum Numismatic Journal* **55**, 10–54.
Arnold, C. J. (1982) 'Stress as a stimulus for socio-economic change: Anglo-Saxon England in the seventh century' in *Ranking, Resource and Exchange*, eds C. Renfrue & S. Shenman, Cambridge-University Press, 124–31.
Arnold, C. J. (1988) *An Archaeology of the Early Anglo-Saxon Kingdoms*, Routledge, London.
Bailey, M. (1990) 'Coastal fishing of south-east Suffolk in the century after the Black Death', PSIA **37**(ii), 102–14.
Ballard, A. (1904) *The Domesday Boroughs*, Oxford.
Barker, B. (1979) *The Symbols of Sovereignty*, Westbridge.
Barlow, F. (1963) *The English Church 1000–1066*, Methuen, London.
Barlow, F. (1970) *Edward the Confessor*, Methuen, London.
Barrow, G. W. S. (1973) *The Kingdom of the Scots*, London.
Bassett, S. (1989) 'In search of the origins of the Anglo-Saxon kingdoms' in *The Origins of Anglo-Saxon Kingdoms*, ed. S. Bassett, London.
Bede, *see* Colgrave & Mynors.
Biddle, M. (1976) 'Towns' in *The Archaeology of Anglo-Saxon England*, ed. M. Biddle, Methuen, London, 99–150.
Bigmore, P. G. (1973) 'Suffolk Settlement: a study in continuity', unpublished PhD thesis, University of Leicester.

Bibliography

Blair, J. (1985) 'Secular minster churches in Domesday Book' in *Domesday Book: A Reassessment*, ed. P. Sawyer, Edward Arnold, London.

Blake, E. O. ed. (1962) *Liber Eliensis*, Camden Society, 3rd ser. **92**.

Bland, R. & Johns, C. (1993) *The Hoxne Treasure*, British Museum Press, London.

Bond, F. (1914) *Dedications to Patron Saints of English Churches*, London.

Boulter, S. (1993) 'Sudbury, All Saints Middle School, Mill Lane', *Medieval Settlement Research Group Annual Report* **8**, 64–5.

Bradley, R. (1984) *The Social Foundations of Prehistoric Britain*, Longman UK.

Brooke, C. (1963) *The Saxon and Norman Kings*, Batsford, London.

Brooks, N. P. (1979) 'England in the ninth century: the crucible of defeat', *Transactions of the Royal Historical Society*, 5th ser., **29**, 1–20.

Brooks, N. P. (1984) *The Early History of the Church of Canterbury: Christ Church from 597 to 1066*, Leicester University Press.

Bruce-Mitford, R. L. S. (1955) *The Mildenhall Treasure*, 2nd edn, British Museum, London.

Bruce-Mitford, R. (1975) (1978) & (1983) *The Sutton Hoo Ship Burial* (3 vols), British Museum, London.

Cam, H. M. (1963) *Liberties and Communities in Medieval England*, London.

Campbell, J. ed. (1982) *The Anglo-Saxons*, Phaidon, Oxford.

Campbell, J. (1987) 'Some agents and agencies of the late Anglo-Saxon state' in *Domesday Studies*, ed. J. C. Holt, 201–18.

Carey Evans, M. (1987) 'The contribution of Hoxne to the cult of St Edmund king and martyr in the Middle Ages and later', *PSIA* **36**(iii), 182–95.

Carr, R. D. (1975) 'The archaeological potential of Bury St Edmunds', *East Anglian Archaeology* **1**, 46–56.

Carr, R. D., Tester, A. & Murphy, P. (1988) 'The Middle Saxon settlement at Staunch Meadow, Brandon', *Antiquity* **235**, 371–7.

Carver, M. (1986) *Bulletin of the Sutton Hoo Research Committee*, 4.

Carver, M. (1989) 'Kingship and material culture in early Anglo-Saxon East Anglia' in *The Origins of Anglo-Saxon Kingdoms*, ed. S. Bassett, London.

Carver, M. O. H. (1992) 'The Anglo-Saxon Cemetery at Sutton Hoo: an interim report' in *The Age of Sutton Hoo*, ed. M. O. H. Carver, Boydell Press, Woodbridge, 343–71.

Charman, D. (1963) 'The documentary evidence', *PSIA* **29**(iii), 301–3.

Chatwin, C. P. (1961) *East Anglia and Adjoining Areas. Memoir of the Geological Survey*, 4th edn, London.

Clare, J. B. (1903) *Wenhaston and Bulcamp*, Halesworth.

Colgrave, B. & Mynors, R. A. B. eds (1969) *Bede's Ecclesiastical History of the English People*, Clarendon Press, Oxford.

Collis, J. (1984) *The European Iron Age*, Batsford, London.

Colman, S. (1976) 'The timber-framed buildings of Ipswich: a preliminary report', *East Anglian Archaeology* **3**, 141–54.

Bibliography

Copp, A. (1989) 'The prehistoric settlement' in *Bulletin of the Sutton Hoo Research Committee* **6**, 15–16.

Corbett, W. M. & Tatler, W. (1970) *Soils in Norfolk: Sheet TM 49* (Beccles North), Soil Survey Record, Soil Survey, Harpenden.

Couchman, C. R. (1980) 'The Bronze Age in Essex' in *Archaeology in Essex to AD 1500*, ed. D. G. Buckley, CBA Research Report **34**, London.

Crossley Holland, K. (1984) *An Anthology of Anglo-Saxon England*, Clarendon Press, Oxford.

Crummy, P. (1979) 'The system of measurement used in town planning from the ninth to the thirteenth century' in *Anglo-Saxon Studies in Archaeology and History* 1, eds S. C. Hawkes, J. Campbell & D. Brown, British Archaeological Reports **72**, 149–64.

Cummins, W. A. (1979) 'Neolithic stone axes: distribution and trade in England and Wales' in *Stone Axe Studies*, eds T. H. McK. Clough & W. A. Cummins, *British Archaeological Reports* **23**.

Cunliffe, B. (1981) *Coinage and Society in Britain and Gaul: some current problems*, CBA Research Report **38**.

Curtis, L. F., Courtney, F. M. & Trudgill, S. (1976) *Soils of the British Isles*, Longman, London.

Darby, H. C. (1952) *The Domesday Geography of Eastern England*, Cambridge University Press.

Davies, J. A., Gregory, T., Lawson, A. J., Rickeff, R. & Rogerson, R. (1992) *The Iron Age Forts of Norfolk*, East Anglian Archaeology **54**.

Davis, R. H. C. ed. (1954) *The Kalendar of Abbot Samson of Bury St Edmunds and Related Documents*, Camden Society, 3rd ser., **84**, London.

Davis, R. H. C. (1955) 'East Anglia and the Danelaw', *TRHS*, 5th ser. **5**, 32.

Davis, W. & Vierck, H. (1974) 'The contexts of the Tribal Hidage: social aggregates and settlement patterns', *Frühmittelalterliche Studien* **8**, 223–93.

Defoe, D. (1991) *Tour through the whole Island of Great Britain, 1724–27*, Yale University Press.

Denney, A. H. (1960) *The Sibton Abbey Estates: Selected Documents, 1325–1509*, Suffolk Record Society **2**.

Dimbleby, G. W. (1962) *The Development of British Heathlands and their Soils*, Oxford Forestry Memoirs **23**.

Dodgson, J. McNeal (1966) 'The significance of the distribution of English place-names in *-ingas, inga-* in south-east England', *Medieval Archaeology* **10**, 1–29.

Dodgson, J. McNeal (1973) 'Place-names from *-ham*, distinguished from *hamme* names, in relation to the settlement of Kent, Surrey and Sussex', *Anglo-Saxon England* **2**, 1–50.

Dodgson, J. McNeal (1985) 'Some Domesday personal names, mainly post-Conquest', *Nomina* **9**, 41–51.

Dodwell, B. (1939) 'The free peasantry of East Anglia in Domesday', *Norfolk Archaeology* **27**, 145–57.

Dodwell, B. (1969) 'The making of the Domesday survey in Norfolk: the hundred and a half of Clacklose', *English Historical Review* **84**, 78–83.

Dougdale, W. (1693) *Monasticon Anglicanum*, eds J. Caley, H. Ellis & D. Bandinel (1846), London.

Douglas, D. C. (1927) *The Social Structure of Medieval East Anglia*, Oxford Studies in Legal and Social History, **9**, Oxford.

Douglas, D. C. (1964) *William the Conqueror*, Eyre & Spottiswoode, London.

Dow, L. (1947) 'A short history of the Suffolk Institute of Archaeology and Natural History', *PSIA* **24**(ii), 129–43.

Drury, P. J. & Rodwell, W. (1980) 'Settlement in the later Iron Age and Roman periods' in *Archaeology in Essex to AD 1500*, ed. D. G. Buckley, CBA Research Report **34**.

Dunmore, S., Gray, V., Loader, T. & Wade, K. (1974) 'The origin and development of Ipswich: an interim report', *East Anglian Archaeology* **1**, 57–67.

Dutt, W. A. (1926) *The Ancient Mark Stones of East Anglia; their origin and Folklore*, Lowestoft.

Dyke, G. *et al.* (1977) *Deben Valley Place Names: Campsey Ashe, Loudham, Eyke, Rendlesham*, Suffolk Local History Council.

Dymond, D. (1985) *The Norfolk Landscape*, Hodder & Stoughton, London.

Dymond, D. & Martin, E. eds (1988) *An Historical Atlas of Suffolk*, Suffolk County Council, Ipswich.

Ekwall, E. (1960) *The Concise Oxford Dictionary of English Place-Names*, 4th edn, Clarendon Press, Oxford.

Ellis Davidson, H. (1992) 'Human sacrifice in the late pagan period in north-western Europe' in *The Age of Sutton Hoo*, ed. M. O. H. Carver, Boydell Press, Woodbridge, 331–40.

Evans, A. C. (1986) *The Sutton Hoo Ship Burial*, British Museum, London.

Evans, M. C. (1987) 'The contribution of Hoxne to the cult of St Edmund king and martyr in the Middle Ages and later', *PSIA* **36**(iii), 182–95.

Everitt, A. (1986) *Continuity and Colonization: The Evolution of Kentish Settlement*, Leicester University Press.

Evison, V. I. (1979) 'The body in the ship at Sutton Hoo', in *Anglo-Saxon Studies in Archaeology and History 1*, eds S. C. Hawkes, J. Campbell & D. Brown, British Archaeologicol Reports **72**, 121–38.

Farmer, D. H. (1982) *The Dictionary of Saints*, Oxford University Press.

Farmer, D. H. (1985) 'Some East Anglian saints' in *East Anglian and Other Studies presented to Barbara Dodwell*, eds M. Barber, P. McNulty & P. Noble, Reading Medieval Studies **11**, 31–50.

Feilitzen, O. von (1937) 'The pre-Conquest personal names of Domesday', *Nomina Germanica* **3**, Uppsala.

Fell, C. (1984) *Women in Anglo-Saxon England and the Impact of 1066*, British Museum, London.

Fellows-Jensen, G. (1974) 'English Field-Names and the Danish Settlement' in *Særtryk af: Festskrift til Kristian Hald*, Copenhagen, 45–55.

Fenwick, V. (1984) 'Insula de Burgh; excavations at Burrow Hill, Butley, Suffolk, 1978–1981' in *Anglo-Saxon Studies in Archaeology and History 3*, eds S. C. Hawkes, J. Campbell & D. Brown, 35–54.

Bibliography

Filmer-Sankey, W. (1992) 'Snape Anglo-Saxon Cemetery: the current state of knowledge' in *The Age of Sutton Hoo*, ed. M. O. H. Carver, Boydell Press, Woodbridge, 39–52.

Finberg, H. P. R. (1964) *Lucerna; studies of some problems in the History of England*, Macmillan, London.

Fleming, A. (1988) *The Dartmoor Reaves: Investigating Prehistoric Land Divisions*, Batsford, London.

Flitcroft, M. (1994) 'Scole', *Current Archaeology* **140**, 322–5.

Fox, C. (1923) *The Archaeology of the Cambridge Region*, University Press, Cambridge.

Freeman, E. (1986) *Sudbury's Story: A thousand years in the history of a small English town*, Freeman, Sudbury.

Frere, S. S. (1974) *Britannia*, 2nd edn, Routledge and Kegan Paul, London.

Galbraith, K. J. (1973) 'Further thoughts on the boar at St Nicholas' church Ipswich', *PSIA* **33**(i), 68–74.

Galbraith, V. H. (1974) *Domesday Book: Its Place in Administrative History*, Clarendon Press, Oxford.

Gardner, T. (1754) *Account of Dunwich, Blythburgh, Walberswick and Southwold*, London.

Garmonsway, G. N. (1972) *The Anglo-Saxon Chronicle*, Dent, London.

Gelling, M. (1977) 'Latin loan-words in Old English place-names' in P. Clemoes, ed. *Anglo-Saxon England*, **6**, 1–14.

Gelling, M. (1984) *Place-Names in the Landscape*, Dent, London.

Gelling, M. (1992) 'A chronology for Suffolk place-names' in *The Age of Sutton Hoo*, ed. M. O. H. Carver, Boydell Press, Woodbridge, 53–64.

Gransden, A. (1981) 'Legends and traditions concerning the origins of the Abbey of Bury St Edmunds', *English Historical Review* **194**.

Green, B., Milligan, W. & West, S. E. (1981) 'The Illington/Lackford Workshop', in *Angles, Saxons and Jutes,* ed. V. I. Evison, Oxford.

Green, C. (1961) 'East Anglian coastline levels since Roman times', *Antiquity* **35**, 21–8.

Green, C. (1963) *Sutton Hoo: The Excavation of a Royal Ship Burial*, Merlin Press, London.

Green, J. (1983) 'The sheriffs of William the Conqueror' in *Anglo-Norman Studies* **5**, 129–45.

Greenway, D. & Sayers, J. (1989) *Jocelin of Brackland: Chronicle of the Abbey of Bury St Edmunds,* Oxford.

Gregory, T. (1977) 'Iron Age Coinage in Norfolk', *Norfolk Museums Service Information Sheet*, Norfolk Museums Service.

Gregory, T. (1981) 'Thetford', *Current Archaeology* **81**, 294–7.

Grove, R. (1976) *The Cambridgeshire Coprolite Mining Rush*, Cambridge.

Hardy, M. (1989a) 'Waveney Valley survey', *Current Archaeology* **115**, 267–9.

Hardy, M. (1989b) 'Flixton', Field Survey, *PSIA* **37**(i), 66–9.

Harper-Bill, C. ed. (1980) *Blythburgh Priory Cartulary, Part 1*, Suffolk Records Society, Suffolk Charters 2, Boydell Press, Woodbridge.

Hart, C. (1966) *The Early Charters of Eastern England*, Leicester.

Bibliography

Hart, C. (1974) *The Hidation of Cambridgeshire*, University of Leicester, Department of English Local History Occasional Paper, 2nd ser., **6**, Leicester.

Hart, C. & Syme, A. (1987) 'The earliest Suffolk Charter', *PSIA* **36**(iii), 165–81.

Harvey, S. P. J. (1971) 'Domesday Book and its predecessors', *English Historical Review* **86**, 753–73.

Haselgrove, C. (1982) 'Wealth, prestige and power: the dynamics of Late Iron Age political centralisation in south-east England' in *Ranking, Resource and Exchange*, eds C. Renfrue & S. Shenman, Cambridge University Press, 79–88.

Hawkes, C. (1949) 'Caistor-by-Norwich, the Roman Town of Venta Icenorum', *Archaeological Journal* **106**, 62–5.

H.E. *see* Colgrave & Mynors.

Hedeager, L. (1992) 'Kingdoms, ethnicity and material culture: Denmark in a European perspective' in *The Age of Sutton Hoo*, ed. M. O. H. Carver, Boydell Press, Woodbridge, 279–300.

Higham, N. (1992) *Rome, Britain and the Anglo-Saxons*, Seaby, London.

Higham, N. (1994) *The English Conquest: Gildas and Britain in the Fifth Century*, Manchester University Press.

Hills, C. (1984) *Spong Hill Part III, Catalogue of Inhumations*, East Anglian Archaeology **21**.

Hines, J. (1984) *The Scandinavian Character of Anglian England in pre-Viking period*, British Archaeological Reports.

Hines, J. (1992) 'The Scandinavian character of Anglian England: an update' in *The Age of Sutton Hoo*, ed. M. O. H. Carver, Boydell Press, Woodbridge, 315–30.

Hirst, J. G. & West, S. E. (1957) 'Saxo-Norman pottery in East Anglia', *Proceedings of the Cambridge Antiquarian Society* **50**, 29–60.

Hodges, R. (1982) *Dark Age Economics: The Origins of Towns and Trade 600–1000 AD*, Duckworth, London.

Hollingsworth, A. G. H. (1844) *A History of Stowmarket*, Ipswich.

Homans, G. C. (1957) 'The Frisians in East Anglia', *Economic History Review* 2nd ser. **10**, 190–206 and in (1945) *Roman Britain and the English Settlements*, eds R. G. Collingwood & J. N. L. Myres, Oxford.

Hooper, N. (1984) 'The housecarls in England in the eleventh century', *Anglo-Norman Studies* **7**, 161–76.

Jessopp, A. (1884) *Norwich: Diocesan History*, Society for the Promotion of Christian Knowledge, London.

Johns, C. (1983) *The Thetford Treasure*, British Museum, London.

Johnson, S. (1976) *The Roman Forts of the Saxon Shore*, London.

Johnson, S. (1983) *Burgh Castle: Excavations by Charles Green 1958–61*, East Anglian Archaeology **20**.

Keys, D. (1992) 'Hunt for farmer's hammer strikes gold', *The Independent*, Friday 20 November, 5.

Kirby, D. P. (1991) *The Earliest English Kings*, Unwin Hyman, London.

Bibliography

Lambert, J. M. *et al.* (1960) *The Making of the Broads*, Royal Geographical Society Memoir **3**.

Lawson, A. (1984) 'The Bronze Age in East Anglia with particular reference to Norfolk' in *Aspects of East Anglian Prehistory*, ed. C. Barringer, Norwich, 141–77.

Lawson, A. J., Martin, E. A. & Priddy, D. (1981) *The Barrows of East Anglia*, East Anglian Archaeology **12**.

Lees, B. A. (1911) 'Introduction to the Suffolk Domesday' in *Victoria History of the County of Suffolk*, **1**, ed. W. Page, London, 358–9.

Lilley, K. D. (1992) *Topographical Frameworks and the Concept of the Morphological Frame*, University of Birmingham School of Geography Working Paper Series **60**.

Loader, T. & Boulter, S. (1993) 'Sudbury: archaeology in Suffolk', *PSIA* **38**(i), 98.

Lobel, M. D. (1935) *The Borough of St Edmund's*, Clarendon Press, Oxford.

Loyn, H. R. (1962) *Anglo-Saxon England and the Norman Conquest*, Longman, London.

Loyn, H. R. (1974) 'The hundred in England in the tenth and early eleventh centuries' in *British Government and Administration*, eds H. Hearder & H. R. Loyn, Cardiff, 1–15.

Loyn, H. R. (1977) *The Vikings in Britain*, Batsford, London.

Loyn, H. (1984) *The Governance of Anglo-Saxon England 500-1087*, Edward Arnold, London.

Loyn, H. (1992) 'Kings, Gesiths and Thegns' in *The Age of Sutton Hoo*, ed. M. O. H. Carver, Boydell Press, Woodbridge, 75–9.

Maitland, F. W. (1897) *Domesday Book and Beyond; Three Essays in the Early History of England*, Cambridge University Press.

Mann, E. (1934) *Old Bungay*, Heath Cranton, London (3rd edn. 1984, Morrow, Bungay).

Margary, I. D. (1973) *Roman Roads in Britain*, 3rd edn, London.

Marshall, W. (1818) *Review and Abstract of the County Reports to the Board of Agriculture . . .* Vol. 3 Eastern Department, Longman, London.

Martin, E. (1975) 'The excavation of a moat at Exning', *East Anglian Archaeology* **1**, 24–38.

Martin, E. (1978) 'A new Iron-Age terret from Weybread', *PSIA* **34**(ii), 137–40.

Martin, E. (1981) 'The barrows of Suffolk' in *The Barrows of East Anglia*, A. J. Lawson, E. A. Martin & D. Priddy, *East Anglian Archaeology* **12**, 64–88.

Martin, E. (1982) 'When is a henge not a henge?', *PSIA* **35**(ii), 141–3.

Martin, E. (1988) 'Burgh: Iron Age and Roman enclosure', *East Anglian Archaeology* **40**.

Martin, E. (1989a) 'Neolithic Suffolk', 'Bronze Age Suffolk' and 'Iron Age Suffolk', Maps 11, 12 and 13 in *An Historical Atlas of Suffolk,* eds D. Dymond & E. Martin, 2nd edn, Suffolk County Council, Ipswich.

Martin, E. (1989b) 'Clare': Archaeology in Suffolk, *PSIA* **37**(i), 60.

Martin, E. (1993) *Settlements on Hill-Tops: Seven Prehistoric sites in Suffolk*, East Anglian Archaeology **65**.

Martin, G. (1954) *The Early Court Rolls of the Borough of Ipswich*, University of Leicester, Department of English Local History Occasional Paper **5**.

Mattingly, H. & Hanford, S. A. trans. (1970) *TACITUS: The Agricola and the Germania*, Penguin, London.

Maxfield, V. A. ed. (1989) *The Saxon Shore: A Handbook*, Exeter Studies in History **25**.

Miller, E. (1951) *The Abbey and Bishopric of Ely*, Cambridge.

Millett, M. (1990) *The Romanization of Britain*, Cambridge University Press.

Moore, I. E. (1948) 'Roman Suffolk', *PSIA* **24**(iii), 163–81.

Moore, I. E., Plouviez, J. & West S. (1988) *The Archaeology of Roman Suffolk*, Suffolk County Council, Ipswich.

Morris, W. A. (1927) *The Medieval English Sheriff to 1300*, Manchester University Press.

Mortimer, R. ed. (1979) *Leiston Abbey Cartulary and Butley Priory Charters*, Suffolk Records Society, Suffolk Charters 1, Boydell Press, Woodbridge.

Murphy, P. (1985) 'The cereals and crop weeds' in *West Stow: The Anglo-Saxon Village*, S. E. West et al. Vol. **1**, 100–8.

Myres, J. N. (1969) *Anglo-Saxon Pottery and the Settlement of England*, Clarendon Press, Oxford.

Myres, J. & Green, B. (1973) *The Anglo-Saxon Cemeteries of Caistor-by-Norwich and Markshall*, London.

Nash, D. (1987) *Coinage of the Celtic World*, Seaby, London.

Newman, J. (1988) 'East Anglian Kingdom survey – interim report on the south-east Suffolk pilot field survey', *Bulletin of the Sutton Hoo Research Committee* **5**, 10–12, Sutton Hoo Research Trust, Woodbridge.

Newman, J. (1990) 'Sudbury, Stour House, Gregory Street; archaeology in Suffolk', *PSIA* **37**(ii), 162–3.

Newman, J. (1991a) 'Ipswich, Boss Hall Industrial Estate; archaeology in Suffolk', *PSIA* **37**(iii), 269–71.

Newman, J. (1991b) 'Sudbury, Walnut Tree Lane; archaeology in Suffolk', *PSIA* **37**(iii), 275–7.

Newman, J. (1992a) 'Boss Hall', *Current Archaeology* **130**, 424–5.

Newman, J. (1992b) 'The late Roman and Anglo-Saxon settlement pattern in the Sandlings of Suffolk' in *The Age of Sutton Hoo*, ed. M. O. H. Carver, Boydell Press, Woodbridge, 25–38.

Newton, S. (1992) 'Beowulf and the East Anglian Royal Pedigree' in *The Age of Sutton Hoo*, ed. M. O. H. Carver, Boydell Press, Woodbridge, 65–74.

Newton, S. (1993) *The Origins of 'Beowulf' and the Pre-Viking Kingdom of East Anglia*, Cambridge.

Oldershaw, A. W. & Dunnett, F. W. (1939) 'A field to field study of 25 parishes in East Suffolk with suggestions for increasing the productivity of the soil', *Journal of the Royal Agricultural Society* **100**, 56–61.

Bibliography

Ozanne, A. (1962) 'The context and date of the Anglian Cemetery at Ipswich', *PSIA* **29**(ii), 208–12.

Painter, K. S. (1967) 'A Roman bronze helmet from Hawkedon', *PSIA* **31**(i), 57–63.

Pálsson, H. & Edwards, P. trans. (1976) *Egil's Saga*, Penguin, London.

Pankhirst, C. (1988) 'The brickmaking industry' in *An Historical Atlas of Suffolk*, eds D. Dymond & E. Martin, Ipswich, 118–19.

Pearson, M. P., Noort, R. van de & Woolf, A. (1993) 'Three men in a boat: Sutton Hoo and the Saxon Kingdom' in *Anglo-Saxon England* **22**, 27–50.

Peglar, S., Fritz, S. & Birks, H. (1989) 'Vegetation and land use history at Diss, Norfolk', *Journal of Ecology* **77**, 203–22.

Penn, K. (1993) 'Anglo-Saxon Settlement' in *An Historical Atlas of Norfolk*, ed. P. Wade-Martins, Norfolk Museums Service, Norwich.

Phillips, C. W. & Rivet, A. L. F. (1962) *Southern Britain in the Iron Age*, Ordnance Survey, Chessington, Surrey.

Phythian-Adams, C. (1978) *Continuity, Fields and Fission: The Making of a Midland Parish*, Department of English Local History Occasional Papers, 3rd ser. **4**, Leicester University Press.

Planche, J. R. (1865) 'The Earls of East Anglia', *Journal of the British Archaeological Association* **21**, 91–103.

Plouviez, J. (1986) 'Archaeology in Suffolk: Pakenham', *PSIA* **36**(ii), 153–4, 160.

Prince, H. C. (1964) 'The origins of pits and depressions in Norfolk', *Geography* **49**, 15–32.

Rackham, O. (1980) *Ancient Woodland: its History, Vegetation and Uses in England*, Edward Arnold, London.

Rainbird Clarke, R. (1939) 'The Iron Age in Norfolk and Suffolk', *Archaeological Journal* **96**, 1–114.

Rainbird Clarke, R. (1960) *East Anglia*, Thames & Hudson, London.

Raven, J. J. (1900) 'The "Old Minster" South Elmham', *PSIA* **10**(i), 1–6.

Raven, J. J. (1907) *The History of Suffolk*, Ipswich.

Redstone, L. J. (1930) *Suffolk*, London.

Redstone, L. J. (1948) *Ipswich through the ages*, East Anglian Magazine, Ipswich.

Redstone, V. B. (1908) *Memorials of Old Suffolk*, London.

Ridgard, J. (1987) 'References to South Elmham Minster in the medieval Account Rolls of South Elmham Manor', *PSIA* **36**(iii), 196–201.

Ridgard, J. (1989) 'Worlingworth c. 1355' Map 31 in *An Historical Atlas of Suffolk*, eds D. Dymond & E. Martin, 2nd edn, Suffolk County Council, Ipswich.

Rivet, A. L. F. & Smith, C. (1979) *The Place-Names of Roman Britain*, Batsford, London.

Rodwell, W. (1989) *English Heritage Book of Church Archaeology*, Batsford and English Heritage, London.

Russell-Gebbett, J. (1977) *Henslow of Hitcham*, Dalton, Lavenham, Suffolk.

Salway, P. (1970) 'The Roman Fenland' in *The Fenland in Roman Times*, ed. C. W. Phillips, London.

Bibliography

Salway, P. (1981) *Roman Britain*, OUP, Oxford.

Sawyer, P. H. (1958) 'The density of Danish settlement in England', *University of Birmingham Historical Journal* **6**(i), 1–17.

Scarfe, N. (1972) *The Suffolk Landscape*, London.

Scarfe, N. (1976) 'The place-name Icklingham: a preliminary re-examination', *East Anglian Archaeology* **3**, 127–34.

Scarfe, N. (1978) 'Blythburgh Holy Trinity Church: excursion', *PSIA* **34**(ii), 155.

Scarfe, N. (1980) 'Rædwald's Queen and the Sutton Hoo Coins', *PSIA* **34**(iv), 251–4.

Scarfe, N. (1986) *Suffolk in the Middle Ages*, Boydell Press, Woodbridge.

Scarfe, N. (1990) 'Notes on an excursion to St Mary's Bramford', *PSIA* **37**(ii), 173–4.

Scull, C. J. (1992) 'Before Sutton Hoo: structures of power and society in early East Anglia' in *The Age of Sutton Hoo*, ed. M. O. H. Carver, Boydell Press, Woodbridge, 3–23.

Selkirk, A. (1976) 'The native towns of Roman Britain', *Current Archaeology* **52** [for September 1975], 134–8.

Seymour Stevenson, F. (1927) 'The present state of the Elmham controversy', *PSIA* **19**(ii), 110–16.

Shenman, S. (1982) 'Exchange and ranking: the role of amber in the earlier Bronze Age of Europe' in *Ranking, Resource and Exchange*, eds C. Renfrue & S. Shenman, Cambridge University Press, 33–45.

Simper, R. (1972) *Woodbridge and Beyond*, East Anglian Magazine, Ipswich.

Sims, R. E. (1978) 'Man and vegetation in Norfolk' in *The Effect of Man on the Landscape; the Lowland Zone*, eds S. Limbrey & J. G. Evans, London, 57–62.

Smedley, N. & Owles, E. (1970) 'Excavations at the Old Minster, South Elmham', *PSIA* **32**(i), 1–16.

Smith, A. H. (1956) *English Place-Name Elements*, 2 Vols, Cambridge University Press.

Sparks, B. W. & West, R. G. (1972) *The Ice Age in Britain*, London.

Spratling, M. G. (1972) 'Southern British Decorated Bronzes of the pre-Roman Iron Age', unpublished PhD thesis, University of London.

Stead, I. M. (1991) 'The Snettisham Treasure' *Antiquity* **248**, Vol. 65, 447–64.

Stenton, F. M. (1922) 'St Benet of Holme and the Norman Conquest', *English Historical Review*, **37**, 225–35.

Stenton, F. M. (1943) *Anglo-Saxon England*, Oxford.

Stenton, F. M. (1958) 'The thriving of the Anglo-Saxon ceorl' in *Preparatory to Anglo-Saxon England*, ed. D. M. Stenton, Oxford, 389–90.

Stenton, F. M. & Clemoes, P. (1959) 'East Anglian kings of the seventh century' in *The Anglo-Saxons, studies presented to Bruce Dickins*, ed. P. Clemoes, 43–52.

Straw, A. & Clayton, K. (1979) *The Geomorphology of the British Isles: Eastern and Central England*, Methuen, London.

Bibliography

Suckling, A. (1846) *The History and Antiquities of the County of Suffolk* Vol. I, (1848) Vol. II, London.

Taylor, C. C. (1975) 'Roman Settlement in the Nene Valley: the impact of recent archaeology' in *Recent Work in Rural Archaeology*, ed. P. J. Fowler, 107–19.

Taylor, C. C. (1983) *Village and Farmstead*, George Philip, London.

Taylor, C. S. (1957) 'The origin of the Mercian shires' in *Gloucestershire Studies*, ed. H. P. R. Finberg, Leicester.

Toynbee, J. M. C. (1964) *Art in Britain Under the Romans*, OUP.

Trist, P. J. O. (1971) *A Survey of the Agriculture of Suffolk*, Royal Agricultural Society of England, London.

VCH Suffolk: *The Victoria History of the County of Suffolk* (1911), ed. W. Page, Vol.1.

Verwers, W. J. H. (1988) 'Dorestad; a Carolingian town?' in *The Rebirth of Towns in the West AD 700–1050*, eds R. Hodges & B. Hobley, CBA Research Report **68**, 52–6.

Wacher, J. S. (1974) *The Towns of Roman Britain*, Batsford, London.

Wacher, J. S. (1978) *Roman Britain*, Dent, London.

Wade, K. (1988) 'Ipswich' in *The Rebirth of Towns in the West AD 700–1050*, eds R. Hodges & B. Hobley, CBA Research Report **68**, 93–100.

Wade-Martins, P. (1975) 'The origins of rural settlement in East Anglia' in *Recent Work in Rural Archaeology*, ed. P. J. Fowler, Moonraker, Bradford-on-Avon.

Wallace-Hadrill, J. M. (1971) *Early Germanic Kingship in England and on the Continent,* Clarendon Press, Oxford.

Wallace-Hadrill, J. M. (1988) *Bede's Ecclesiastical History of the English People: A Historical Commentary*, Clarendon, Oxford.

Warner, P. M. (1982) 'Blything Hundred: a study in the development of settlement AD. 400–1400', unpublished Ph.D thesis, University of Leicester.

Warner, P. M. (1985a) 'Documentary Sources', *Bulletin of the Sutton Hoo Research Committee*, No. **2**, 7–8.

Warner, P. M. (1985b) 'Documentary Survey', *Bulletin of the Sutton Hoo Research Committee*, No. **3**, 16–21.

Warner, P. M. (1986) 'Shared churchyards, freemen church builders and the development of parishes in eleventh–century East Anglia', *Landscape History* **8**, 39–52.

Warner, P. M. (1987) *Greens, Commons and Clayland Colonization: The Origins and Development of Green-side settlement in East Suffolk*, Department of English Local History Occasional Papers, 4th ser. 2, Leicester University Press.

Warner, P. M. (1988) 'Pre-Conquest Territorial and Administrative Organization in East Suffolk', in *Anglo-Saxon Settlements*, ed. D. Hooke, 9–34, Blackwell, Oxford.

Webster, G. (1978) *Boudica: The British Revolt against Rome AD 60*, Batsford, London.

Webster, L. & Backhouse, J. eds (1991) *The Making of England: Anglo-Saxon Art and Culture AD 600–900*, British Museum, London.

231

Welch, M. (1992) *English Heritage Book of Anglo-Saxon England*, Batsford English Heritage, London.

West, S. E. (1956) 'A Roman road at Baylam, Coddenham', *Antiquaries Journal* **35**, 73–5.

West, S. E. (1963) 'Excavations at Cox Lane (1958) and at the Town Defences, Shire Hall Yard, Ipswich (1959)', *PSIA* **29**(iii), 233–303.

West, S. E. (1970) 'The Excavation of Dunwich Town Defences, 1970', *PSIA* **32**(i), 25–37.

West, S. E. ed. (1973) *Ipswich: The Archaeological Implications of Development*, Scole Committee, Suffolk.

West, S. E. (1976) 'The Romano-British site at Icklingham', *East Anglian Archaeology* **3**, 63–126.

West, S. E. (1983) 'A new site for the martyrdom of St Edmund?', *PSIA* **35**(iii), 223–5.

West, S. E. (1985) *West Stow, the Anglo-Saxon Village*, East Anglian Archaeology, 24 (2 vols).

West, S. E. (1988) *Westgarth Gardens Anglo-Saxon Cemetery Catalogue*, East Anglian Archaeology, **38**.

West, S. E. & Barrett, D. (1985) 'South Elmham St Cross, The Minster', *PSIA* **36**(i), 52.

West, S. E., Scarfe, N. & Cramp, R. (1984) 'Iken, St Botolph, and the coming of East Anglian Christianity', *PSIA* **35**(iv), 279–301.

Whitwell, B. (1991) 'Flixborough', *Current Archaeology* **126**, 244–7.

Whitelock, D. (1930) *Anglo-Saxon Wills*, Cambridge Studies in English Legal History, Cambridge University Press.

Whitelock, D. (1945) 'The conversion of the eastern Danelaw', *Saga-Book of the Viking Society* **12**, 159–76.

Whitelock, D. (1969) 'Fact and fiction in the legend of St Edmund', *PSIA* **31**(iii), 217–33.

Whitelock, D. (1972) 'The pre-Viking Age Church in East Anglia', *Anglo-Saxon England* **1**, 1–22.

Williamson, T. (1989) 'Ancient landscapes', in *An Historical Atlas of Suffolk,* eds D. Dymond & E. Martin, 2nd edn, Suffolk County Council, Ipswich, 40–1.

Williamson, T. (1993) *The Origins of Norfolk*, Manchester University Press, Manchester.

Williamson, T. & Bellamy, L. (1987) *Property and Landscape*, George Phillip, London.

Wormald, P. (1990) 'Domesday Lawsuits: a provisional list and preliminary comment' in *England in the Eleventh Century*, ed. C. Hicks, Harlaxton Medieval Studies **2**, Proceedings from the 1990 Harlaxton Symposium, King's England Press, Barnsley.

Wymer, J. (1984) 'East Anglian paleolithic sites and their settings' in *Aspects of East Anglian Prehistory*, ed. C. Barringer, Geo Books, Norwich.

Wymer, J. (1988) 'Solid geology' Map 2 in *An Historical Atlas of Suffolk*, eds D. Dymond & E. Martin, 2nd edn, Suffolk County Council, Ipswich.

Index

Index

Index

Index

Index